TRUTH AND POWER:

ROBERT S. HARDIE AND LAND REFORM DEBATES IN THE PHILIPPINES, 1950 – 1987.

PAUL M. MONK

Monash University
Centre of Southeast Asian Studies
Monash Paper Number 20
1990

Published by
Centre of Southeast Asian Studies
Monash University, Clayton, Victoria, Australia 3168
 Truth and Power: Robert S. Hardie and Land Reform Debates in the

Philippines 1950–1987

HD
906
. M66
1990

©1990 Paul Monk
I.S.B.N. 0 7326 0152 5
I.S.S.N. 0727 6680

Typeset by
Rosemary Burns
Computer Services Unit
Monash University

Printed and bound by
Aristoc Press Pty. Ltd.
Glen Waverley, Victoria Australia 3168

Front cover shows a cartoon published on the front page of the Manila
Daily Mirror of 3rd January 1953

For further information on other publications from the Centre, write to:

The Publications Officer
Centre of Southeast Asian Studies
Monash University
Clayton, Vic. 3168
Australia

TABLE OF CONTENTS

ACKNOWLEDGEMENTS

This small contribution to Southeast Asian studies and the study of American foreign policy owes much to four individuals for different reasons.

It was David Chandler, of the Monash University Southeast Asian Studies Centre, whose expression of interest in my work on the Hardie Report first generated the idea of the monograph in July 1988. He has been an unstinting and vigorous editor. His new publications editor, Linda Syme, has worked with admirable professionalism on the task of turning a couple of dissertation chapters into a presentable and attractive monograph.

The other two individuals to whom acknowledgements are due go back much further in the history of the material and the authorship of the monograph than 1988. Mr Robert Hardie himself, long since retired and living quietly in Springfield, Missouri, generously responded to my intrusive and persistent questioning over three years. Without his willingness to testify to events of three, four and even five decades ago, much of the history that is related herein would have remained far more tentative and puzzling than it has become through my correspondence with him.

Finally, I must once more express my gratitude to and affection for my companion in heart and mind, Jeanne Illo, whose love and intelligence have contributed to this investigation in numerous ways almost from its beginning.

MAPS AND TABLES

INTRODUCTION

This is a small part of a larger investigation which has, so far, reached the stage of a completed doctoral dissertation. To become a major inquiry in its own right, the material herein requires amplification from U.S. archives and further treatment of Philippine agriculture and rural affairs. I hope to so amplify it in the next few years. In the meantime, publication of this monograph serves two purposes. To begin with, it tells, for the first time, in enough detail to confound the usual glib or polemical accounts of it, the history of U.S. involvement in Philippine agrarian politics since the formal decolonization of the Philippines in 1946. In the second place, it initiates a discourse analysis of the American debate on land reform in the Philippines, thus challenging the implicit self-understanding of participants in that debate over many years, rather than simply marshalling "facts" in support of a particular position, based on a perhaps equally challengeable self understanding.

These are, perhaps, bold claims for what is little more than an extended essay on a controversial subject. Unfortunately, in the present context, I cannot reproduce the broader theoretical and historical frame of reference which, in my doctoral dissertation, lends richer meaning and greater weight in argument to much of what I have set down in the material on the Philippines in this monograph. It seems important, therefore, to offer a brief account of the context provided in the dissertation for the treatment given to U.S. debates on land reform in the Philippines, which has here been separated from that context.

The doctoral dissertation is entitled *Civilization and the Typhoon: America, Land Reform and "Irrational Revolution" in the Philippines, Vietnam and El Salvador 1950-1984*. Its title and theme are derived from the outlook of Woodrow Wilson, President of the United States of America from 1912 to 1920, concerning the political and social upheavals of the 1910s in Mexico, China and Russia. Alarmed by the destructive violence of these "revolutions", which he saw as the fruits of European imperialism, Wilson told his private secretary, Colonel Edward House, that "civilization" was in danger of being swamped by a "tidal wave of ultra-radicalism" if conditions in the world colonized by the Europeans were not altered peacefully and "rationally". The conservatives, he averred, do not know what forces are loose in the world. On his way to the Versailles Conference, in December 1918, he told House, "liberalism must be more liberal than ever before, it must even be radical, if civilization is to escape the typhoon".

President Wilson believed that American wealth, power and political ideals could remake the world of the imperial era into a world of liberal polities "safe for democracy". He failed to win either European statesmen or American politicians to his view of things and died in 1924 (the same year as his radical rival V. I. Lenin) with his dreams in tatters. In the generation that followed his death there came typhoons of upheaval such as even he can scarcely have imagined in his darkest dreams. By 1950, after tens of millions of violent deaths, the world appeared to be polarized between the power bloc of the "totalitarian" revolutionaries, led by Stalin's USSR and Mao's China, and the conservative power bloc of the European empires and "Third World" elites, led by the United States of America. Under the shadow of an ever more horrendous nuclear balance of terror, "irrational revolutions" threatened to break out in many places. The United States set its face, its wealth and power against them. What remained in question was whether American political ideals suggested or might provide some alternative to this balance of terror and bloody counterrevolution, while dispelling the shibboleth of "totalitarianism".

The first chapter of *Civilization and the Typhoon*—Revolution— concluded with this invocation of the vision of Woodrow Wilson. The major part of the inquiry explored the fate of American political ideals, as expressed in proposals for sweeping, democratic land reform in "developing" countries, in the contest with the interests of American wealth and power and its clients and allies around the world, throughout the Cold War era. Three major case studies were chosen—the Philippines, Vietnam and El Salvador—because between them they spanned the whole era of terror from 1950 to 1984. In addition, they were all well-known and controversial cases in which the United States had underwritten counterinsurgency operations against radical-led peasant rebels. Vietnam, for obvious reasons, was the pivotal case. The discovery of the Hardie Report and its fate made the Philippines of the early 1950s a most fruitful, as well as otherwise natural, prelude to the Vietnam case study. The "New Society" land reform charade of the Marcos years in the Philippines was an obvious post-Vietnam study. The civil war in El Salvador had broken out when I was in the middle of my undergraduate studies. It seemed the most obvious case to bring the inquiry forward into the 1980s. The fall of Marcos in 1986 was a bonus for the inquiry and rekindled the land reform issue in the Philippines in the years during which I was completing my doctoral research and writing. It provided, of course, a propitious set of circumstances for publication of this selection from my findings.

At the very beginning of my doctoral investigations, I came across the work of Wolf Isaac Ladejinsky, the son of a Ukrainian grain farmer and miller, who had fled the Soviet Union in 1922 as a young man and found his way to the United States. Teaching himself English while working at humble jobs, Ladejinsky had finally qualified for Columbia University, studied agricultural economics and, on graduating, went to work in the U.S. Department of Agriculture's Office of Foreign Agricultural Relations in the late 1930s. His work on Japanese agriculture led to a leading role in drafting plans for a major land reform in Japan when the Americans occupied it after the Pacific War.

Shaken by the collapse of the Chiang Kai-Shek regime in China in the late 1940s, in the face of peasant armies led by the Communist Party, Ladejinsky became an outspoken proponent of land reform in Asia as an American initiative to outbid the Communists in the long-suppressed revolutions breaking out in many places in the wake of the Second World War and its shattering effect on European colonial empires. "The American agrarian tradition of forty acres and a mule, or an Asian variant thereof" he wrote in 1950, should be exported by the United States in order to demonstrate to the peasant masses of Asia that the U.S.A. was not a defender of "agrarian feudalism" or a mere status quo power in the Cold War. Instead, he found himself sacked from the Department of Agriculture in 1954 by American Secretary of Agriculture, Ezra Taft Benson, and denounced as a "socialist" and a "national security risk" whose land reform work in Japan had been at odds with "American farm methods".

Even earlier than 1954, American conservatives had attacked the land reform as something "far to the left of anything now tolerated in the United States". I decided to pursue this theme through the years of the Cold War, to discover whether this sort of conservative response to land reform calls from American liberals had been consistent; whether liberals had stuck to their "guns"; and what implications the conservative versus liberal confrontation had had for counterinsurgency, in countries where radicals had taken up guns because of the obstinate resistance of conservatives to serious reform.

Robert S. Hardie was born in the United States, in a rural town in Nebraska wholly dependent on agriculture. He studied agricultural economics in the early 1930s and graduated just in time to join the Department of Agriculture headed by Henry Wallace and Rexford Tugwell during the first New Deal administration of President Franklin D. Roosevelt. This was a time of rural crisis in the United States, with hundreds of thousands of poor farmers and migratory labourers cast adrift by the economic and ecological troubles of the Great Depression. By the late 1930s, Hardie had become the regional director for California, Nevada, Arizona and the Dakotas of the Resettlement Administration's network of relief camps for displaced rural people—a world made famous by John Steinbeck's novel of 1939, *The Grapes of Wrath.*

Like Ladejinsky, Hardie was sent to Japan to work on the land reform there and between 1946 and 1949 he was the chief administrator of that program. After two years of economics studies at Cambridge University, England, between 1949 and 1951, Hardie was sent to the Philippines with a mandate to undertake a major study of land tenure conditions and make recommendations for a systematic land reform in that country, the principle of which had, so he was informed, already been agreed upon by the Philippine and American governments, under the Quirino-Foster Agreement of 1950. When he did so, however, he, too, found himself attacked as a "Communist" and a subversive. After two years in the Philippines, he returned to the United States a disillusioned man. The Americans had manoeuvred Ramon Magsaysay into the office of President of the Philippine Republic, but had backed away from the controversial problem of land reform with the accession to office in the United States of President Dwight Eisenhower and his Secretary of State John Foster Dulles, in March 1953. Very early in the course of my investigations, it became clear to me that the aborted work of Robert Hardie offered a great connecting link between the attack on Wolf Ladejinsky's land reform work in Japan and the enduring, bitter controversies over the American role in Vietnam, between 1950 and 1975. This monograph is still offered as such a link.

In Washington D.C., in December 1984, I found and talked with John Cooper, an agricultural economist of the same vintage as Ladejinsky and Hardie, who had worked with them in Japan and with Hardie in the Philippines, and also, in the mid-1960s, as land reform advisor within the U.S. mission in South Vietnam. Hardie, he told me, had been bitterly upset by the American government's retreat from land reform in 1953 and had retired to a small farm and a teaching job at a university in Missouri, never working for the U.S. government again. Reflecting on the events of 1953, Cooper told me of a cartoon that had appeared in the

Manila press at the height of a public debate over the Hardie Report in January 1953. It showed the Hardie Report being burned at the stake, he told me, and pleading "What have I done?". A hunchbacked figure, about to set fire to the pyre, retorted "You spoke the truth".

John Cooper could not remember which paper the cartoon had appeared in. Two years later, in the precincts of the Philippine National Library in Manila, I unearthed the old cartoon on the front page of the 3 January 1953 issue of the long defunct Manila *Daily Mirror*. It is, of course, the cartoon that adorns the front cover of this monograph. The cartoon, I found, in December 1986, was headed sardonically "A Serious Offence". The picture of the Hardie Report, which I had read in 1985, being burned at the stake in 1953 for speaking the truth seemed to me a beautiful epitomization of the themes of my own inquiries. It is with implicit reference to the long histories of struggle between truth and power evoked by the stake that I give this monograph its title.

Perhaps, in the predominantly Catholic culture of the Philippines, the symbol of the stake has more meaning than elsewhere in Asia. In the current political climate of ideological confrontation and religious radicalization in the Philippines, the association between the Hardie Report and the stake made by the cartoonist of the *Daily Mirror* back in January 1953, has a great deal of meaning. The meaning of the Hardie Report and its fate within the long history of American involvement in Philippine affairs ought to become much clearer through this exposure than it has been. Since genuine land reform in the Philippines remains a heresy as far as the entrenched ruling elites are concerned, it may be an opportune time to revive the Hardie Report from the ashes of the stake as a challenge to the repressive conservatism of the heirs of those who condemned it to death thirty six years ago, because it had spoken the truth.

Paul Monk
Canberra
September 1989.

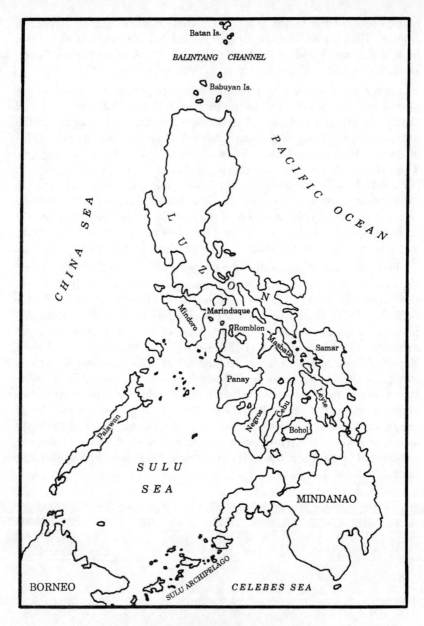

**MAP 1: THE PHILIPPINE ISLANDS:
AS PRESENTED IN THE MCMILLAN/RIVERA REPORT, 1952**

Source: Robert T. McMillan/Generoso F. Rivera, *The Rural Philippines,* MSA, Manila, October 1952, p.8.

PART ONE

The Hardie Report and Its Fate:
1950–1954

Chapter One

Colonization And Rebellion

"I will make a new song for Filipinos/... Where the peasants are asking questions, thinking of unity/Where the workers are organizing, knowing the strength of solidarity/Where the leaders are pointing the way to freedom/Where the Hukbalahaps are fighting for liberation/Where the Communists and Socialists are vanguarding the revolution/... Till my heart breaks with anger/Till the conscience of America awakes—/I will hurl this democratic song to where it all began."

— Carlos Bulosan (c. 1948)

The history of rebellion in the Philippines was already a long one before the Americans invaded the country in 1898–1900. The numerous revolts which occurred from the time of the Spanish invasion of the archipelago, in the sixteenth century, until the American invasion at the end of the nineteenth, are both discernible and important, as the roots of conflicts and debates which have filled Philippine political history in the decades since 1900 and are now, it seems, coming to a head. Together they suggest a process of internal social transformation in the Philippines, punctuated by violent upheavals. There was a long process of indigenous cultural resistance to the Spanish, marked by a series of revolts: by Lakan Dula (1574), Magalat (1596), Tamblot (1621), Bankaw (1622), Sumoroy (1649), Maniago (1660), Malong (1661), Dagohoy (1744), Palaris and Silang (1762), against Spanish rule, forced labor and imposition of Catholicism[1]. Gradually, however, Catholicism itself became a cultural zone of conflict and revolt with Apolinario de la

Cruz (1840), Jose Burgos, Mariano Gomez and Jacinto Zamora (1872), Papa Isio (1896) and Gregorio Aglipay (1902)[2]. Transcending Catholicism and turning modern European ideas in turn into a zone of conflict and revolt, becoming both more critical and more cosmopolitan, Philippine resistance clothed itself in the language of liberal dissent with Jose Rizal, Graciano Lopez Jaena, Marcelo H. del Pilar and Antonio Luna and of liberal or social revolutionism with Andres Bonifacio and Apolinario Mabini, culminating in the archipelagic rebellion against the Spanish in the late 1890s. The Philippine rebels set up the Malolos Republic in 1898, but it became divided and was defeated by the American invaders. The rural-based social revolts of Vicente Lukban and Miguel Malvar, Simeon Ola and Macario Sakay (1901–1903) were afterglows of the Malolos Republic and its unresolved inner tensions[3]. The social critical activities of Lope K. Santos, Isabelo de los Reyes and Aurelio Tolentino (1902–1906) prefigured the emergence of labor organizations and socialist political agitation in the 1920s and 1930s led by Pedro Abad Santos, Jacinto Manahan, Crisanto Evangelista and Benigno Ramos. Out of all this, in the 1940s, grew the Hukbalahap Movement, under the influence of the Communist Party of the Philippines[4] and out of the Hukbalahap Movement and its defeat in the 1950s there emerged in the late 1960s the New People's Army.

When the Americans annexed the Philippines from Spain[5] and crushed Philippine resistance, between 1898 and 1903, they inherited an archipelago which was demographically and commercially as well as culturally and politically just beginning to become a part of the world economy. The chief features of internal transformation bearing on the rural crises that later erupted, were the internal colonization of the land frontier, notably on the Central Luzon plain in the late nineteenth century, and the beginnings of sugar cultivation in the Visayas; both supporting the growth of a landlord class and a burgeoning population of peasants without land titles[6]. The Americans presided over the accelerated development of these trends and at no point thoroughly came to terms with their implications. Early attempts to redistribute land, by buying and breaking up the half million acres held by the religious orders around Manila[7], and to rationalize the land ownership situation, by introducing the Torrens titling system, seem to have contributed more to an accentuation than a mitigation of the social trends at work.

The ideological self-perceptions of the Americans in the Philippines seem from the beginning to have centred on a need to believe themselves benevolent in bearing and beneficent in their impact on the Filipinos[8].

Dean Worcester, of the Philippine Commission, which governed the colony in the first decade of the American era, embodied this sense of benevolence when he wrote in 1914:

> "Never before in the history of the world has a powerful nation assumed toward a weaker one quite such an attitude as we have adopted toward the Filipinos."[9]

Worcester fulminated against the Malolos Republic, which had resisted U.S. conquest, describing it as ruled by an upstart clique, "a Tagalog oligarchy, in which the great mass of the people had no share."[10] He asserted that the American protectorate alone stood between an arbitrary and corrupt oligarchic regime and progress toward broad-based democracy in the Philippines[11]. The most telling criticism of Worcester's outlook is that while he claimed American policies served to check the Filipino oligarchy and strengthen broadbased democracy, in sombre fact the policies pursued by the U.S. in the Philippines served on balance to check broadbased democracy and strengthen the Filipino oligarchy. Glenn May, in his persuasive study of the early American period, tells us:

> "American colonial policy during the Taft era did *not* have a dynamic impact on the Philippines. Educational reforms, viewed by many policymakers as a key instrument of social engineering, brought Filipinos only marginally better schooling than they had received at the end of the Spanish period. Americans effected few significant changes in the Philippine economy: the ambitious economic programs of the Commission were not realized, primarily because of Congressional opposition. At the end of the Taft period, as at the beginning, Philippine society was dominated by a landed elite. Moreover, by giving *principales* political power (which they had lacked under Spanish rule) and by allowing easy access for their crops to the American market, American policymakers effectively reinforced the dominance of that elite over Philippine communities. The net effect of American policies was not to implant popular government, but to nurture an oligarchy."[12]

May's conclusion regarding the period of the Philippine Commission is that "American policymakers were unable to agree" on whether or how to change Philippine society[13]. If this was true in the earliest years of American rule, it became more pronounced later.

During the Governorships of Francis Burton Harrison and Leonard Wood, in the 1910s and 1920s, the United States relinquished much of the administration of the country to the Filipino oligarchs, led by Sergio Osmena and Manuel L. Quezon, and debated among themselves the utility of the Philippines as a possession.[14] Since the formation of the League for Peace and the *Partido Federal* in 1900, the Filipino *ilustrados*, largely a class of landowning patricians, had formed an alliance of convenience with the Americans as a bulwark of political order against the prospect of social revolution. The Americans for their part sought in such an alliance the stabilization of their impulsive conquest. This was dubbed the "policy of attraction". There was thus constructed a major obstacle to broad-based democratic development. For the *ilustrados* held land, wealth and power in such manner and such measure as to block both political and economic democracy and, as Peter Stanley puts it, "there was no tackling the core problems of land tenancy, labor and the distribution of wealth without alienating the Filipino elite and subverting the policy of attraction."[15] Thus it was that, in the words of George Taylor, "the United States... made no serious or effective effort to build a sound economic base for democracy in its half century of rule."[16] In this regard, both U.S. colonialists and Filipino *ilustrados* prepared the ground for the social rebellions of the years since 1945.

The paternalistic claims of Dean Worcester notwithstanding, the period of American administration in the Philippines was marked by the thorough entrenchment of the Filipino landed oligarchy within the "democratic" institutions the Americans set up. Commodity exports soared, while landlessness and tenancy increased steadily. The population began to increase rapidly, without concomitant social or economic reforms to accomodate such an increase in numbers. All this was becoming evident even in the 1920s and 1930s, though it was to become much more acute in the 1940s and thereafter, but American ideological delusions cast something of a veil over it all. There were concerned Americans who observed the social significance of the peasant revolts of the early 1930s[17], but to do very much about the situation, the Americans would have had to "reach outside the whole existing structure of political participation."[18] That was not work for men such as American Governors General Taft, Forbes, Harrison or Wood and no serious effort was made by the Americans to enfranchise or otherwise encourage and draw into the political arena the peasant masses, whose slow

TABLE 1: POPULATION EXPLOSION IN THE PHILIPPINES (1799-1950)
COINCIDENT WITH ITS INCORPORATION INTO THE
EUROPEAN WORLD ECONOMY.

POPULATION OF THE PHILIPPINES
1799 - 1948

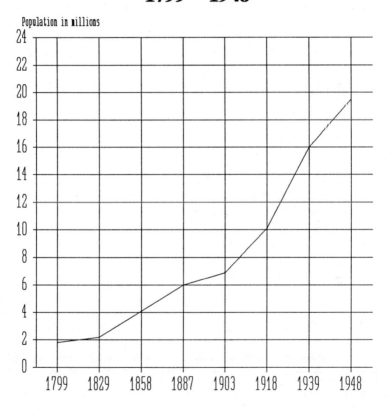

Source: Robert T. McMillan/Generoso F. Rivera, The Rural Philippines, MSA, Manila, October, 1952, p.13. Extrapolated to cover the period since 1948, the curve would become almost vertical, as the population has trebled in these forty years

TABLE 2: RISING LEVEL OF SHARE TENANCY IN THE RURAL
PHILIPPINES DURING THE AMERICAN COLONIAL PERIOD.

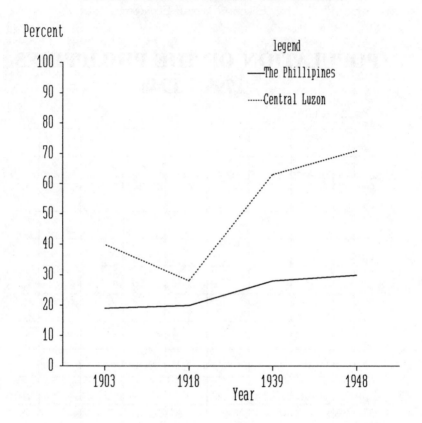

Chart 1. Incidence of farm tenancy, 1903-1948: Central Luzon and national averages compared. Central Luzon average based on official census data for Bulscan, Nueva Ecija, Pampanga, and Pangasinan.

Source: F. L. Starner, *Magsaysay and the Philippine Peasantry,* University of California Press, 1961, p.14.

awakening to political consciousness and a sense of class grievance has been described as the "most significant sociopolitical development of the American period."[19] In the two decades before the Second World War, the Philippine Socialist Party, led by Pedro Abad Santos, the Workers and Peasant Union founded in 1930 by the same man; the Philippine Communist Party led by Crisanto Evangelista and Jacinto Manahan; the Sakdal movement led by Benigno Ramos, all organized around the cause of worker and peasant emancipation. Blocked by the landlords, unaided if not condemned by the Americans, driven to more and more searching theories of the frustration of reform in the Philippines, the labor organizers began to read and quote Karl Marx and to think in terms of armed revolt[20].

The "awakening" of the Philippine peasant masses was hardly a process uniform throughout the archipelago or univocal in its "class consciousness". It was partial, regional, often backward-looking in its normative orientation. It was, however, rooted not in centuries old *traditional* relations so much as in the *crisis* of those relations induced by "progress", as Kerkvliet has argued[21]. The accumulation of grievance and the stirrings of revolt were centred in those areas where both demographic pressure and the gradual commercialization of agriculture were greatest: Central Luzon and the Visayas. Moreover, the peasant leaders were more and more conscious of the national economic and international dimensions of their situation and attempted to use the political institutions established by the Americans to advance their cause. The Sakdals in 1934 and the Socialists and Communists in 1946 tried the method of electoral politics but, being thwarted by conservative domination of the state and political culture, and seeing the United States as the guarantor of the oligarchic regime, they then sought outside help from such international rivals of the U.S. as Japan, in the 1930s, and the U.S.S.R.

Interviewed in Tokyo in May 1935, Sakdal rebel leader Benigno Ramos told the *New York Times*: "We know the American government in the islands is so strong that revolt against it means suicide. But what else can we do?"[22] The outlook of these people is well-expressed by Brian Fegan:

> "Peasant members held syncretic folk-Marxist ideas, adapted
> through the earlier idiom of folk-Catholic ideas. Except on
> the issue of sources of external support — critically a source
> of arms — both strands shared a view that the landlords

and America were the enemy, and had such a hold on the
political system that peaceful reform was impossible. The
first stream (Benigno Ramos' Sakdals) looked to Japan as a
source of arms. The urban intellectual leaders of the second
more Marxist stream felt a rising was out of the question, but
ordinary members and middle-level leaders had vague hopes
of guns from Russia." [23]

The Sakdals were crushed when they rose in 1935. Their heirs, the
Hukbalahap, having begun to organize before the Second World War,
distinguished themselves in fighting a guerrilla war of resistance against
the Japanese between 1942 and 1945. However, when the Americans returned, the Huks found themselves set upon as an enemy and disarmed,
even executed out of hand, while the Americans released and established
in power Manuel Roxas and other members of the old elite, who had col-
laborated with the Japanese. In 1946, the Huks formed the Democratic
Alliance and stood candidates for the new Philippine Congress, six of
whom were elected. However, Manuel Roxas barred the Democratic
Alliance representatives from assuming their seats in Congress and hit
squads assassinated two of them. After some efforts at mediation, the
Hukbalahap leaders, with thousands of angry followers in Central Luzon, where tenancy had reached particularly high levels among the rural
poor, raised the flag of revolt. [24]

Chapter Two

A New Dealer In The Domain Of Landed Oligarchs

"Chronic economic instability and political unrest among farm tenants has culminated in open and violent rebellion. The rebellion derives directly from the pernicious land tenure system; it is but the latest in a long and bitter series...In championing the cause of tenants, Communism wins their sympathies—just as governments (or the supporters of governments), careless of causes, whose actions are limited to the suppression of symptoms and maintenance of the status quo, are bound to win their enmity...Continuation of this system fosters the growth of Communism and harms the U.S. position. Unless corrected, it is easy to conceive of the situation worsening to a point where the U.S. would be forced to take direct, expensive and arbitrary steps to ensure against loss of the Philippines to the Communist block in Asia—and would still be faced with finding a solution to the underlying problem."

—Robert S. Hardie (1952).

The Huk Rebellion was the best organized and most nearly successful rural rebellion in the long history of such rebellions in the Philippines[25]. It was, of course, only one of many such movements against the pre-war order in Asia in the late 1940s. In early 1950, a few months before the outbreak of the Korean War, two American survey missions travelled through Japan and Southeast Asia to assess the economic and political situation. One was sent by the Army Department and consisted

of Deputy Under Secretary of the Army, Robert West, and Director of
the Department of Agriculture's Office of Foreign Agricultural Relations,
Stanley Andrews. The other was sent by the Department of State and
was headed by R. Allen Griffin, a former deputy director of the ECA mission in China and a friend of conservative California Republican Senator
William Knowland[26]. The West/Andrews team, in the words of Michael
Schaller, "worried that radical, anti-colonial insurgencies, especially in
Indochina, imperiled regional integration," and urged that the U.S. help
restore internal order in Southeast Asia lest it go the way of China and
so that it could serve as a source of food and raw materials for Japan.[27]
The Griffin Mission placed more emphasis on the social and economic
side and resisted the efforts of Army Deputy Secretary Tracy Voorhees to
secure U.S. military control of the proposed aid programs in Southeast
Asia. It was the Griffin Mission's proposals, backed by Dean Acheson,
which became the basis of aid policy to the region from as early as
March 1950.[28] The Bell Mission was sent by President Truman to the
Philippines, where President Elpidio Quirino had requested further U.S.
assistance[29]. The Mission arrived in the Philippines on 10 July 1950[30]
and submitted a 107-page report, along with nine technical memoranda,
to President Quirino three months later[31]. The Bell Report called for
reforms in the Philippines as a condition of U.S. aid[32], including adjustments of the rural relations of production to render them both more
equitable and more efficient[33]. Just what form such adjustments were
expected to take remained unclear.

There was considerable debate within the Department of State in
1950 over land reform in Southeast Asia. A memorandum from the
Pacific and Southeast Asian Affairs (PSA) office to Dean Rusk at the
Office of Far Eastern Affairs (FE) dated 13 October 1950 and headed,
"Land Reform in South East Asia," noted that

> "Mounting interest in 'land reform'... gives rise to the
> following observations. I wish particularly to offer them in
> view of the notion in some quarters that PSA (or FE) is
> unregenerate on these questions..."
>
> "It is often asserted that either without limit or "when-
> ever practical" we must make every effort to shape our foreign
> policy, including but not confined to our aid programs, in
> order to effect agricultural reform. This is necessary, it is ar-
> gued, either to steal the Commies' thunder or in its absence
> to create a society in which independent small proprietors
> will have the will and the strength to resist Communism. It is

generally implied that the position in South East Asia is such
that a policy of this nature is both necessary and in general
(together with technical assistance for the peasants) almost
sufficient to withstand Communism. I should like to confront
the thesis (which is largely derived from experience in Japan,
Korea, China and India) with certain observations which are
of at least equal validity regarding S.E. Asian countries..."[34]

The author of the memorandum went on to argue that in Indochina and
Thailand the Communists were not using land as an issue or working
with the peasants and that, therefore, land reform was not urgent. This
is significant in itself, as a way of approaching the problem, but of more
immediate interest here is his conclusion that the Communists were using
land as an issue and stirring up the peasants in the Philippines, so that
"here the thesis is sufficiently sound to warrant political application".

Pursuant to the Bell Report findings, on 14 November 1950, President Quirino and ECA Administrator William C. Foster signed a formal agreement, the so-called Quirino-Foster Agreement, in which the Philippine President, in expectation of U.S. assistance, pledged "total economic mobilization and the bold implementation of measures to fulfil the aspirations of the Filipino people"[35]. Meanwhile, U.S. Agricultural Attache in Manila, Merrill W. Abbey, was closely in touch with the complexities and difficulties of the rural Philippines. During 1950 and into 1951, in a series of cables to Washington, he urged upon his superiors the need for systematic study and thorough tackling of a situation he described as grave and even intolerable. "*Without proper direction*", he informed them "*the underdeveloped areas can easily become another Luzon.*" [36] [emphasis added]. In cables throughout the first half of 1951, Abbey pressed Washington to send to Manila agrarian experts able to pull the various Philippine rural affairs bureaucracies together, since they seemed uncoordinated and noncooperative[37]; objected that "*no qualified American has made an exhaustive study of the subject with the view of correcting an intolerable situation;*"[38] [emphasis added]; and insisted:

> "Land policy problems will require the best technical assistance available from the U.S. Much of the success of U.S. aid programs are contingent upon the ultimate solution to several land settlement matters confronting the country."[39]

Abbey sent clippings from the Manila press to impress upon his superiors in Washington the agitated state of rural Central Luzon. One such clip-

ping, from the *Philippines Herald* ran the headline: "Lack of Land Dis-
tritution System Under ECA Aid Program Deplored." Abbey described
the piece as "self-explanatory." Of an article in the *Manila Times* in August 1951, pointing up discontent in Central Luzon as rooted in tenant
grievances, he commented "Such reports are appearing constantly in the
press."[40] He reaffirmed the Bell Report's finding, however, that there
was "great inertia in the part of the [Philippine] Government to give really serious consideration to agriculture's many besetting handicaps and
longstanding maladjustments."[41]

While Abbey pressed for positive action on land reform, the debate
on the subject within the Departments of State and Agriculture in Washington was vigorous. Early in 1951, Richard Ely of PSA, who had been
in the Philippines at the time of the Sakdal uprising sixteen years before,
and who had written on American land tenure problems in the 1920s[42]
wrote up a memorandum for his PSA colleague Leonard Tyson in which
he remarked

> "I believe we should think in the direction of impressing
> on the landholding classes that they are sitting on dynamite,
> and unless they themselves bring about reform in the treat-
> ment of tenants, they cannot hope to survive; but *I doubt if
> you can radically change the land system in the Philippines
> in our time except by Communist Revolution. . .*"[43] [emphasis
> added]

Around the same time, in March 1951, an agricultural economist named
Ferber, in the Far East Division of the Office of Foreign Agricultural
Relations (OFAR), drew up a memorandum under the heading "Land
Reform in the Philippines," which his Division chief Wilhelm Anderson
edited and then circulated within State and Agriculture. The memorandum and Anderson's conservative emendations are strikingly indicative
of the political scope of the debate on land reform within the bureaucracies at that point and provide a fascinating prelude to the dramatic
events that were to follow

The Ferber memorandum was unequivocal in its summary account
of Philippine agriculture

> "In all respects, the peasants are in a disadvantageous
> position as regards the moneylenders and landowning class.
> They are largely illiterate, unorganized (except for the leftist
> groups) and susceptible to intimidation and deception.

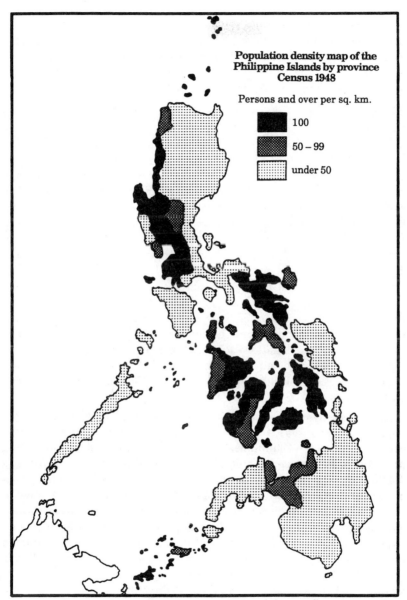

MAP 2: POPULATION DISTRIBUTION IN THE PHILIPPINES AT THE TIME OF THE HARDIE REPORT

Source: Robert T. McMillan/Generoso F. Rivera, *The Rural Philippines,* MSA, Manila, October 1952, p.9.

Consequently, they are commonly deprived of their civil and
economic rights. The prosperity engendered by the development of export crops has not proportionately increased the
real income or prosperity of the peasant producers. In fact,
the gap between the rich and poor is growing wider."[44]

The author observed that tradition, inertia and avarice sustained both
the "landowning class" and the status quo. "In the political sphere,"
he added, "a landowning class maintains its ascendancy, running the
government in its own interests." Moreover, "costly efforts to eradi-
cate agrarian unrest by military action have proven futile" and there
was an urgent need "to induce the governing Filipino class...to bring
about fundamental changes in the Philippines' traditional agrarian relationships." Wilhelm Anderson edited the text massively at this point.
He crossed out "landowning class" and substituted "large estate owners." He crossed out "a landowning class" and substituted "economically
powerful group." He struck out the phrase "running the government in
its own interests" and pencilled a question mark over it. He crossed
out "the governing Filipino class" and substituted "those governing the
Philippines." Whether, in fact, the Philippine government in 1951 had
the degree of autonomy from the interests of the large estate owners
that Anderson's emendations to the Ferber analysis suggest was what
stood to be revealed by any vigorous espousal of land reform in the baili-
wick of that economically powerful group on the part of the American
government.

In the midst of all this debate and in response to Merrill Abbey's
requests, in early 1951, the ECA put together a small team of agrarian
experts to go to the Philippines to tackle the deep-rooted and worsening
problems of Philippine agriculture. A "qualified American", in Abbey's
phrase, was sent by the ECA specifically to examine land tenure conditions, making "an exhaustive study of the subject with the view of
correcting an intolerable situation". This was Robert S. Hardie. Hardie
was an agricultural economist who had grown up during the 1920s in a
rural Nebraska town solely dependent on agriculture. He had graduated
as Bachelor of Science in agriculture in 1933 and had been immediately
recruited to the New Deal's fledgling Federal Emergency Relief Administration. He had become, by 1938, regional director of the community and
family services section of the Farm Security Administration's Migratory-
Labor Camp-and-Community Organization, for Utah, Nevada, California and Arizona, a body whose work has been immortalized in the form
of the Weedpatch Camp, in John Steinbeck's The Grapes of Wrath[45].

After war service, he had been trained and dispatched to Japan[46], in late 1945, to work for the Economics Unit, Agricultural Division, Natural Resources Section, G.H.Q., SCAP in Tokyo, on the land reform program. As head of the Economics Unit, from July 1946 until July 1949, Hardie was a driving force in the administration of the land reform in Japan. In writing his history of the land reform in Japan a decade later, Laurence Hewes singled out Hardie for special praise.

> "Robert S. Hardie...set the terrific pace of work which finally got the program in motion. His tremendous physical endurance and drive pushed through a daily output that taxed everyone around him, and forced many of the Japanese to the point of exhaustion. This contribution was essential in the face of all sorts of shortages, both in material and personnel..."[47]

Hardie brought the same qualities with him to the Philippines, but with less fortunate results, and it may be that Hewes, writing in 1958, singled out Hardie, his friend and colleague, for praise in part to balance the rough treatment Hardie received for his work in the Philippines.

Following his work in Japan, Hardie went to Cambridge University, to take a tripos in economics, and it was as he concluded his studies there, in early 1951, that he received a letter from his old colleague, Raymond Davis, by then head of the Agricultural Section of the MSA (as the ECA had by then been renamed), asking him to go to the Philippines on a two year assignment "to advise the Philippine Government on the formulation and administration of a thoroughgoing land reform program." Having no interest in accepting a job that might prove futile, Hardie pressed Davis on the seriousness of the Philippine government regarding land reform. "Following receipt," he recalled in 1986, "of assurances that the Philippine Government was genuinely interested in carrying out such a reform, I answered in the affirmative."[48] The basis of Raymond Davis's assurances to Robert Hardie was the Quirino-Foster Agreement of November 1950. While the U.S. Government may have been serious about land reform on the basis of this agreement, the commitment of the Philippine Government of President Elpidio Quirino was another matter, as Hardie was to discover.

Upon his arrival in the Philippines, Hardie, with his customary energy, "immediately began a study, as thorough as possible under the circumstances, involving an examination of all available records and reports, interviews with responsible public officials and concerned private sources and extensive field trips."[49] It is evident that Hardie proceeded on the firm conviction that the assignment he had been given was to initiate the prompt design and implementation of "a land reform program of a scope and depth necessary for achievement" of the goals set down in the Quirino-Foster Agreement[50]. Of all people, however, it was Merrill Abbey who found the assignment and singlemindedness of Hardie unsettling, as a private letter he wrote in November 1951 to Ambassador Myron Cowen, then in Washington, makes clear.

> "Dear Mr. Ambassador,
> Just prior to your departure you will recall your request to have me look over the submitted Land Reform Proposal by Robert Hardie, Land Tenure Specialist, ECA, and to pass an opinon along to you. In as much as *neither myself nor anyone in the Economic Section or for that matter in the Embassy, except the Chief of the Political Section, have been consulted,* I feel that it is rather futile to pursue the subject when basic policy objectives have apparently already been predetermined.
>
> "I believe Land Reform is of monumental importance from the U.S. political and economic point of view. Therefore, it behooves the Department to proceed slowly, as wrong policy or incorrect implementation would have far-reaching repercussions... there is no simple solution.
>
> "Mr. Hardie did an excellent piece of work in Japan and worked hard to prepare a Philippine prospectus... however, my chief criticism of the project to date is that it is <u>almost a one man program</u> (underscored in the original), namely Hardie's..."[51]

The letter is interesting, given Abbey's persistent calls for thorough measures to be taken to deal with "an intolerable situation" in the Philippines. What is noteworthy is Abbey's apparent concern that the sending of Hardie had been a political decision made according to policy objectives set in Washington and insufficiently coordinated with the U.S. economic and agricultural specialists in the Philippines itself.

Within six months of his arrival in Manila Hardie had drafted a land reform proposal and sent it back to Washington for circulation and discussion. That his proposal received endorsement at that time is clear from the cable traffic. Writing to Leonard Tyson at PSA, in late January 1952, OFAR's Wilhelm Anderson, whose conservative emendations to the Ferber memorandum of March 1951 have been noted above, commented concerning the Hardie draft proposal:

> I have gone over Mr. Hardy's proposals with some care and find them *sound, feasible and adequate* for the tasks at hand. In saying this, I am not speaking for the Dept. Agriculture, which is vitally interested in the matter, but only for the Far East Division of OFAR. My ideas in this regard are shared by Messers. Marshall D. Harris and Arthur F. Raper, the land tenure and land reform experts of the Bureau of Agricultural Economics, both of whom have read the report...
>
> "...I would urge you most strongly to encourage our Embassy at Manila to support Mr. Hardy's proposals by all available means. Time is of the essence. If political stability is to be achieved in the Philippines, the Government must be actively encouraged to take positive action to improve the lot of the rural masses. As far as Mr. Hardy's paper is concerned, I could suggest some refinements in language and construction, but these are minor matters. It does not seem to me we need concern ourselves with the minute details of land reform legislation. This will be discussed in great detail by the committees of the Philippine Congress, and can be influenced effectively by our officials in Manila.
>
> "My recommendation is that you and your associates in State support fully our Embassy and STEM officials in Manila to *bring about rapid implementation of Mr. Hardy's proposals.*"[52] [emphasis added]

As the review of the proposal continued, Secretary of State Acheson cabled the Embassy in Manila:

> "...In view strong U.S. interest and support land reform in PHILS along gen lines Hardie Report and in view PHIL commitment to broad recommendations Bell Report...
>
> "...What actions has ADMIN or Congress taken, and who constitutes support and opposition?
>
> "...What are probabilities enactment?
>
> "...What progress made on corollary measures such as rural credit and marketing?
>
> "...What further action do you suggest by U.S. GOVT at this time?"[53]

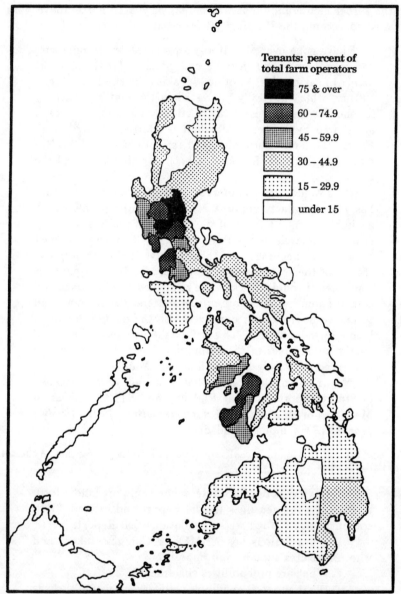

MAP 3: DISTRIBUTION FO FARM TENANCY IN THE PHILIPPINES BY PROVINCE AT THE TIME OF THE HARDIE REPORT
Source: F.L. Starner, *Magaysay and the Philippine Peasantry,* University of California Press, 1961, p.11.

This last question by Acheson became the leading one from April 1952 through into 1953, for as a long cable from Ambassador Spruance to Acheson dated 9 April makes very clear, the U.S. Embassy in Manila had few illusions as to the enthusiasm of the Quirino Administration for land reform.

Spruance informed Acheson that the Embassy was pressing Quirino and his cabinet on a number of agrarian reform issues, and running into considerable resistance. As for action by the Quirino Administration, there had been none, save a "very weak statement" by Quirino in his State of the Nation message. Concerning the political and legislative context into which the Hardie proposal was about to be thrust, Spruance informed Acheson:

> "General opinion here that large part House and a num-
> ber of Senators will oppose liberalizing tenant rentals, other
> major land reform measures unless brought into line by other
> considerations than their own convictions and interests. Some
> feeling here that newspapers may give support to good ten-
> ancy legis and that if admin is prevailed upon to introduce
> bill...there is some prospect of passage. Consider no prospect
> enacting this session land transfer program covering substan-
> tial part of tenant farmed land."
>
> "A large number of bills dealing with landlord-tenant re-
> lationships now in Congress. None has reached point of en-
> actment and likelihood is that most will not have serious
> support. Probable effectiveness these bills in solving basic
> problems range from completely negative to very doubtful.
> MSA PHILCUSA bill considered much superior to any of
> those under consideration.."[54]

Ambassador Spruance had few illusions concerning the willingness of the Philippine oligarchs to legislate a serious land reform and considered that to get such a program into being the United States would have to press them very hard. He cabled Acheson on 9 April 1952

> "...Fundamental reforms in such matters as land tenure,
> farm credit, etc. will, if effective, adversely affect interests
> property-owning classes who for all practical purposes at
> present run country. These groups will act only under pres-
> sure and we may expect no real reforms will come about as

long as they observe that they can procastinate on such questions without jeopardizing flow of U.S. assistance. If, fearful
of charges of invasion of sovereignty, we continue loans and
assistance of all kinds without even suggesting or intimating
that we expect some positive action on part of Phil Govt then
nothing will be done. If we meet every request for assistance
with counter-inquiry on progress being made on reforms recommended to Phil Govt and insist on discussing such things
first we may hope to get reluctant action on some but not
all of reforms we envisage as necessary. This is the strategy
now being followed by Emb MSA. Public statements of U.S.
officials either in Washington or Manila which touch on our
program in Phils shld invariably include this theme."[54]

Washington, however, was undeterred at that time. On 18 April
Acheson cabled Spruance

"Now that Inter-Agency COMITE on Land Reform has
approved general terms Hardie Report, we consider it appropriate for AMB and Renne to communicate to Quirino and
PHIL GOVT U.S. gratification for interest shown in this
problem by Quirino ADMIN, *U.S. conviction that reform
essential to future PHIL. progress and stability*, and U.S.
GOVT desire to support PHILS in meeting this problem...
You may wish *urge PRES estab necessary machinery for implementing land reform along Hardie Report lines* including
drafting of necessary legislation and also point out that improvement of lot of farmers is necessary and effective part of
overall anti-COMMIE campaign."[55] [emphasis added]

Taking up the very phrasing of Wilhelm Anderson, Acheson, in the same
cable, advised Spruance and Renne:

"The [Hardie] Report is *sound, feasible and adequate* for
that segment of land reform which it deals with, namely conditions of land tenure...It is strongly recommended that the
EMB and the STEM at Manila *support by all possible means
the recommendations of the report...*" [emphasis added]

Thus, some months before the completion of Hardie's report on land
tenure and land reform in the Philippines, the program that he was

drawing up had been reviewed carefully and strongly approved both in Manila and in Washington

Robert Hardie's report, as completed in September 1952, ran to nearly three hundred pages, forty two of these making up the body of findings and recommendations, while the remainder consisted of appendixes of statistical and documentary material. It was entitled *Philippine Land Tenure Reform: Analysis and Recommendations*, but became known at once as the Hardie Report. On account of this piece of work, Robert Hardie was to be denounced as a "Communist" by Philippine conservatives; one American critic was to describe the report as "the most impractical and intemperately written" report ever done for MSA in the Philippines[56], while another suggested that Hardie "showed almost no understanding of [the] political realities involved"[57]. Still other critics have asserted that Hardie's work was part of a counterinsurgency scheme, that Hardie's aim was to pacify the Philippine peasantry "through the application of land reform as a technique of social control."[58]; that "the progressive aspects of his program were based on a technical assessment of the minimum requirements for defeating Communist-led insurgency"[59]. Yet the whole of Hardie's analysis was in terms of market economics and political liberty, not centralized state or collective ownership or political power; his sense of the realities of the situation does not appear to have diverged much from that of Spruance or Acheson and his recommendations went far beyond any minimum calculation of social control or counterinsurgency.

Hardie twice cited the Roman maxim *salus populi suprema lex*, the good of the people is the highest law, which seems rather like an allusion to John Locke's second treatise of government, where the same maxim is invoked in pressing the case for the openness of government to correction and reform[60]. He was to find the Philippine government less amenable to reform or correction than he had perhaps hoped, but he withdrew in discomfort and frustration, not in cynicism, and the ungenerous estimates of his work by his critics have served to consign to oblivion what was in fact a provocative and ill-fated proposal for "rational revolution" in the Philippines. As a proposal for thoroughgoing land reform, the Hardie Report leaves all Philippine legislation on the subject, before or since, far behind. As a bold and lucid commitment to land reform, it makes subsequent American involvement in land reform in the Philippines look timid, inconsequential and equivocal. It constitutes a matchless point of departure for those who would criticize both Philippine land reform legislation and American involvement in the matter, while reluctant to lapse into the language of Leninism.

Hardie made a vigorous effort to pull together the data on the Philippine rural sector that was available in 1951-52. His chief source of statistical data was Vol. 2 of the 1938 Census of the Philippines. "Compilation and publication of the 1948 census data respecting agriculture, long delayed for lack of funds, is progressing with the aid of ECA assistance," he remarked in a note at the beginning of the Report[61]. Congressman Diosdado Macapagal of Pampanga was to assert, in early 1953, that Hardie's recommendations were based on out of date census figures, but this was a superficial and diversionary remark. Hardie consulted all those with updated knowledge and, as the problems he addressed had worsened during the years after 1938, not improved, his figures were, if anything, conservative, contrary to Macapagal's insinuation. That Hardie was a Communist or fellow-traveller, as Eugenio Perez and other conservative Filipino officials were to allege, is sufficiently confuted, one might think, by the second paragraph of his opening, summary statement:

> "In the Philippines, agriculture furnishes a livelihood to nearly three fourths of the population and accounts for about three fifths of the national income. The industry is plagued, however, by a pernicious land tenure system which thwarts all efforts for technological improvement in agriculture. Chronic poverty and unrest among tenants has culminated in open and violent rebellion which the Communists are exploiting to the full. That tenants seek to become owners of the land they cultivate is *prima facie* evidence against their adherence to, or their understanding of, the basic principles of communism. This knowledge affords little comfort, however, for the fact remains that misery and unrest among tenants is being used to advance the goal of communism in Asia. The problem is not a post-war phenomenon; it has been developing for years, deeply rooted in feudal customs."[62]

There was, moreover, nothing "minimal" about Hardie's analysis or recommendations.

> "The causes of rural poverty and consequent unrest are not far to seek. (a) The smallness of farms acts to limit potential gross income. As a national average, the tillable land area per farm is 3 hectares. Farms containing less than 2 hectares of tillable land, constituting more than 1/2 the

total farms, occupy less than 1/5 the tillable land area. (b)
Tenant frequency is high, averaging about 35% for the nation
as a whole and soaring to more than 70% in those areas where
unrest is greatest. (c) Farm rentals are oppressive. Most tenants pay 50% of the gross product... as rent. (d) Net family
incomes derived from farm operations are woefully inadequate for a decent standard of living. Farm family income
from outside sources is insignificant. (e) Interest paid by tenants on borrowed money is grossly onerous. Annual rates of
100% are common and rates of 200% and even higher are
not unusual. The majority of small farmers borrow regularly from year to year. (f) A lack of adequate and economic
storage, marketing and buying facilities forces farmers to sell
in a low price market and buy in a high. (g) Guarantees
against ruinous prices are non-existent. (h) The development
of institutions conducive to the growth and strengthening of
democratic principles hs long been neglected in the rural areas. (i) Other factors bearing on economic instability include
minimum wages, taxation and inheritance."[63]

Hardie's picture of the Philippine rural economy recalls the indictment of American agrarian ills by Tugwell and Wallace, as by Steinbeck and Caldwell, in the 1930s—the background of his own work and
experience—and one has only to read his report to find the allegation
that he was pre-occupied with "techniques of social control" or with
minimal defence of American interests simply untenable:

"The land tenure system affects every phase of the nation's social, economic and political life. Its correction is a
matter of vital importance to numerous interests other than
tenant farmers alone. (a) Political Stability: Open and violent rebellion, rooted in and fed by tenant discontent threatens the very existence of the Republic. (b) Agricultural Production: Generally speaking, in the Philippines concentration of land ownership is inimical to maximum production;
abilities and incentives for efficient management tend to decrease as the size of holdings increase; tenants grow indignant
of the marginal effect when half the gains derived thereby
accrue to the interests of others. (c) Industry: Development
suffers so long as rentier wealth lies dormant in land and is
thus denied to the needs of industrial investment. (d) Fiscal Management: Tax burdens mount with increasing costs

for maintaining law and order while initiation of fiscal policies vital to the entire economy must be held in abeyance for
want of funds. (e) Morale: And then there are the effects of
misery and unrest and violence on the individual citizen, his
family, his church, which history will for many years continue
to measure."[64]

Hardie was forthright, concise and unsparing in his criticism of prior
efforts at or evasions of land reform in the Philippines:

"...the term "social justice" has seen much service in
written and spoken form. But all...implementing laws are
weak in structure and limited in scope. They have been rendered ineffective by legal tests for ambiguities, by judicial
practices inspired by feudal culture, by lax enforcement, and
through failure on the part of Congress to provide funds necessary for the accomplishment of stated aims.
"Responsibility for the enforcement of existing legislation
is scattered through several Departments with little or no
coordination of related interests. Administrators, strained
by efforts to enforce ambiguous and piecemeal legislation, often appear to have adopted apathetic and indolent attitudes
respecting remedial action."[65]

Pursuant to this, Hardie trenchantly summarized decades of American
awareness of and inaction on the land tenure problem in the Philippines:

"Numerous studies and reports on the Philippine Land
Tenure problem have been prepared by qualified and properly
constituted bodies since the origin of American Government
interest in the Philippines. All have noted its pernicious character, recognized its implications and recommended remedial
action. None have found to the contrary."[66]
"...The land tenure pattern is an integral part of Philippine culture. The Americans inherited the situation from
the Spaniards who, in the beginning of the 17th century,
had carefully adjusted their colonial methods to harmonize
with the social and economic structure of an earlier Asiatic
form of feudalism. *Although not satisfied with the situation,
the Americans failed to take effective measures to correct it.*"
[emphasis added][67]

Finally, Hardie stressed that pioneer land settlement, or the "Mindanao first," slogan was no better than a distraction from the chief problem. In this respect, he was refreshingly candid by comparison with many disquisitions on Philippine agrarian problems before and since:

> "The thought that the solution to Philippine agrarian unrest is to be found in the settlement of underdeveloped areas, is based on a false appraisal of the problem. Firstly, world experience proves that increases in population will alone serve to neutralize the planned effects of emigration. Secondly, the acquisition of and settlement of such land by one in the status of a typical Luzon tenant requires cash reserves he does not have. Lastly, and most basic, is the fact that these newly developed areas are after all a part of the Philippines and subject to the laws and customs of the land. If not corrected, pernicious land tenure practices which have led to violent rebellion in Luzon will continue being transported to the newly developed area, thus spreading the misery and unrest. *Land tenure reform is needed quite as much for Mindanao as for Luzon.* Settlement of new areas is an imperative, but it is no substitute for land tenure reform..."[68][emphasis added]

The political implications of Hardie's findings were such that out of conservatism or delicacy he might have muted or softened the conclusions he drew from them. That he did not do so was the single reason for the criticism and even abuse levelled at him from both right and left. Read in the light of subsequent developments, his conclusions seem, in 1989, prescient and incisive. The passages that follow were the most "controversial" in the Hardie Report, simply because Hardie showed himself to be neither a Communist nor prepared to indulge the prejudices and sensitivities of anti-Communist conservatives, nor willing to engage in wishful thinking.

> "Chronic economic instability and political unrest among farm tenants has culminated in open and violent rebellion. The rebellion derives directly from the pernicious land tenure system; it is but the latest in a long and bitter series. Communists have acted quickly and directly to exploit the situation as a part of the general movement against capitalism in Asia—as they did in China and Korea. In championing the cause of tenants, communism wins their sympathies— just as governments (or supporters of governments), careless

of causes, whose actions are limited to the suppression of symptoms and maintenance of the status quo, are bound to win their enmity...Taking into consideration the landless as well as tenant farmers, it is possible that the sympathies off at least 35 percent of the population are open for bid—and this in the rural areas alone[69].

"...There is no reason to believe, unless the cause be remedied, that rebellion will not spread. Neither is there any reason to believe that the rebellious spirit, nurtured by years of poverty and strife, will be broken by the force of arms or appeased by palliatives in the form of a questionable security in Mindanao. Relief from the oppressive burden of caciquism has been too long sought—and too long denied. Years of privation, suppression, and empty promises, have served apparently to endow tenant demands with a moral as well as an economic character. Tenants demand correction of the basic inequities which characterize the agrarian pattern. Growth and development of a peaceful and democratic rural economy will come into existence only when these basic inequities have been eliminated[70].

"...Unless corrected, *it is easy to conceive of the situation worsening to a point where the United States would be forced to take direct, expensive and arbitrary steps to insure against loss of the Philippines to the Communist block in Asia—and would still be faced with finding a solution to the underlying problem...*[71]

"Suggestions for "further study of the problem" and *fears of "hastily conceived remedies" ring hollow* and as something less than original in light of the fact that officially constituted bodies have been recommending remedial action since the time of Taft; and that, even now, open rebellion threatens the very existence of the democracy in the Philippines. This is hardly a time when, to borrow from Tacitus, "indolence stands for wisdom"...Any action (or inaction) capable of interpretation by tenants as more procastination would be an aid to the Communists."[72][emphases added throughout]

At the conclusion of Part III, Para 23 of his report, under the heading "Is Immediate Land Reform Justified?" Hardie stated categorically: "The evidence favoring an immediate and thorough land reform in the Philippines is overwhelming." He then proceeded to an extended dis-

TABLE 3: AMERICAN LAND TENURE ADVISERS IN
THE PHILIPPINES 1951-1960

1. For the Land Tenure Project:

Robert S Hardie Joe R Motheral Frate Bull	July 1951 to August 1953 September 1954 to August 1955 December 1955 to April 1957* --- * on the title page of the Report Bull designates himself as Land Tenure Adviser December 1955 to April 1958.

2. For the Land Development Project

Ray E Davis	November 1952 to February 1957

Source: Frate Bull, *Land Reform in the Philippines 1950-1958*, ICA, Manila, 1958.

3. US Technicians Assigned to Land Tenure and Development Project:

Robert S Hardie Ray E Davis Joe R Motheral Frate Bull Eddie Daniel	August 1951 to August 1953 November 1953 to February 1957 September 1954–September 1955 December 1955–April 1958 August 1958 to September 1960

Source: AID Manila memorandum W.C. Tucker 28 March 1962, p.1.

cussion of the concept, order of priorities, legislative and financial organization and public information aspects of implementing such a reform. Of his numerous observations under various headings in the ensuing fifteen pages, perhaps the most interesting and most pertinent to analysis of Philippine land reform debates fall under the heading "Inadequacy of Existing Concepts:"

> "In reviewing the record respecting the need for the abolition of tenancy and the establishment of owner farmers on privately owned tillable lands, one is struck by the fact that the thought behind such consideration has been confined almost exclusively to "landed estates." The term (and concept) permeates Philippine law and even writers of the Bell Report incorporated it into what might otherwise have been a specific recommendation. However satisfying the phrase may be to those who would "abolish feudalism," the term is absolutely ambiguous and has in the past served only to becloud apparently benevolent legislation with charges of discrimination. Existing law respecting the subject is, therefore, totally ineffective. Aside, however, from the ambiguity of the term "landed estates," the concept is subject to much more basic criticism. In the first place, it places the whole idea of reform in an extremely negative light—it would destroy large (?) estates rather than create owner-cultivators—the idea becomes one of "soaking the rich" just because they are rich and to help the poor just because they are poor. Secondly, it would confine opportunities for becoming an owner-cultivator to those "fortunate" enough to have leased from an estate owner. Aside from other faults involved in this criticism, the proposition becomes even more disturbing when one remembers that it is no more glorious to be a tenant of a small owner than of a large—that as a matter of fact, tenants of the larger and more economically secure owners the world over are usually subject to much more favorable treatment than are those who rent from small owners whose meager incomes make benevolence to their tenants a luxury they can ill afford. Thirdly, it limits what should be a vital and necessary reform to a haphazard, piecemeal discriminatory program. The courts have quite justly questioned the validity of considering such law as serving to improve "public welfare," have condemned it as a measure to satisfy few and

selfish interests, and have, therefore, named action under it
unconstitutional. Fourthly, the concept would not eliminate
tenancy—but only "landed estates." A great deal of land
capable for use as a source upon which to establish owner-
operators of family-sized farms would be left untouched... "[73]

This offers a most instructive commentary on the whole debate concerning "retention limits" and "smaller landowners" which has for decades
been a feature of land reform debate in the Philippines at the expense
of concentrating on the abolition of tenancy and, as Hardie argued, "a
positive program aimed at creating the maximum practicable number of
owner-operated family-sized farms."[74]

Having examined all existing legislation and the bureaucracies involved in Philippine rural affairs, Hardie urged a clean sweep and the
setting of things on a new and sound footing. The laws governing acquisition of privately owned farm land should be repealed and replaced by
a new code based on detailed recommendations as set out in Part IV of
the report, he wrote. Laws respecting landlord-tenant relations "should
be combined into one single law, purged of ambiguities, *extended to include all crops... and geographical areas in the Philippines*" and so on[75].
The bureaucratic machinery "scattered through three Departments with
little or no coordination" and mandated under "piecemeal and impotent
legislation" was, in his judgement, inadequate to the major tasks of
agrarian reform and ought to be superseded by "an Authority created
specifically for the purpose, working directly under the President."[76]
The work ought and could be accomplished expeditiously, he argued.
The land transfer could be accomplished within two years from the enactment of enabling legislation. Title registration would require another
three years; amortization of tenant payments and retirement of bonds
granted in compensation for land expropriated under the law "should
require about thirty years."[77] It is of some interest to note that Hardie's
computed timetable for a comprehensive land reform would have seen
it enacted in 1953, and completed not later than 1985[78]. Considering
that these years brought no such reform and that by 1985 the Philippine
state and economy were in major crisis, from which the 1986 overthrow
of Ferdinand Marcos has proven no more than a respite, this timetable
is worth entering into the record.

At Para 32, "What Would Be the Educational and Informational
Requirements For a Tenure Program?", Hardie stressed the need for
wide and thorough dissemination of the objectives and progress of a

TABLE 4: ROBERT HARDIE'S TIME SCHEDULE FOR
LAND REFORM IN THE PHILIPPINES AS OF 1952

"Paragraph 30. What estimate can be given as to the time required to carry out the tenure reform envisaged in this paper?

The answer to this question is *dependent on many variables,* but in our opinion, in deference to political as well as administrative considerations involved, such an answer should be strongly influenced by a policy of speed. Experience in other countries would indicate that the land transfer phase of the reform—the purchase and sale of lands affected by the law—*could,* be accomplished within about two years from the date of enactment of enabling legislation. Completion of title registration will probably require in the neighbourhood of another three years. Amortization of tenant payments and retirement of bonds should require about thirty years, though the law should make provision for an extension of this period in instances of adversity beyond the control of land purchasers. *Assuming,* that principles to characterize reform legislation are decided in the relatively near future, and in accordance with the foregoing, it would appear that the following time schedule is possible of attainment:

(a) *Assuming,* early settlement of policies and principles and establishment of an appropriate administrative authority, legislation could, be drafted in time for consideration by the Congress convening in January 1953;

(b) *Provided* legislation is enacted during the session opening in January 1953, a Land Commission System could be established and ready to start operations by July 1953;

(c) *Provided* that above schedule is met, land acquisition *could* be accomplished by July 1955.

(d) *Then,* title registration could be completed by July 1958

(e) And bonds should be retired and purchase contracts settled by about 1980—the latter *not later than 1985*"

Source: Hardie Report pp. 21–22 [emphases added].

genuine land reform program. This was to become an immediate bone
of contention between the land reformers anad President Quirino and,
of course, it remains an issue of enormous significance. Hardie's characteristically lucid and plainspoken observations on this point, therefore,
merit being registered:

> "One half of the people in the Philippines are illiterate;
> the number of small farmers (particularly tenants) with expe-
> rience in being able to decide their own questions—let alone
> to act officially in the solution of those of others—is negli-
> gible; many are without experience as members of organiza-
> tions; few have access to current periodicals; many are awed
> by the law; many will be subject to the sabotaging arguments
> and acts to be expected from some landlords and all commu-
> nists. And yet it is this very group who must be made to
> understand what the program holds for them—of the need
> for vigilant and intelligent cooperation if the program is to
> be successful.
>
> "Land reform cannot be carried out in Manila. Deci-
> sions respecting status of individual land parcels and farm
> operators must be made on the spot by persons thoroughly
> acquainted with the real situation...
>
> "Furthermore, the record shows public officials to have at
> times been subject to graft, and that the acts of Congress,
> although ostensibly favoring land reform, have been weak
> and ambiguous. Inasmuch as a majority of the public appear
> to favor reform, continuing and widespread publicity on the
> nature and accomplishments of the program is mandatory if
> the program is to accomplish its objective."[79]

On the basis of this prospectus, Hardie elaborated in seventeen pages
his specific recommendations for a land reform:

> "(1) To abolish insofar as practicable, the institution of
> tenancy in Philippine agriculture
> "(2) To establish to the maximum practicable degree a
> rural economy based on owner-operated family-sized farms
> "(3) To establish fair tenancy practices for that portion
> of farmers who continue to work the land as tenants
> "(4) To eliminate hindrances to the fruition of objectives
> set forth in (1), (2) and (3) immediately above.'

The whole reform, under the direction of the proposed
Land Reform Authority, should be guided at all times by the
principles of

"(1) The fundamental dignity of man, and "(2) Private
rather than state, individual rather than collective ownership
of land."[80]

While arguing zero-retention for absentee landlords and 4 to 8 hectares
for owner-cultivators, Hardie stressed that precise retention ceilings, subject to the objectives of the comprehensive land reform, "are questions to
be settled by appropriate officials within the Philippine Government."[81]

"My report... was completed, published and ready for distribution,
by the fall of 1952," Hardie recalled thirty five years later:

> "Heading the second paragraph of its Prefatory State-
> ment was advice that it was 'intended to serve as the basis for
> policy discussion and program planning'. Copies of the Re-
> port were formally delivered by Dr. Roland R. Renne, Head
> of Mission (STEM) to Mr. Jose Yulo, Dr. Renne's counter-
> part in the Philippine Government. Though as far as I know
> the Government of the Philippines received the Report in a
> congenial manner, it never made an official response—neither
> by way of acceptance, rejection or suggestion for modifica-
> tion of the recommendations it contained. I was informed
> only that President Quirino did not want the Report made
> public. Though this request by the President violated an ex-
> tremely important condition contained in the Quirino-Foster
> Agreement, the Mission chose that it was to be honored and
> I was so informed."[82]

A copy of the Hardie Report was also delivered by Ambassador Spruance to Philippine Foreign Secretary Joaquin Elizalde at the Foreign Office on 12 September 1952. Attached to it was a brief Aide Memoire
which read in part as follows:

> "It is the firm conviction of the Government of the United
> States that in most countries in the world, including the
> United States, economic progress and political stability are
> closely related to the prevailing systems of agricultural eco-
> nomic institutions...

"...The Ambassador of the United States and the Chief of the Mutual Security Agency Mission in Manila have been instructed to emphasize that it is the view of the Government of the United States that land reform is essential to the economic progress and political stability of the Philippines without which the menace of Communism cannot be permanently checked.

"The American Embassy and the MSA will be happy to provide further technical assistance to the Philippines in formulating a definite program of land reform. Furthermore, when the Government of the Philippines is prepared to move ahead with a positive land reform program, the MSA is prepared to provide funds and personnel in addition to those already being provided to aid in rapid and thorough cadastral surveys, title registration and clearance, and other measures needed to correct this major course of agrarian unrest in the Philippines.

"The Government of the Philippines is urged to give early consideration to the questions raised and the suggestions made in the attached report with the assurance of continuing interest and encouragement of the Government of the United States in any effort to bring about improvement."[83]

Chapter Three

Auto-da-fe

"(There was a) major shift in the official policy of the United States toward foreign assistance in 1953, which was reflected in the recommendations of the mission in Manila concerning land reform. Whether the repudiation of Hardie's recommendations on land reform and the adoption of a more cautious approach to agrarian reform in general were directly connected with the change of administration in Washington is not clear. Certainly, Hardie's departure from Manila and Roland Renne's replacement as head of the Mutual Security Agency in the Philippines paved the way for a general reexamination of America's assistance there, and for a sharp shift in the official attitude toward rural reform ... by the time Magsaysay assumed office, it was observable that the complexion of the Mission had changed on questions of tenancy regulation and reform there was not a single United States policy, but rather a number of policies, dictated in part by the inclinations of the individuals assigned to the operations mission at different times ... "

—Frances L. Starner (1961)

Ambassador Admiral Raymond Ames Spruance, a great naval commander in the Pacific War, was a man of few words, but effective action, and proved to be an excellent ambassador, "unusually adept at achieving agreements and understanding with quiet conversations."[84] Not by temperament an interventionist, and in this respect differing from his predecessor Myron Cowen[85], Spruance "made few statements for public release during his stay in the Philippines"[86] and was described by the

Manila Daily Bulletin on his departure from the Philippines in March
1955 as "the quiet ambassador."[87] An old "Jeffersonian" American and
admirer of Henry George, Spruance was repelled by the corrupt and
patrician character of the Quirino Administration. In a letter to his
daughter of late 1952, he remarked:

> "All we can do out here is to point out what we think is
> wrong and the remedies, and hope to get enough honest and
> patriotic Filipinos in the Government to correct conditions.
> We can bring pressure to bear on the Government to pass
> the laws we think are necessary, but we cannot get the laws
> enforced against the wealthy minority who are now in control
> ... all this is discouraging ..."[88]

Spruance's tact and patience were tested by Quirino throughout late
1952, as the Ambassador waited for the Philippine President to comply
with prior understandings and respond to or release the Hardie Report.
In mid-October, Hardie and MSA STEM chief Roland Renne were invited to meet with President Quirino and his advisors at Malacanang,
but at the meeting Hardie found himself "neither questioned nor consulted" and no comment was made on his Report[89]. While awaiting
a response to the Report during September, October and November
1952, Hardie "formulated and supervised the drafting of two legislative
proposals, both of which were vital to a comprehensive land reform:
one, a measure to regulate landlord-tenant agreements, the other designed to regulate agricultural labor relations." These proposals were
duly submitted to the Quirino Administration, and were "treated in the
same manner as the Report had been and was being treated."[90] In mid-
December, Ambassador Spruance decided that suppression of the Hardie
Report by the Quirino Administration did not accord with the terms of
the Quirino-Foster Agreement or conduce to achievement of the reforms
envisaged therein, as in the Bell Report, and he decided to act.

By mid-December 1952, the Hardie Report had become the subject of
rumor in Manila press circles, and Spruance decided to break a controlled
story on 16 December. He called in a UPI journalist based in Manila,
discussed the matter of land reform with him and encouraged him to
file a story in New York publicizing the main arguments of the Hardie
Report. The journalist, seeking a headline, seized upon the phrase on
page 8 of the Hardie Report in which Hardie had warned of the possibility of deterioration of the situation in the Philippines "to a point where

TABLE 5: MSA AGRICULTURE DIVISION STAFF ROSTER 1951–55.

AGRICULTURE DIVISION ROSTER, August 1955
TECHNICAL ASSISTANTS

POSITION	OCCUPANT
Chief	RAY G. JOHNSON (August 1952–July 1955)
	Edward J. Bell (September 1951–August 1952)
Deputy Chief	JAMES P. EMERSON (February 1955–present)
	Acting Chief (August 1955–present) and
	Assistant to the Chief (July 1952–February 1955)
	Mark B. Williamson (May 1951–July 1952)
Agriculture Production Advisor	HOWARD W. REAM (October 1954–present)
	Joseph E. Walker (April 1953–June 1954)
	Ilay G. Johnson (January 1952–August 1952)
Agriculture Information Specialist	HAROLD E. CHRISTIE (August 1954–present)
	James P. Emerson (October 1951–December 1953)
Animal Production Specialist	FRANK E. MOORE (September 1952–present)
	Paul A. Grant (July 1951–September 1953)
Animal Husbandry Advisor	JAMES A. ROBINSON (May 1952–present)
Irrigation Engineer Advisor	Theodore R. Thompson (June 1953–July 1955)
	Position transferred to Public Works Division, May 1954
	Vernon W. Baker (January 1952–July 1953)
	Fred H. Larson (January 1952–July 1952)
Pump Irrigation Engineer	William Reeves (November 1954–present)
	Position transferred to Public Works Division, May 1954
Entomologist	J. ALEX MUNRO (April 1955–present)
	Henry K. Townes (July 1952–June 1954)
Fertiliser Distribution Specialist	Forrest H. Turner (June 1953–March 1954)
	Ivan E. Miles (December 1951–May 1953)
	Duties now combined with Soils Management Advisor
Rice Advisor	LAWRENCE C. KAPP (August 1953–present)
	Loren L. Davis (February 1952–December 1952)
Agricultural Extension	LAURENCE W. DORAN (April 1952–present)
	John V. Hepler (February 1950–November 1954)

TABLE 5: MSA AGRICULTURE DIVISION STAFF ROSTER 1951–55.
(CONT'D)

AGRICULTURE DIVISION ROSTER, August 1955
TECHNICAL ASSISTANTS

Home Economics Extension Advisor	BEATRICE BILLINGS (March 1952–present)
Rural Organization and Youth Advisor	HARPER S. JOHNSON (April 1952–present)
Agricultural Extension Advisor	LEONARD NEFF (Scheduled to arrive September 1955)
District Agricultural Extension Advisor (Cebu)	HENRY L ALSMEYER (December 1953–present)
District Agricultural Extension Advisor (Tarlac)	STUART C. BELL (April 1954–present)
District Agricultural Extension Advisor (Naga)	EDWIN C. BOOTH (October 1954–present)
District Agricultural Extension Advisor (Cagayan de Oro)	VIRGIL M PROFFITT (October 1954–present)
District Agricultural Extension Advisor (Ilagan)	MOSHER D. BUTLER (October 1954–present)
District Home Demonstration Advisor (Cebu)	JEANETTE C. HOSBACH (August 1953–present)
District Home Demonstration Advisor (Naga)	ALICE ELISABETH SMITH (March 1955–present)
District Home Demonstration Advisor (Cagayan de Oro)	CHARITY B. SHANK (April 1955–present)
District Home Demonstration Advisor (Ilagan)	WILLIE VERMILLION (Scheduled to arrive September 1955)
Agricultural Research Advisor	LELAND E. CALL (September 1951–present)
Fiber Research Advisor	Otto A. Reinking (May 1950–May 1952) (Consultant November 1954–March 1955)
Soils Management Advisor	(To be filled) Clement L. Orrben (July 1951–March 1955)
Forest Management Advisor	PAUL W. BENARD (August 1952–present)

TABLE 5: MSA AGRICULTURE DIVISION STAFF ROSTER 1951–55.
(CONT'D)

AGRICULTURE DIVISION ROSTER, August 1955
TECHNICAL ASSISTANTS

Forest Products Utilization Advisor	GEORGE HUNT (April 1954–present)
	(Employed by Food and Agriculture Organisation of the United Nations)
	Winslow L. Gooch (July 1951–July 1953) Deceased May 1954
Rural Credit and Co-operatives Advisor	JOHN L. COOPER (September 1951–present)
Land Settlement Advisor	RAY EWELL DAVIS (November 1952–present)
	Milton C. Cummings (June 1951–December 1951)
Land Tenure Advisor	Joseph R. Motheral (September 1954–August 1955)
	Robert S. Hardie (July 1951–August 1953)
Cadastral Engineer	Leonard M. Berlin (October 1951–February 1952)
Agricultural Economist	CLARK C. MILLIGAN (May 1955–present)
	Claud F. Clayton (November 1952–November 1954)
Social Science Advisor	ROBERT T. McMILLAN (October 1951–present)
	(Position transferred to Economic and Industrial Development Staff, October 1953)

CONSULTANTS

Rice Price Policy	John D. Black (November–December 1954)
Fisheries	Herbert E. Warfel (May–June 1952, September 1952–January 1953)
Foot–and–Mouth Disease	Charles U. Duckworth (March–April 1954)
Land Reform	John Baker, Edwin Johnson. V. Webster Johnson (October–November 1952)
Agricultural Extension	M.C. Wilson (January–February 1955)

AMERICAN SECRETARIES

Miss Dorothy Sherman (May 954–present)
Miss Miriam E. Fricken, Administrative Assistant
Mrs. Helen C. Dahl, Administrative Assistant
Mrs. Thelma E. Carroll
Mrs Patricia Hamilton
Mrs. Charlotte Selz
Miss Ann Wright
Miss Barbara A. Meylor
Miss Helen Brownell

FILIPINO STAFF

Mrs. Asuncion M. Nepomuceno	(August 1952–present)
Miss Maxima B. David	(January 1952–present)
Miss Isabel C. Regalado	(June 1952–present)
Mrs. Fortunata T. Vasquez	(October 1952–present)
Mrs. Rosa E. Rasgonio	(July 1951–April 1955)
Miss Salome O. Moreno	(January–November 1953)
Mrs. Amparo G. Celestino	(February–September 1952)
Mr. Mariano Concepcion, Statistician	(February 1952–October 1953)

CORNELL CONTRACT GROUP

Name	Field of Specialisation
A.M. Brunson	Agronomy
Maralin G. Cline	Project Leader
S.N. Fertig	Botany
Paul R. Hoff	Engineering
Delmar C. Kearl	Economics
J.G. Matthyss	Entomology
Lyle E. Nelson	Soils
A.G. Newhall	Plant Pathology
Almon J. Sims	Publications and Extension
Kenneth L. Turk	Animal Husbandry
Horst Von Oppenfield	Economics
Thomas York	Agronomy

Source: R.G. Johnson, The Philippines ICA Agriculture Program 1955. VSOM/ICA Manila 1955. Annex.

the United States would be forced to take direct, expensive and arbitrary steps to insure against loss of the Philippines to the Communist block in Asia." When the story was filed in New York, inquiries were made of the Department of State concerning its authenticity. There was a flurry of cables between the Embassy in Manila and Department of State and Spruance took steps to balance and fill out the story for further press treatment. Efforts were made to suppress the story and on 20 December a modified version appeared in the *Philippines Herald*, datelined Washington 18 December. From there the story was taken up by the *Manila Bulletin, Daily Mirror, Manila Times, Manila Chronicle* and *Philippines Free Press*. The U.S. Embassy received a rush of requests for copies of the Hardie Report "from all quarters, including social science, agriculture and economics teachers and students."[91] The press and public reaction was overwhelmingly favorable. Having failed to smother the Hardie Report with silence, President Quirino and those around him were embarrassed by its release and sought to deflect its impact.

When, on 17 December, the Department of State cabled Spruance inquiring about the UPI story, Spruance responded that the Embassy considered it "lurid and sensational and not (rpt not) conducive to securing Philippine cooperation in solving this basic problem." His account of the press "leak" is an interesting study in diplomatic-press relations:

> "...Emb learned that such a story was in making and arranged mtg yesterday between Symonds and Amb. at which time the whole land reform program was discussed, including Bell Mission and Hardie reports and two Phil Comite reports. Special emphasis was put on desirability of approaching land distribution realistically, *excepting sugarlands* from small individual holding breakup. Symonds' attention called to delay in issuing land titles and other pertinent and correctable phases of problem, but these which would have made a strong straightforward account left out in favor of sensational treatment. When Symonds left, Amb. believed a hard-hitting, constructive, factual story wld be outcome and deplores story as transmitted ..."[92]

Spruance contacted Foreign Secretary Elizalde, encouraged him to contact the Philippine Ambassador in Washington, Carlos P. Romulo, in an effort to suppress the story "if not (rpt not) already disseminated" and suggested Department of State "take parallel action if possible."[93] The Department of State responded that the story was already out but that the U.S. press "does not seem particularly interested." It was on 20 December that the first summary of the Hardie Report appeared in the Manila press, with a long article in the *Philippines Herald*, with which the Embassy expressed satisfaction. Concerning this summary of the recommendations of the Hardie Report, Spruance cabled Acheson:

> "Writer obviously has access to complete Hardie Report. Embassy of opinion Philippine Government well-conditioned for the first public account of Hardie Report by Embassy consultations with Elizalde ... and Quirino and feels no (rpt no) serious repercussions will be forthcoming. Other local newspapers have as yet made no (rpt no) mention of subject."[94]

If Elizalde and Quirino were "well-conditioned" to deal with the release of the Hardie Report, it was due to more than consultations with the U.S. Embassy. They were tough political animals and they fought back against Spruance's quiet, persistent pressure by singling out the language of the Hardie Report as objectionable and raising precisely the issue Spruance had anticipated in his 9 April 1952 cable to Acheson— Philippine sovereignty and U.S. intervention therein. Spruance cabled Acheson on 22 December:

> "When Elizalde discussed Hardie Rpt Dec. 18 with Emb. officer, he took exception language of report which he said was insulting to independent nations. He said that when report originally scrutinized by Quirino, Pres. became irate and refused to study document seriously. Elizalde said Phil Govt could not use Hardie rpt as basis discussions land reform problem with U.S. While this remark made in heat of discussion, engendered by revelations in Symonds' art ... it can nevertheless be taken as indication attitude Phil Govt toward land reform in general and Hardie rpt in particular."[95]

On 23 December, Quirino arranged a "meeting" at Malacanang with a group of tenants and farmers from Pampanga, led by Congressman Diosdado Macapagal, at which these tenants told him, according to the official Malacanang press release, that the Hardie Report was misleading and there was no unrest in Pampanga. The release went on:

> "They pointed particularly to that part of the report which recommended that all estates be bought by the government

and then distributed among the people. They told the President that *this is exactly what the Huks are preaching and they expressed grave concern about the matter*" [96]. [emphasis added]

Quirino had hit upon a red smear as a way to deal with the Hardie Report and though careful not to compromise himself by personally and publicly denouncing the Report, he seems to have encouraged others to do exactly that.

The foremost spokesman for the anti-Hardie smear campaign was House Speaker Eugenio Perez. Even as the *Manila Bulletin* serialized a condensed version of the Hardie Report on 24, 25 and 26 December, Perez publicly denounced what he called the "many radical ideas in the report which can be regarded as leftist in inclination," charged that MSA experts were getting their information from "unreliable sources with communist tendencies," and declared that there ought to be more thorough screening of MSA experts by the U.S. and Philippine Governments to ensure that radicals like Hardie did not come to work in the country. The release of a second MSA report, the McMillan/Rivera Report on rural living standards, at this point, raised conservative Philippine tempers even higher. Speaker Perez, in the words of Teodoro Locsin of the *Philippines Free Press*, "really hit the ceiling." [97] He called the McMillan/Rivera Report "malicious" and, along with the Hardie Report, an attempt to "incite the Filipino people against their government." Both were "communist-inspired" Perez asserted, deploring what he called the MSA's "program of hate" against the Philippines. Have they come here "to help or to criticize?" he asked [98]. He announced that he would ask President Quirino to file a formal note of protest with the United States Government against the MSA's activities [99]. If the U.S. wants to assist the Philippines, he declared, it should eschew sending *"men of doubtful persuasions"* and simply supply the Philippine Government with money to fund its own, perfectly adequate rural programs. Commented Locsin: "And, presumably, no questions asked. No accounting to be made."

Not all Filipino politicians joined the governing Liberal Party men in attacking the MSA Reports. Liberal Senator Quintin Paredes, as reported in the Christmas Day edition of the *Manila Times*, rebuked Perez for his insinuations that the U.S. had sent experts of Communist persuasions or with other than benign intent. The Nationalist Party bosses were especially forthcoming in defence of the MSA Reports, seeing in the embarrassment of the Quirino Administration a chance to throw it off balance for the upcoming Presidential election of 1953. Senator

Gil Puyat and Senator Cipriano Primicias, both Nacionalistas, were reported as repudiating the language and substance of Perez's remarks. Senator Primicias informed MSA chief Roland Renne that the Nacionalista senators as a group applauded the veracity of the MSA Reports. He told Renne that the Hardie Report was not intervention in Philippine affairs and was opposed by Malacanang *"because it had told the truth."* Jose B. Laurel, Jr. was reported as saying he would "place the opposition in the vanguard of the *general agitation for implementation* of the MSA-PHILCUSA Reports."[100] Senate President Eulogio Rodriguez described the Hardie Report as providing "a true picture" of Philippine agrarian affairs. Nacionalista Congressman Numeriano Babao, of Batangas, observed, in response to Perez's diatribe: "To my knowledge, these American experts ...(came) ...with no other intention than to assist our country in its multifarious economic and social problems so that we could stand on our own feet.'"[101] The U.S. Embassy drew encouragement from all this. Spruance cabled Acheson on 6 January 1953:

> "...I believe current public discussion of these problems is very beneficial. It looks as if Nacionalistas might approve measures we feel essential to welfare Philippines and necessary to eliminate conditions producing recruits for Communists. Quirino as you know refused opportunity to take this side. A division on basis of principle between Liberals and Nacionalistas would be very healthy development in political life of Philippines."[102]

A breach between Elpidio Quirino and Raymond Spruance had been opened even before release of the Hardie Report, prompting the American Ambassador and Edward G. Lansdale, the CIA's counter-insurgency specialist in the Philippines, to single out Elpidio Quirino's Defense Secretary, Raymond Magsaysay, in November 1952, as a US-backed candidate for the 1953 Presidential elections. That move appears to have firmed up strongly in January and February 1953.

On 7 January 1953, the U.S. Embassy staff and the leading members of the Quirino Administration held a conference at Malacanang "to discuss the situation created by the publicity of the Hardie Report on land reform and the McMillan/Rivera report on living conditions in the barrios."[103] Present at the meeting on the American side were Ambassador Spruance, DCM William Lacy, MSA Chief Roland R. Renne, Deputy MSA Chief Edward Prentice, Economic Counsel to the Embassy Daniel M. Braddock, and possibly others. Neither Robert

Hardie nor Robert McMillan seems to have been there. On the Philippine side were President Quirino, Foreign Secretary Joaquin Elizalde, Secretary of Finance Aurelio Montinola, Governor of the Central Bank Miguel Cuaderno and Senator Tomas Cabili. The meeting was summarized in a long despatch by Braddock to the Department of State two days later. Describing the conference as having been "rather tense, but not unfriendly," Braddock noted that Quirino was prepared to approve of the two reports as "studies" but remonstrated strongly "against the implication which he regarded as contained in the reports that his administration was responsible" for the rural conditions described in them. Quirino burst forth against the "threat" of American "intervention in case the land tenure situation was not corrected," regarding which Spruance "replied to the effect that if conditions continued to provide a breeding ground for Huks, U.S. military aid to the Philippines would probably have to be increased." Braddock added: "The President again with much feeling, asked, 'You subscribe to that statement (about "direct, expensive and arbitrary steps")'? Then, getting better control of himself, the President said in effect, "you offer to help us maintain our internal stability, but in case we fail, *because of lack of money*, you believe the U.S. should take direct, expensive and arbitrary steps." The U.S. Ambassador responded that the U.S. only wanted to help the Philippines and reaffirmed "the need for effective land reform."

The character of the conference is captured best in Braddock's record of a part of the dialogue, in which the parading of nationalist pique is somewhat denuded of credibility by the evident and express desire of President Quirino to suppress the hard-hitting reports and with them both political damage to his cultivated public image and the pressure for a comprehensive agrarian reform:

CABILI:	The publication was not sufficiently gone over. Can't we arrange a meeting to study it?
QUIRINO:	That is what this meeting is for.
SPRUANCE:	The Report has been gone over carefully and officially as a study.
QUIRINO:	As a study it is excellent.
CABILI:	Was its publication approved by MSA and the Embassy?
SPRUANCE:	Yes, I ordered it.
QUIRINO:	Factual studies I like. It is the manner in which the Report was presented that I object to.

MONTINOLA:	The Bell Mission said many of the same things, but said them in a more acceptable fashion.
PRENTICE:	Was not the Aide Memoire that transmitted the Report the official document?
ELIZALDE:	As an MSA study, the Report contains many things that should have been left out. It is most undiplomatic.
SPRUANCE:	We tried to eliminate things which were likely to affect Philippine sensibilities.
ELIZALDE:	Who said anything about sensibilities?
QUIRINO:	The MSA is free to suggest anything if it wishes, but it is not free to criticize the Government. This Report is a threat.
CUADERNO:	This kind of situation is why Sukarno didn't want MSA in Indonesia.
QUIRINO:	As a study I accept it, but why publicize it? It should be a tool, a modus operandi, to help us carry out our objectives.
CABILI:	We were not consulted about this Report.
MONTINOLA:	It is destroying public confidence in the Government.
QUIRINO:	Certain references to Government indifference and apathy in the Reports are having a bad effect on the public. These reports should not, for this reason, be treated as public documents.
SPRUANCE:	Is not land reform of public interest?
ELIZALDE:	But it is the *language* of the Report.
QUIRINO:	I want to thank you for letting me get this out of my system. This matter should not come between us. *These Reports are for us who have to solve the problems, but they are not for the newspapers and not for the working people...* From now on I shall request that all these reports be kept confidential, which are controversial in nature and which put the Government on the defensive[104]. [emphasis added].

The "bad effect on the public" that so concerned Quirino was compounded of the chorus of approval for the Hardie Report from his political rivals within the establishment, liberal critics of corrupt elite politics in the press, provincial reformers and labor organizations. Congressman Edmundo Cea (Nac., Camarines Sur) actually commended the "brutal

TABLE 6: DIRECTORS OF THE U.S. AGENCY FOR INTERNATIONAL
DEVELOPMENT IN THE PHILIPPINES 1951–76

Roland Renne	July 1951–May 1953
Harry Brenn	August 1953–March 1957*
Paul D. Summers	October 1957–May 1962**
James H. Ingersoll	May 1962–May 1965***
Wesley Haraldson	May 1965–December 1970****
Thomas Niblock	January 1971–August 1975*****
Garnett Zimmerly	August 1975–November 1976

Source: Lewis E. Gleeck, Jr. 'Twenty Five Years of U.S.A.I.D. in the Philippines', Bulletin of the American Historical Collection, Manila, Vol. V, No. 2 (19), April 1977, pp. 46-68.

Note: Zimmerly was killed in a helicopter crash in *November* 1976 and replaced by Peter Cody.

---

* Transferred from Manila to ICA in Iran, at that time a bigger mission than the Philippines ICA.

** Previously deputy director and then director of ICA's Office of Far Eastern Relations (1953–57)

*** Prominent Chicago businessman. Became close to Alejandro Melchor.

**** Fresh from a highly successful tour as USAID Mission Chief in Taiwan. He encountered an upsurge of anti-Americanism. Faced increasing Washington demands for evidence that the assistance being given in fact brought development— refused to be intimidated by either Manila or Washington. Critical of the Mrcos land reform performance in the 1960s as mere political gimmickry.

***** Career USAID officer. Worked in Afghanistan, Korea, at IBRD. Presided over AID Manila funding from \$2.72 million (1970) to \$6.27 million (1972). The police training program terminated 'by an ideological tantrum on the part of the United States Congress'.

frankness" of Hardie. Jesus Bigornia, writing for the *Manila Bulletin*, chided "a touchy Philippine officialdom" for expressing "violent exception to a few hard truths."[105] Pablo Manlapit of the United Labor Political Action Committee told the *Manila Times* on 2 January that ULPAC had examined the Hardie Report and found "nothing which could justify the spirited criticism of the report coming from certain local political quarters." Manlapit described the Hardie Report as "factual, forthright, sincere, precise and accurate," declared that the conclusions arrived at were based on the facts found and that the recommendations "for improvement of an undesirable situation are well thought out, thorough and farseeing"[106]. One Leon S. Cruz of Caloocan, Rizal, writing to the editor of the *Philippines Free Press*, rebutted Eugenio Perez's and Elpidio Quirino's assertions that what was needed was American money: "Speaker Eugenio Perez said that what the Filipinos need is money and more money. No, sir, he is wrong! What they need are honest and efficient leaders who can save democracy in this country, and can put into effect the good recommendations of the Hardie Report"[107]. Nowhere was Perez better scouted that in the columns of the *Philippines Free Press*, which took him to task, as it did Quirino, for his diatribes against the MSA:

> 'Exaggerated', President Quirino said. 'A true picture', says Senate President Rodriguez. 'Rather than criticize the MSA Report,' he says, 'We must find means to implement its recommendations.' Those who would know the truth have merely to go to the barrios to find out who is lying. Or, to put it more gently, who is misinformed.
>
> Is it true that, as Speaker Perez phrased it, the American aid program has been converted by 'men of doubtful persuasions' into a 'program of hate' against the Philippines? Is it further true that, as the Speaker put is, 'America wants to exact its pound of flesh for every half-pound that it gives to the Filipinos? "In the first place, it may be noted that the Speaker involves himself here in a contradiction. The first question implies that America means well by the Philippines, is ready to help for the sake of helping, but that its program of aid has been converted by American subversives into a program of hate against the country. Yet in almost the same breath the Speaker accuses America of being a murderous usurer (the Speaker's reference is to Shylock) demanding twice for what it gives, squeezing the heart's blood out of the Filipino

people, shrieking for its pound of flesh. The Speaker should
get together with himself"[108].

Accompanying the *Philippines Free Press* article by Teodoro Locsin, in
which these remarks were made, was a photograph of General Douglas MacArthur. The writer compared the Hardie Report with SCAP's
land reform in Japan, and under MacArthur's picture placed the caption "Communist inspired?" Perhaps Locsin might have been given food
for thought had he asked Ezra Benson, or Harry Kern and James Lee
Kauffman of the American Council on Japan was SCAP's land reform
"Communist inspired?"—for they believed it to be precisely that.

The anti-Hardie lobby was extensive. As the *Manila Bulletin* noted in
late December 1952, the views of Eugenio Perez were shared by Rep. Jose
Y. Feliciano (Lib., Tarlac) of the House Committee on Agriculture, Rep.
Diosdado Macapagal (Lib., Pampanga), chairman of the Committee on
Foreign Affairs, and Rep. Jose O. Corpus (Lib., Nueva Ecija), chairman of the Committee on Agrarian and Social Welfare[109]. PHILCUSA
chairman, the wealthy Jose Yulo, at odds with his deputy, Dr. Amando
Dalisay, broke his silence on the subject on 7 January by, on the one
hand, defending the McMillan/Rivera Report from attacks by Quirino
and Perez, but washing his hands of the Hardie Report as an MSA document which was no responsibility of PHILCUSA[110]. Meanwhile, in a red
rap that was to last for months, Tito V. Tizon (Lib., Samar), chairman
of the House Committee on UnFilipino Activities *(sic)*, having secured
a copy of the Hardie Report from Jose Yulo at PHILCUSA, denounced
it as "a gross misrepresentation of actual conditions"[111]. On 3 January
1953, Amando Dalisay appeared before the CUFA and, in response to
its questions regarding the charges levelled at Hardie by Eugenio Perez,
told the Committee that Hardie had no Communist leanings. Pressed by
Committee member Senator Francisco Delgado, Dalisay "asked the committee to invite Hardie for a full determination of the facts surrounding
the conclusions and recommendations arrived at" in the MSA Report[112].
The culmination of Tizon's campaign against Hardie came, however, in
April 1953, when he urged the Quirino Administration to insist that
all copies of the Hardie Report be withdrawn from circulation and to
"study the possibility of criminally prosecuting all persons responsible
for the preparation, release and publication of the Hardie land reform
paper"[113]. The nature of the case was magnificently captured in a cartoon published on the front page of the Manila *Daily Mirror* on Saturday,
3 January 1953, under the caption "A Serious Offence." The cartoon

depicted the Hardie Report about to be burned at the stake and a hunch-backed figure, bearing the torch of bigotry, representing the CUFA and the landed interests. Bound to a stake and looking dismayed, the Hardie Report pleads: "What have I done?" The hunchback's cynical answer says it all: "You spoke the truth!"

The U.S. Embassy and MSA had anticipated resistance from Philippine conservatives to Hardie's land reform proposal, as Spruance's cables make clear. They were not especially daunted by the initial vehement attacks on the Hardie Report. The conclusion to Braddock's 9 January despatch summarizing the meeting at Malacanang indicates that they saw themselves as having delivered an enlivening push against conservative inertia, while fully appreciating that such inertia remained a major obstacle to reform of any thoroughgoing kind:

> "The Embassy is not encouraged to believe that the Mala-canang conference will help much in settling the fundamental issue. It does not believe that the Quirino Administration is likely to undertake a genuine land reform program designed to liquidate the large landed estates.*(sic)* Some gain, how-ever, has probably been made ...The issue of land reform has been put plainly before the people, and will certainly play a part in the coming elections. The opposition party, if only to embarrass the Administration, has hailed the Reports as exposing the Government's neglect of a situation crying for attention, and to some extent has thereby committed it-self to a reform program if and when it should come to power. Our insistence on the need for land reform has undoubtedly put some strain on our general relations with the Quirino Government. Some of the language of the Reports has pro-vided the Government with an excuse to charge the United States with a threat of intervention, and this aspect is cur-rently receiving prominent play in one of the newspapers, the *Manila Chronicle*. But the harm done is not regarded as se-rious or permanent, and *on balance the Embassy believes that the best interests of the United States have been served by the publicity which has attended the two Reports*"[114]. [emphasis added]

Under the bold heading "U.S. Intervention" on 17 January 1953, the nimble and tireless Teodoro Locsin wielded his pen once more with sin-gular dexterity against Speaker Perez and the anti-Hardie lobby:

" ..... When the United States sent economic aid and military equipment, it was intervening in Philippine affairs. Of course. But the Philippine Government liked that kind of intervention; nobody made a squawk. Many officials got rich from the economic aid, if the country did not. And American arms not only contained Communism, they froze the feudal system that inspired the revolt in Central Luzon.

The 'era of good feeling' lasted quite a while. This month it came, more or less abruptly, to an end. The Hardie Report on the tenancy system ... produced outcries of American intervention. Not only that. The documents were, according to one critic, Speaker Perez, "communist inspired." The MSA documents had only one purpose: to discredit the administration and help bring about the government's fall—to the Reds. Protest must be made to Washington. This is, if not war, gentlemen, intervention ... "[115].

Writing for the *Christian Science Monitor* in April 1953, David Sternberg, the paraplegic American journalist, resident in Quezon City since 1939 and an American intelligence agent in the 1950s and '60s, wrote that charges of U.S. intervention came chiefly from Quirino and the Liberals around him, including Diosdado Macapagal and Tito Tizon. "All other sources," he averred, "including the Manila press" regarded the MSA Reports with favor[116]. Diosdado Macapagal, who as President in 1963 was to claim that his land reform legislation would complete an "unfinished revolution" in the Philippines, was an outspoken critic of the Hardie Report. There were, to be sure, problems with the country's agriculture, he said on 27 December 1952, but *"to say that the system threatens the very existence of the Republic is to be unduly alarmed, like being before a candle-light and seeing a conflagration."*[117] (emphasis added). The Huk rebellion might have required action of some kind, but it had, Macapagal asserted, been quelled by Defense Secretary Ramon Magsaysay and no longer threatened the Republic.

It was Defense Secretary Ramon Magsaysay, in fact, who became the centerpiece in efforts by Spruance to oust Quirino and bring to power a reform-minded Philippine regime. In a controversial move that has still not received proper historical examination, the U.S. Embassy, with the clear encouragement of Washington, decided to back Magsaysay against Quirino in the 1953 Philippine Presidential elections. It was a covert operation, with Lansdale and his team handling the candidate and funnelling hundreds of thousands of American dollars into the Magsaysay

TABLE 7: PRINCIPAL US DIPLOMATIC AND AID PERSONNEL IN THE PHILLIPPINES, 1946–1980

Date	Ambassador	Political Section	Public Safety	USIA/USIS
1946	Paul P Steindorf Consul General	-	-	-
1948	Emmet O'Neal	Thomas H. Lockett	-	-
1950	Myron Melvin Cowen	Vinton Chapin	-	-
July 1952	Raymond Ames Spruance	H. Merrell Benninghoff Daniel Braddock Richard Ely	- - -	John Nalley, PAO
October 1954	Raymond Ames Spruance	Charles R. Burrows, FSO-1 William Lacy, FSR-1 Carl Boeringer Daniel Braddock Richard Ely, Att FSR-2	- -	
July 1956	Albert F. Nufer	Charles R. Burrows	-	William W Copeland, PAO
July 1958	Charles E. Bohlen	Carl H Boehringer Richard Ely, Att FSR-1	-	Richard Barnsley, PAO
July 1960	John D. Hickerson	Henry L.T. Koren Paul Kattenburg John Gordon Mein, Cons O-2 Henry L. T. Koren	Carl A. Betsch, Chief Police Adviser, R-4 Robert H. Whitmer	Richard Barnsley, PAO

TABLE 7: PRINCIPAL US DIPLOMATIC AND AID PERSONNEL IN THE PHILIPPINES, 1946-1980 (CONT'D)

Date	Ambassador	Political Section	Public Safety	USIA/USIS
July 1962	William E Stevenson	Max V Krebs	Carl A. Betsch	Lewis C.Mattison,PAO
July 1964	William McC. Blair Jr	Richard E. Usher	William Simmler, Jr Chief Public Saf Adv, R-3 / Harry B. Hambleton, PSA, FC-4	John H. Esterline, CR-2, PAO
May 1967	William McC. Blair Jr / James M. Wilson Jr, DCM	Richard E. Usher	William Simmler Jr Chief PSA, R-3 / Elliot B Henzell / Walter E. Kreutzer	Harold G McConeghy, PAO
September 1968	William C. Mennen / James M. Wilson Jr DCM	Richard E. Usher / Stanley W. Guth,	William Simmler Jr Chief PSA, R-3 / Elliot B. Henzel, Franklin S. Hoyle, Paul T. Riley, Frank R. Smith, William C. Smith	Henry L. Miller Jr, PAO
January 1970	Henry A. Byroade	Francis Underhill	William Simmler Jr Chief PSA R-3 / Stanley W. Guth	Henry L. Miller, Jr. PAO
June 1972	Henry A. Byroade / William C. Hamilton, DCM	Thomas A. Donahue, R-1 Ronald D. Palmer Pol/Mil Affs		Henry L. Miller Jr, PAO

TABLE 7: PRINCIPAL US DIPLOMATIC AND AID PERSONNEL IN THE PHILIPPINES, 1946–1980 (CONT'D)

Date	Ambassador	Political Section	Public Safety	USIA/USIS
June 1974	William H. Sullivan	Eiler R. Cook Labor/Pol Off, O-3	Edward R. Bishop	Maurice E. Lee, PAO
	Lewis M. Purnell, DCM George T. Kalaris Pol Off, R-2	Shepard C. Lowman Pol Off, O-3		
July 1976	William H Sullivan Lee T. Stull, DCM	Robert H. Wenzel		Maurice E. Lee, PAO
July 1978	Richard W. Murphy Donald R Touissaint, DCM	Robert H. Wenzel	-	Horace G. Dawson, PAO
September 1980	Richard W. Murphy James D. Rosenthal	Herbert S. Main	-	

TABLE 9: PRINCIPAL US DIPLOMATIC AND AID PERSONNEL IN THE PHILLIPINES, 1946–1980 (CONT'D)

Date	AID Director	AID	Other
1946	-	-	Clarence Boonstra, Agricultural Attache John M. Beard, Senior Economic Analyst
1948	-	-	Temple Wanamaker, 2nd Sec, Vice Consul, FSO-5
1950	Vincent C. Cherchi	-	Edward E. Rice, 1st Sec, Consul, FSO-3 Merrill W. Abbey, Agricultural Attache
July 1952	Roland R. Renne	-	James D. Ball, 1st Sec, Consul, FSO-3
October 1954	Harry A. Brenn	Edward S Prentice FOA-3, Dep Dir John L. Cooper, Rural Credit Coop, FSS-2 Ray E Davis, Income Tax Adv FSS-2 Ray Ewell Davis, Land Settlement Adviser	James P. Emerson, Asst, Agric. Chief, FSO-3 Ray G Johnson, Dir Agr Div, FSS-3 Herbert K. May, Econ Adv Robert T. Mc Millan, Social Sc Adv, FSS-2 Joseph Motheral, Land Adv, FSS-2 Warren W. Wiggins, Asst Dir Econ Pol, FOA-3
July 1956	Harry A. Brenn	Edward S. Prentice, Dep Dir FOA-3 Robert T. McMillan, Social Sc Kurt Nathan, Chief Econ Dev Staff, FSS-1	Frate Bull, Land Tenure Adv, FSS-2 Ray E. Davis, Inc Tax Adv, FSS-1 Raymond Ewell Davis, Land Sett Adv, FSS-2

TABLE 7: PRINCIPAL US DIPLOMATIC AND AID PERSONNEL IN THE PHILLIPPINES, 1946–1980 (CONT'D)

Date	AID Director	AID	Other
July 1958	Paul D Summers	Daly C. Lavergne, Dep Dir, R-1 Frate Bull, Land Tenure Adv, 5-2	Richard L. Hough, Prog Analyst, R-6 Eddie F. Daniel, Agri, Ec Adv, R-3
July 1960	Paul D Summers	Leland A. Randall, Dep Dir, R-1	Eddie F Daniel, Agri, Ec Adv, R-3 David B Bales Rural Youth Adv, R-4
July 1962	Paul D. Summers James H. Ingersoll	Leland A. Randall, Dep Dir	Lewis E. Gleeck Jr, Cons Sect 1st Sec, O-2 Burl Stugard, Agri Att William C. Tucker, Food Agr Off, R-3
July 1964	James H. Ingersoll	Richard V. Bernhart Frank D. Ozment,	Lewis E. Gleek Jr, Cons Gen, O-2 Lee Parramore, Agr Att
May 1967	Wesley C. Haraldson	Ernest E. Neal, Dep Dir, R-1 David Christenson Lee Parramore, Agr Att	Lewis E Gleek Jr, Cons Att, O-2 Bernard Zagorin, ADB Dir
September 1968	Wesley C. Haraldson	Ernest R. Neal, Dep Dir James Brady, Rur Adv Off, R-4 David Christenson, Asst Prog Off, Rural Affs, R-5	Lewis E. Gleek Jr, Sup Cons Off, O-2 Bernard Zagorin, ADB Dir Frederick W. Traeger, Agr Att
January 1970	Wesley C. Haraldson	Thomas Clinton Niblock Dep Dir, R-1	Bernard Zagorin, ADB US Dir etc Frederick W. Traeger, Agr Att Harold D. Koone, Rur Dev Off, R-3

TABLE 7: PRINCIPAL US DIPLOMATIC AND AID PERSONNEL IN THE PHILLIPPINES, 1946–1980 (CONT'D)

Date	AID Director	AID	Other
June 1972	Thomas C Niblock	Christopher Russell, Dep Dir	Thomas L. Rose, Area Dev Adv, R-2 Frank R. Smith
June 1974		David Christenson, Land Reform Adv Thomas L. Rose, Area Dev Adv, R-2 Michael Korin Land Reform Facilitator Keith W. Sherper Chief Land Reform Advisor	Frank R. Smith, Pub Saf Electronics Spec.
July 1976	Garnett A. Zimmerly	Glenn R. Samson, AGR Michael Korin Chief Land Reform Advisor	Paul Rex Beach, ADB
July 1978	Peter M. Cody	Glenn R. Samson, AGR	John E. Mellor, ECOL Comm Lester E. Edmond, ADB US Dir
September 1980	Anthony Schwarzwalder	John E. Riesz, AGR	Lester E. Edmond, ADB US Dir

campaign chest. Though denounced ever since by Philippine nationalists as an imperialist conspiracy, this covert operation was not, in itself, a conservative move, but one which must be seen as an effort to avoid the sort of problem that Chiang Kai-shek had posed in China. Certainly, it involved blatant intervention in Philippine affairs, but that intervention needs to be kept in the perspective of a clear American perception that unless major reforms were implemented in the Philippines its tenuous democratic institutions were likely to collapse under the strain of increasing class conflict. The decision to back Magsaysay appears to date from early 1952, but was precipitated in November 1952 as the Quirino Administration stone-walled the Hardie Report.

American as well as Philippine conservatives appear to have seen a direct link between the support for Magsaysay and the Hardie Report, for it was just as the conservative attack on the Hardie Report was coming to a head in the Philippines that there appeared, on 10 March 1953, an editorial in the *Wall Street Journal* belittling the report and linking it to American partisanship in the coming Philippine elections:

> "There is an election coming up in the Philippines next November and a United States aid agency is just where it ought not to be—right in the middle of it. We got there by way of a little report on land reform...President Quirino took particular objection to a little phrase hidden in the report, written by Mr. Robert Hardy *(sic)*. This special little phrase warned that the United States might have to take direct, expensive and arbitrary action to save the Philippines from Communism, unless poverty and unrest among tenant farmers were alleviated. How? By land reform, of course; by the Philippine government buying land and divvying it up among the farmers...but...the Philippine government just hasn't got that kind of money..."[118].

The inauguration of the Eisenhower Administration, which occurred just before this editorial appeared, brought with it a conservative shift in America's foreign aid policies. This was made clear in the Philippine case by a retrenchment on the land reform issue even before Magsaysay had been elected. From February onward Hardie felt support ebbing for the major land reform initiative he had espoused[119]. According to Raymond Davis, writing to Gary Olson in 1972, the Quirino Administration demanded Robert Hardie's recall in early 1953 and, when Washington refused to stand by him, Hardie resigned in disgust[120]. John Cooper's recollection of the matter in 1984 was even more poignant. Hardie, he reflected, "believed in his heart that this had to be done in the Philippines. He was determined to help the Filipino people." The vitriolic attacks on his Report and the abandonment of it by the U.S. government "nearly broke him emotionally and ruined his career with the Federal Government", inducing him to retire to a small farm and a teaching job in Missouri[121].

Actually, Hardie did work again for the U.S. government. In 1962 he was engaged by Robert Nathan & Associates for A.I.D. to do a study of rural development in another country where the United States was then concerned about political stability and rural development—El Salvador[122]. Clearly, however, the vigor of his work did not conform to the foreign policy priorities of the Eisenhower Administration. While reluctant to interpret his experience in terms of the American conservative reaction of the 1950s, the attacks on the China hands Vincent, Service, Davies, Lattimore, or the attacks on Wolf Ladejinsky[123], Hardie still had strong feelings, more than thirty years later, about the abortion of his work in the Philippines:

> "Convinced that all hope for a meaningful Philippine Land Reform Program had been effectively stifled, with completion of my contract, I returned to the U.S. in mid-summer 1953 and made no request for its renewal, having no desire to continue on with a once noble effort reduced to a charade and waste of public funds. In retrospect, I am firmly convinced that my decision thus made in 1953 was not alone the right one, but the only possible honorable one. Subsequent developments would seem to have supplied an abundance of proof in support of this opinion" [124].

Hardie's work deserves more prominent recognition in the history of the Philippine Republic than the hegemonic patrician memory or anti-American leftist historiography have accorded it. And it has a significance within the broader context of American policy transcending Hardie's personal fate. For in the best American traditions of both political prudence and democratic faith, the policy thrust behind the Hardie Report in 1951-52 was a recognition of the social, economic and political needs of the Philippine Republic beyond the narrower concerns of American strategic policy. Had Communism proved more benign or successful than it had by the 1950s and not assumed the frightful character stamped on it by Stalin (who died in late March 1953), the warnings of Hardie about the menace of Communism to the Philippines might justly be dismissed as merely conservative. Such was not the case and anti-Communism in the likes of Hardie must be considered as a rejection of totalitarianism, not of democratic modernization. When, however, in March 1954, the U.S. Mission in Manila drafted a land tenure study to replace the Hardie Report, the commitment to land reform was all but eliminated and all Hardie's emphases shifted to a concern with conservative political stability alone, accompanied by fatuous expressions of confidence in the capacity of the Philippine government to cope with the situation in the long run. This retreat was endorsed by Secretary of State John Foster Dulles, in cables to the Embassy of May 1954, and despite much fanfare about the popular Magsaysay, there was no strong American push behind land reform after 1954 and what there was dissipated completely after Magsaysay's death in 1957. The passage of time in the Philippines would do much to fulfil the predictions of Robert Hardie, but his work was not remembered by Americans who came after him, or even by critics of American policies in the Philippines. A veteran of the American New Deal, Robert Hardie had gone "over the top" in the Philippines in 1952-53, only to find himself stranded in the political no-man's land between entrenched conservatives and totalitarian revolutionaries. He himself survived, but the Hardie Report fell into a shell crater and was forgotten, as the Cold War swept around and past it, fought out from deep trenches on both sides.

Testifying before the Senate Armed Services Committee, in March 1951, concerning the effects of the American occupation on Japan, General Douglas MacArthur described the land reform that had been pushed through by the occupation authorities as the most effective land reform since that legislated by the brothers Gracchus "in the days of the Roman Empire". His allusion to the Gracchi was vague and whimsical, omitting all reference to the fact that the brothers Gracchus had been assassinated because of their efforts at major reforms within the Roman Republic. Moreover, their violent deaths had brought on a major social crisis which climaxed with the overthrow of the patrician Republic and the instauration of the Empire of the Caesars. If, however, one were to mimic MacArthur and refer to ancient history by way of setting the abortive land reform work of Hardie in classical perspective, the analogue would have to be the defeat of a land reform proposal advanced by Scipio Aemilianus, kinsman and predecessor of the Gracchi, after the Third Punic War (149-146 B.C) Scipio's was not "a piece of narrow class legislation, directed primarily against the nobility or in support of the people" wrote historian Hugh Scullard; "it was *an attempt to restore the balance in the interest of the whole community* "[125]. Scipio was a friend of the historian Polybius and had learned from him the Aristotelian theory of the cycle of growth and decline of states [*politeion anacyclosis*], according to which the most stable polity was one in which a balance was preserved between oligarchy and democracy.

The analogy between this episode in Roman history and the defeat of Hardie's efforts in the Philippines becomes notable where Scullard observes:

> "But apparently he [Scipio Aemilianus] misjudged the selfishness of the *optimates* [patrician landowners] and rather than provoke a major crisis which would merely hasten the process of *anacyclosis*, he desisted. Thwarted in one way, Scipio may have acted in another, we cannot tell. But if he did take any action it was clearly not sufficient to meet the needs of the day and the position gradually deteriorated until Gracchus demanded reform and precipitated revolution."

Scipio had desisted from pushing for reform for fear of provoking social strife and actually precipitating the downfall of the republic, the preservation of which had been the object of his policy. Coming after him, the brothers Gracchus refused to desist and were assassinated. Their deaths, as Theodor Mommsen long ago observed[126], made it evident that only a Gracchus armed—or a "prophet" armed, to invoke the famous passage from Machiavelli's *The Prince* which inspired the titles to Isaac Deutscher's monumental biography of Trotsky[127]—could hope to break the hold of the patricians on the state. The armed struggle ended, just as Scipio Aemilianus had feared, not in the renovation of the Republic, but in the downfall of its representative institutions and the triumph of the despotism of the Caesars. Yet Scipio Aemilianus also had failed in his very moderation, one must reflect. Lacking either a creative vision or the political determination to insist on reform, he failed even as a conservative. In the aftermath of the Hardie Report, much the same might be said of U.S. policy in the Philippines.

As the more and more cynical and corrupt Ferdinand Marcos squandered the freedom and resources of the Philippine Republic in the 1970s, those responsible for United States policy in its former colony might well have reflected on Robert Hardie's warning of 1952:

> "Unless corrected, it is easy to conceive of the situation worsening to a point where the United States would be forced to

take direct, expensive and arbitrary steps to ensure against
loss of the Philippines to the Communist block in Asia and
would still be faced with finding a solution to the underlying
problem"[128].

In between the demise of the Hardie Report and the dictatorship of Ferdinand Marcos, the United States took direct, enormously expensive and arbitrary steps across the South China Sea from Manila, in a sustained attempt to ensure against loss of Vietnam to the Communist bloc in Asia. It stumbled, finally, to a sorry debacle in Vietnam, precisely because it could not find, or would not attempt, a solution to the underlying problems in that country. Both the forgotten warnings of Hardie and the disasters of the Vietnam War provide a sombre background against which to view the debates over land reform in the Philippines which took place in the 1970s. They did not inform those debates, but they give them their larger meaning.

PART TWO

A Charade And A Waste
Of Public Funds
1954–1987

Chapter Four

Memory Yields

"From the time of President Garcia, there has been what amounts to a stalemate between the landlords and their allies in Congress and in the executive departments and the elements favoring land reform. Apart from the peasants themselves, these elements consist of most of the press, perhaps most of the businessmen, a growing body of opinion which in the past few years has included technocrats inside and outside the government service and student groups. The most significant development during this later period has been the growth of disillusionment approaching the mutinous with the political system as it exists and functions today and with its capacity to achieve not only justice for the farm tenants but to move society in the direction that modernization requires."

— *Lewis E. Gleeck Jr. (1970).*

Robert Hardie's departure from the Philippines in August 1953 was followed by a major retrenchment in U.S. commitment to land reform in the Philippines. Distaste for sweeping measures that would involve major transfers of property ownership and the preference for programs of technical assistance with an emphasis on production rather than land reform can be observed to predominate within the U.S. Mission after the departure of Robert Hardie. These value orientations were especially evident in the positions taken by Raymond Johnson and James Emerson, the director and deputy director of the MSA/FOA Agriculture Division in Manila during 1954–55.[1] The political implications of such positions were clearly conservative. It was with reference to just such positions that New Deal and AID land reform veteran Laurence Hewes reflected, in 1965, on his return to the United States from India, that, for land reformers such as himself, there was no real future in the foreign aid program of the United States. Robert Hardie had reached a similar conclusion as early as the northern summer of 1953.

Robert Hardie's disillusionment by mid-1953 leaves little room for doubt that, in his judgement at least, the retrenchment on land reform occurred within the U.S. Mission some months before Ramon Magsaysay was elected President of the Philippines in November 1953, with massive covert U.S. support. This did not become immediately apparent, especially since Magsaysay stood for election on a platform of agrarian improvement [2]. There remained within the U.S. Mission until well into 1955 men whose commitment to land reform in the Philippines was genuine and serious. In March 1954, however, a report was prepared within the Mission which articulated the retrenchment from the land reform position staked out by Hardie. This report was not made public as the Hardie and McMillan/Rivera Reports had been, so that its implications only gradually became apparent. When Magsaysay presented the first of his agrarian bills, the Agricultural Tenancy Act, to the Philippine Congress in early 1954, it struck entrenched resistance in the landlord-dominated House of Representatives and much debate ensued over its provisions. A turning point was reached when it became known that the U.S. FOA Mission was content to see the bill emasculated.[3] Thereafter, the Magsaysay agrarian program as a whole lost whatever force it might have had and while various steps were taken to reorganize and perhaps strengthen rural affairs administration, no significant land reform was ever envisaged. What needs to be put in clearer perspective is the nature of and reasoning behind the American decision to retrench on land reform in this fundamental manner even after the American candidate had won office with something of a mandate for agrarian reform.

Early in January 1954, Joseph Dougherty, who had replaced Merrill Abbey as Agriculture Attache in late 1953, cabled the State Department that the Philippine Secretary of Agriculture, Salvador Araneta, had drafted a land reform bill and had asked Robert McMillan "to take the draft with him to the Mission, review it and make appropriate suggestions" to be considered by Araneta before the bill was submitted to the Philippine Congress[4]. Dougherty commented that the draft bill impressed him as "progressive and vigorous, practical and comprehensive" in its grasp of the land reform problem. Washington's response was to urge the setting up of a joint working group in the Mission to study the matter and draw up a position paper for the U.S. Embassy and the FOA.

It was suggested that the "special knowledge and experience [of Claud] Clayton, [Raymond E.] Davis and [John] Cooper should be useful."[5] Claud F. Clayton was the Mission's agricultural economist; Raymond Ewell Davis its land settlement adviser and John Cooper its rural credit and cooperatives adviser. There was, at that time, no land tenure adviser, as, following Hardie's departure in August 1953, more than a year elapsed before Dr. Joseph R. Motheral arrived to take his place, in September 1954. The joint working group, formed in late January 1954, consisted of Cooper, Davis and McMillan for FOA and Daniel M. Braddock and Herbert K. May from the Embassy. Of these, McMillan had shown already that he regarded land reform to be urgent and important. The outlook of the other four is rather difficult to judge on the basis of anything but the evidence of the report the group produced some seven weeks after its formation. Chairman of the group was land settlement adviser, Raymond Davis[6] and it could be that the emphasis on pioneer land settlement, rather than land reform within the group's report reflected his chairmanship and perhaps the anti-land reform views of Raymond Johnson and James Emerson behind him. Certainly, the report warrants close attention, as marking an almost complete abandonment of all the emphases and recommendations of the Hardie Report.

The working group submitted its report to Ambassador Spruance and FOA Mission director Colonel Harry A. Brenn on 19 March 1954, under the title *The Philippine Agricultural Land Tenure Study*, with a covering memorandum. This is the document that became "known" as the Cooper Report, but I shall henceforth refer to it as the *Davis Report*, in the belief that this is a more accurate description of its authorship. Unlike the Hardie and McMillan/Rivera Reports, this paper was never made public. Its departures from the positions advanced by those reports were, however, dramatic. The authors specifically rejected as unfeasible any nationwide land transfer program[7] and, in the covering memorandum, struck an astonishing note of discord with the whole tenor of the 1952 MSA Reports:

> "In preparing this report, the committee has substituted the words 'land tenure improvement' in place of 'land reform'. This change was made because it is believed that the former term states the problem in a positive manner and conveys more accurate description of the Philippine situation. Also, *some local officials have indicated that connotations associated with the word 'reform' make its use for land tenure purposes in the Philippines undesirable.*"[8]. [emphasis added]

In the body of the Davis Report one finds total abandonment of Hardie's recommendations regarding the rationale for and proposed scope of land reform in the Philippines and its priority over tenancy regulation or land settlement schemes.

There was no attempt made in the Davis Report to debate or confute Hardie's arguments; the Hardie Report was simply ignored and its recommendations replaced by altogether narrower and more conservative prescriptions. Yet, looking back on the episode thirty years later, John Cooper observed:

> "If they had financed and put through that program of Hardie's that they burned at the stake, the Philippines would be immeasurably further ahead today than it is. Instead they've been at it thirty years and they still haven't got it done"[9].

The concluding sentence here might better have been phrased: "Instead, they've avoided doing it for thirty years and have allowed every move in its direction to be thwarted by entrenched interests, so that, of course, it has never been done"[10]. And Cooper might have added that, after Hardie, U.S. land tenure advisors in the Philippines for thirty years held to a passive, if not a complicit, attitude towards Philippine travesties of land reform; beginning quite clearly and specifically with the Davis Report, of which he had been a co-author.

The Bell Report had noted that growing public sentiment in favor of land reform in the Philippines in 1950 might prove all too transient once the Huk Rebellion was beaten down. Robert Hardie had noted that the Huk Rebellion constituted "*a material shift in power*" between landlord and peasant forces as compared with pre-war years and was thus a useful, if dangerous, impetus to change. The Davis Report noted only that rural conditions were used by the Huks "*as an excuse for their dissident activities.*" [11]. Its authors went on to make the notable observation, utterly at odds with the Hardie Report, that:

> "...even under current tenancy practices, provinces with under 30% tenancy have virtually no unrest except as dissidents come in from adjacent communities and utilize undeveloped areas for their operations. In provinces with tenancy rates ranging from 30 to 50%, unrest is not a significant problem. In provinces with 50 to 60%, instances of unrest present a continuing problem, and provinces with over 60% of the farmers in a tenancy status have serious social unrest conditions requiring frequent military action."[12].

Displaying a confidence in the qualities and capacities of the Philippine government which analysts such as Ely, Abbey and Hardie had clearly not held, the authors of the Davis Report went on to assert:

"In brief, by vigorously enforcing an equitable landlord-tenant policy, pushing land settlement, purchasing cultivated lands in overcrowded high tenancy areas and carrying out certain supporting measures tenure difficulties can be reduced to a minimum. *Such accomplishments will meet the present social unrest challenge. They will not provide a permanent solution to all land tenure difficulties in the Philippines, but they will bring the situation under control. If this is done, there is every reason to believe that the government can cope with future needs in this field.*"[13] [emphasis added].

It is not hard to understand why impatient critics of U.S. policy in the Philippines, such as McCoy and Olson, writing in the early 1970s, found the Davis [Cooper] Report to be "cynical" and the above passages to be a calculus of counterinsurgency[14]. Nor is it necessary to share the somewhat indulgent and optimistic assessment by those authors of the achievements of communist revolutions in order to see the Davis Report as marking and defining a signal retreat from the nerve and imagination, the "rational revolution", embodied in the Hardie Report.

Retrenchment on land reform was formalized by Secretary of State John Foster Dulles, in cables to the Embassy dated 6 May and 21 May 1954. In the first of these, Dulles informed Spruance:

"State, Agriculture and FOA concur findings, recommendations FOA/ *Embassy memorandum on land tenure improvement.* Will support you and USOM in assisting Magsaysay in manner which you deem advisable re. achievement objectives of program."[15][emphasis added].

Given the unequivocal support for Hardie's recommendations from both State and Agriculture less than two years earlier, this endorsement of the Davis Report requires explanation. In the 21 May cable, Dulles spelled out what amounted, whether he knew it or not, to a point by point abandonment of the findings and recommendations of the Hardie Report. Whereas Hardie had found all existing Philippine land tenure law "weak in structure and limited in scope" and "rendered ineffective by legal tests for ambiguities, by judicial practices inspired by feudal culture, by lax enforcement"[16], Dulles advised that "the primary emphasis should be placed on uniform and forceful enforcement of *existing rice share tenancy legislation*"[17]. The explanation offered by McCoy and Olson in 1971 and 1974 was that the waning of the Huk rebellion relieved the reluctant American foreign policy-makers of the apparent need for sweeping land reform and enabled them to fall back on the "infinitely preferable"[18] conservative posture enunciated in the Davis[Cooper] Report. This is only part of the truth. Both McCoy and Olson wanted to include the Hardie Report in a continuous and seamless web of American counterinsurgency planning. It would seem to be more accurate to describe the Hardie Report as representing the liberal side of American thinking and the Davis Report the more conservative, with the two being not in a continuum but at odds. John Foster Dulles at State, like John Hollister at FOA, stood on the conservative side.

Given the process of analysis and inquiry that had occurred throughout 1951-52 concerning Philippine agrarian maladjustments and possible reforms to remove them, the position of Dulles in May 1954 must be described as a very conservative one. That position, moreover, far more than the recommendations of the Hardie Report, may be said to have defined the scope of FOA/ICA/AID approaches to land reform in the Philippines *from 1954 down to the present* . It was economically summarized in Dulles' 21 May cable to Manila:

> " ...implementation of recommendations ...will require political and administrative support heretofore largely lacking. Such support is also essential for enforcement of existing legislation, failing which there is not much point in fostering new legislation perhaps no more palatable to political leaders than that extant. *Existing reports, studies, surveys, findings and recommendations have had little useful effect due to lack of sustained will to action.* It is most essential now to make certain that there exists or is brought into being adequate political and administrative support effectively to enforce existing legislation. Therefore, *careful consideration should be given to what can be done now, in the light of all competing and conflicting political forces, to marshal support for such enforcement.* The use of limited resources, which tend to be dissipated if spread too thinly on too many fronts, can be more effective if concentrated on fewer programs. From experience elsewhere, it appears that *rent reduction, if properly enforced, can be a most effective phase of a larger land tenure improvement program.* After successful implementa-

tion of one or two major improvement programs such larger programs can be undertaken."[19] [emphasis added]

It simply is not possible to reconcile these observations with the findings and recommendations of the Hardie Report, but they parallel the recommendations of the Davis Report of March 1954 and, as we shall see, it was not until the 1970s that any U.S. land tenure specialists took issue with this approach to the land reform issue. Even then, they did so as dissenting voices within policy-making circles and had no more positive impact on official policy than had the Hardie Report a generation before them. The decisions of 1954 became, in effect, the plot point for a generation of FOA/ICA/AID involvement in "land reform" in the Philippines. That "plot point" may be described as setting what I shall refer to as the "Dullesian agenda": a policy of geopolitical and social conservatism, tempered by lip-service to the need for reforms.

The realization that the United States had pulled back from strong advocacy of land reform in the Philippines in 1954 was registered by Senator Emmanuel Pelaez, sponsor of the Agricultural Tenancy Act, in the Philippine Senate in August of that year. Referring to the Davis Report, which he apparently knew only by hearsay, Senator Pelaez observed:

> "It was stated in the only report of the FOA that it is not possible to legislate over night and change from one system to another. This new report of the FOA took into account the lack of facilities—the fact that these tenants have to be nurtured into self-confidence and that this cannot be done over night.Why did PHILCUSA change its stand? The PHILCUSA has been working hand in hand with FOA. FOA, the former MSA, you will remember, Mr. President, issued the famous Hardie Report and the McMillan Report and other similar reports and ...the originators of Senate Bill No. 98 were the experts of PHILCUSA, but the FOA issued another study ...and practically *reversed itself on many of the opinions stated in the Hardie Report.*"[20] [emphasis added]

"Reversed" is not too strong an expression to describe what the Davis Report did with the "opinions stated in the Hardie Report". Whereas Hardie had called for comprehensive legislation to set rural social relations on a new footing in order that the rural economy might develop vigorously, the Davis Report blurred the entire issue of reform of tenurial practices in stating:

"The Philippines is a new and undeveloped nation, especially
with respect to its agricultural resources. This means that
agricultural planning must *allow sufficient flexibility* to per-
mit the agricultural segment of the national economy to develop in the Philippines."[21] [emphasis added]

This "flexibility" consisted, in effect, of leaving the tenancy system
to work itself out in relation to the technical and commercial modernization of food and export agriculture and of taking what amounted to
a *laissez-faire* approach to the social character of land settlement in the
"undeveloped" areas of the country. Such a prescription could not have
been further removed from the recommendations of the Hardie Report.

Robert Hardie had urged a land reform "extended to include all crops
and geographical areas in the Philippines" and a retention ceiling of 4 to 8
hectares for owner-cultivators, zero for absentee landlords. The collapse
of the land reform initiative after Hardie's departure from the Philippines becomes evident in considering that when President Magsaysay
finally presented his Land Reform bill [Republic Act 1400] to the Philippine Congress, it called for the expropriation or government purchase
of private lands in excess of 144 hectares. By the time the bill had
passed Congress in September 1955, that retention ceiling had risen to
300 contiguous hectares of private ricelands, 1,024 hectares for private
lands devoted to other crops and 600 hectares for corporations [22]. Of
this "Land Reform Act", one Philippine historian has written:

"Other provisions of the law which served the cause of the
landlords rather than the tenants were: the estates could only
be expropriated on the petition of the majority of the tenants
(who, of course, could easily be coerced against making such a
petition) and the manner of compensation to landowners was
in cash and contingent on the capability of the Central Bank
to underwrite the land certificates. Judging from the P60
million total disbursement for the purpose during the first
five years of the expropriation program, those who shaped
the law into final form succeeded in incorporating into it
enough loopholes to guarantee its failure"[23].

Yet of the program of which this was the coping stone, Robert Hardie's
replacement, Dr. Joseph R. Motheral, felt able to remark, in May 1956:

"In his struggle to emerge from a feudalistic tradition and
centuries of colonial rule, the Philippine tenant is now offered

genuine economic alternatives for the first time. The land reform *(sic)* program fashioned for him is the *most complete and best integrated in the world today.* Despite the *striking accomplishments already recorded,* much of it is still on the drawing boards. To convert these plans into action will call for all the energies, talents and integrity that can be brought to bear in this young republic."[24] [emphasis added].

The contrast between Hardie's bitter disillusionment and the fatuous enthusiasm of Motheral for the U.S./Magsaysay agrarian program of 1956 should not be underestimated because of the superficial similarities in their language. Their arguments were, in fact, antithetical. What Hardie had proposed may have been foredoomed to encounter strenuous political opposition from entrenched interests. What Motheral endorsed was a hollow, propagandistic sham, foredoomed to futility.

The Land Reform Act of 1955 was foredoomed to futility for reasons other than the absurdly high retention ceilings that it set[25]. Before it even came before the Congress, President Magsaysay had failed to secure a realistic land assessment scheme or a hike in the land tax sufficient to finance the requirements of any sort of serious land reform law and to shift the basis of land ownership from criteria of social prestige, speculation and parasitic rentier "feudalism" to one of sound investment. The failure of land taxation reform was reflected in the fate of a report on land ownership and real property values prepared for the Philippine Department of Finance in 1954-55 by one Arturo Sorongon, under ICA auspices. Entitled *A Special Study of Landed Estates in the Philippines,* this report was based on a survey conducted between 18 January and 30 April 1954, covering every province except Sorsogon and every chartered city except Tagaytay, which was intended to tabulate, for taxation purposes, reliable evidence of the extent of land ownership concentration in the country[26]. The author, in his preface, acknowledged the assistance and advice of a number of ICA's technical staff in Manila: Dr Orville McDiarmid and Warren Wiggins (successive assistant directors for Economic Policy), Melville Monk (chief of the Finance and Trade Policy staff), Albert Noonan (Local Government Tax Advisor) and Dr. Joseph R. Motheral (Land Tenure Advisor).

Sorongon concluded that the data collected and presented in the large statistical annex to his report indicated the scope for a major taxation reform. He reported that, of a land area of 29,741,290 hectares in the Philippines, some 19% was classified as farm land in the *1948 Census of Agriculture*: a total of 5,726,584 hectares. Of this area, he related, some

42%, or 2,407,939 hectares were owned in holdings of 50 hectares or above
and that these lands were owned by no more than 0.36% of rural families
in the Philippines [27]. Like the Hardie Report before it, however, this
report, which may be referred to as the Sorongon Report, was put aside
and for all practical purposes consigned to oblivion. None of Sorongon's,
Hardie's or McMillan's data or arguments were included in any of the
ICA's "land reform progress" reports in the Philippines between 1955
and 1960. No effort seems to have been made to use them as a benchmark
for monitoring the rural scene in the Philippines. The Hardie Report,
the McMillan/Rivera Report and the Sorongon Report became dead
texts by no later than 1957 and only scattered copies survived, gathering
dust in various archives and libraries, while tenancy and landlessness,
rural poverty and exploitative use of the agricultural resources of the
Philippines worsened in the 1960s and 1970s. Following Magsaysay's
death in a plane crash in March 1957, even his attenuated rural program
bogged down completely under his successor, President Garcia [1957-61],
paralleling the bogging down of President Diem's rural program in South
Vietnam in the same years.

A far more accurate summation of the "achievements" of the Magsaysay program and the aspirations for it of the FOA/ICA Mission than that
offered by Dr. Joseph Motheral was that delivered by deputy director
of the Agriculture Division, James P. Emerson, in his 1956 end of tour
report:

> "Drastic and sudden changes in ownership at huge cost to the
> public treasury, with attendant economic and social chaos
> have been avoided to date" [28].

Perhaps, when he described the Magsaysay program as "the most complete and best integrated in the world", Motheral had meant simply that
it had avoided the sort of perils that Emerson associated with sweeping
land reform. Certainly, Emerson put the case more clearly. Clearer still
and articulating a dissenting opinion from the position of Emerson—to
say nothing of Motheral—was the judgement of Robert McMillan, the
FOA Mission's sociologist and co-author of the 1952 McMillan/Rivera
Report, which had stated:

> "In the Philippines, economic and political power is concen-
> trated in the hands of a relatively small minority. Most of the
> responsibility for existing conditions and most of the moral
> obligation for initiating amelioration programs to improve

TABLE 8: TRENDS IN PHILIPPINE RICE PRODUCTION

YEAR	PRODUCTION	AREA (000 ha)	YIELD kg/ha	NPK/ha kg	%area MV	%area irrigated
1961-62	3,861	3,185	1,212	7.18	0	31
1965-66	4,053	3,153	1,293	7.15	1	35
1981-82	7,859	3,381	2,326	39.18	81	80

Source: Eduardo C. Tadem *Grains and Radicalism: the Political Economy of the Rice Industry in the Philippines 1965-1985.* Third World Studies Center. UP Diliman. September 1986 p.19.

TABLE 9: BREAKDOWN OF PHILIPPINE ARABLE LAND OWNERSHIP IN PROPERTIES 50 HECTARES AND ABOVE

According to A.P. Sorongon: *A Special Study of Landed Estates in the Philippines. Analysis and Findings. Manila 1955.*

Area category (Hectares)	Number of Owners	% Rural Families	Area Owned	%Total Farm Area
50-200	11,770	0.29	1,142,196	20.0
201-800	1,445	0.04	435,257	7.6
801-1000	423	0.02	286,885	4.9
1,000 and over	221	0.01	515,466	9.0
Totals	13,859	0.36	2,379,804	41.5

TABLE 10: LAND OWNERSHIP IN THE PHILIPPINES ACCORDING TO THE 1948 CENSUS OF AGRICULTURE

Type/Area	% Population Owning Land
A. Agricultural Land	
100 ha and above	0.18
20-99 ha	1.68
15-19 ha	6.00
below 5 ha	26.00
none	65.00
B. Non-Agricultural Land (including mineral land, forest, swamp)	
With	3.0
Without	97.0

the welfare of the generally inarticulate majority rests largely
with this group. Should this responsibility and obligation be
met with indifference, neglect or opposition, the possibilities
are remote for achieving social and economic changes through
peaceful means"[29].

That McMillan may have been a dissenting voice in the preparation of
the Davis Report is suggested by his critical response to the passage of an
emasculated Philippine Agricultural Tenancy Act, in a paper delivered
in Urbana, Illinois, in September 1954, at the annual general meeting of
the American Rural Sociological Society.

In contrast with the prescriptions of the Davis Report and in clear
contradiction of the [later] statements by Emerson and Motheral as to
the state of affairs in the Philippines and how satisfactory it was, McMillan reaffirmed the urgency of land reform in the Philippines to modernize
relations of production, market structures and farming methods, in order to improve the country's prospects for coping with problems arising
from rapid population growth in the deeply impoverished rural sector.
He concluded, as he had two years earlier, that since most political and
administrative leaders in the Philippines were either landlords, akin to
landlords, or ideologically and socially tied to landlords, *"it is apparent that they will continue to assist landlords in maintaining the status
quo."*[30] The suppression of the Huk rebellion by the Philippine armed
forces "with American aid" had served, he said, to decrease the felt need
on the part of many landlords "for changes in the tenure system". He
then told his fellow American rural sociologists:

> "It appears inevitable that land reforms will be achieved
> sooner or later in the Philippines, either through evolution
> or revolution. The short-sighted landlords and large-scale
> farmers can retain their present stranglehold on Philippine
> agriculture only so long as the armed forces of the Republic can suppress dissidents effectively. On the other hand,
> unfair rental agreements, usury, widespread unemployment,
> rapid growth of population, relative lack of self-government
> among other factors provide fertile soil for sowing seeds of
> revolution."[31]

In the political climate of 1954 in the United States, this was a stand
notable for its candor and its challenge to conservatism. What has to be
emphasised, of course, is that McMillan, in stating these opinions, was a

more and more isolated voice in FOA/ICA circles, as far as land reform in the Philippines was concerned. The candid and vigorous language, in which he cast his opinions on the subject at the conservatives, contrasts sharply with the language of Emerson and Motheral and all but a very few American voices, on the margins of official policy, for the following twenty years and more, as we shall see in some detail in the balance of this study. The language of Emerson and Motheral and their many colleagues over the years may be dubbed the *language of inertia*. Its futilities and circularities came to constitute the ingrained character of American policy discourse on land reform in the Philippines.

Adoption of the Dullesian agenda from 1954 limited American involvement in "land reform" programs in the Philippines to technical tinkering and cosmetic measures. Nothing fundamental was seriously attempted. It is not surprising that, in consequence, the biting MSA reports of 1952 lapsed not only from policy relevance but also from institutional memory. Nevertheless, the extent to which this occurred, under circumstances in which the problems addressed by these reports not only were not solved but worsened appreciably, is surely an important aspect of policy history over the years after 1954—its shadow, as it were, or to use the phrase Daniel Ellsberg coined to describe *The Pentagon Papers*, its "hidden history". Mnemonically selective reference to the Hardie Report is already notable in the omission of all mention of it from the Davis Report and in the brief and false statement by James Emerson, in his 1956 end of tour report, that release of the Hardie Report to the press in December 1952 had been "unauthorized"[32], whereas it is clear that Ambassador Spruance had ordered its release. Frate Bull, in his end of tour report as land tenure adviser (successor to Motheral) in 1958, glossed over the whole matter, again with nary a mention of the Hardie Report or its substance, while casually admitting that no land reform properly so-called had occurred in the Philippines to that time [33].

Perhaps there is no more remarkable testimony to the institutional amnesia that relegated the Hardie Report to the "memory hole" than the flattened and misleading account of U.S. policy on land reform in the Philippines in the 1950s given by noted American foreign aid historian John D. Montgomery, in an essay entitled "United States International Advocacy of Land Reform" which appeared in a book he edited under the title *International Dimensions Of Land Reform*, published in 1984:

> "American efforts to introduce land reform to the Philippines
> brought the problem to the attention of Ramon Magsaysay,

TABLE 11: TENANCY AND CONCENTRATION OF RURAL LAND OWNERSHIP
IN THE PHILIPPINES CIRCA 1960

Province	Total Families	%Families Landless	%Tenancy (1960 census)	No. 50+ ha	%Total families	Harvest area to foregoing
Bataan	17,972	89.3	54.4	34	0.18	25.0
Batangas	100,043	70.6	55.2	334	0.33	47.0
Bohol	101,112	42.8	20.6	800	0.29	21.8
Bulacan	74,138	84.4	69.1	152	0.21	20.8
Capiz	81,290	62.8	67.3	607	0.74	71.0
Caute	80,942	79.5	55.8	205	0.40	27.3
Cebu	213,156	89.0	47.8	229	0.11	8.5
Iloilo	44,238	72.5	88.8	844	0.58	43.8
Laguna	64,957	69.8	54.5	100	0.15	16.5
Leyte	185,853	89.0	44.1	293	0.16	17.0
Negros Occ.	172,173	91.5	61.5	1,041	0.66	71.8
Nueva Ecija	84,201	80.3	76.2	645	0.77	58.9
Pampanga	70,788	94.8	85.2	553	0.78	72.5
Pangasinan	173,943	60.8	50.2	334	0.19	17.9
Rizal	120,767	88.0	50.6	111	0.09	-
Tarlac	60,511	80.5	62.2	412	0.68	60.5
Zambales	24,490	16.8	53.2	103	0.42	53.7

Source: Dante C. Simbulan *A Study of the Socio-Economic Elite in Philippine Politics and Government 1946-1965.* PhD 1965 p.88

TABLE 12: HECTARES PURCHASED BY THE GOVERNMENT FOR LAND
TRANSFER 1933–70

Period	Hectares Purchased for Transfer
1933–55	4,643
1955–63	19,155
1963–70	3,857

Source: Joel E. Rocamora/Corazon C. Pangniban *Rural Development Strategies: The Philippine Case.* Final Report I.P.C. Quezon City. 1975

who used rural development as a major issue in his successful 1953 Presidential campaign. The Philippine government
did pass a land reform bill after the United States had indicated its intention to offer aid for this purpose. *Later,
the United States sent Robert S. Hardie, a veteran of the
Japanese reform, to help implement the Philippine venture.
But Magsaysay's untimely death reduced American influence*
and Philippine interest in land reform and further action was
delayed for about two decades."[34] [emphasis added]

Montgomery implies here that Hardie arrived in the Philippines in 1955,
after the passage of Magsaysay's agrarian legislation, "to help implement the Philippine venture". The termination of his work is attributed
to Magsaysay's "untimely death" and consequent reduction of American influence in the Philippines. No suggestion enters the picture that
a serious debate occurred within American circles over the land reform
issue, or that there were Americans who were by no means enthusiastic
about serious land reform. Given that Montgomery's essay was a reflection on the *advocacy of land reform* in the international arena by the
United States, one can only find its muddled chronology and conceptual
opacity on the subject of the Hardie Report and its fate disconcerting.
Yet it is not simply one historian's error. It forms part of a peculiar
pattern of institutional amnesia, in which the Hardie Report and its significance were, for all practical purposes, suppressed from the collective
memory of Americans responsible for monitoring Philippine rural affairs
and "internal security".

Quite as notable as Montgomery's failure to recall the nature, tim-
ing and frustration of Hardie's work in the Philippines, was the failure of
men who had worked in or on the Philippines at the same time as Hardie
to recall these things at all, when questioned about them in 1986-87.
John Melby, Philippines Desk Officer at the State Department in 1951-
52, wrote to the author: "I know nothing about the Hardie Report"[35].
Edward Lansdale, leading CIA officer in the Philippines, with Charles
Bohannan, between 1950 and 1954, wrote: "The name 'Hardie' does not
ring a bell at all. Are you sure you have it right?"[36]. The "institutional amnesia" at work here becomes significant for the policy process,
of course, only where it can be found to affect those with a direct role in
more recent land reform work in the Philippines. It is, therefore, of particular significance, perhaps, that Michael Korin, who was AID's land
reform "facilitator" and then chief land reform adviser in the Philippines at the height of the land reform program under President Marcos,

from October 1973 until October 1977, was entirely unaware, as late as December 1987, of the very existence, to say nothing of the substance or history, of the Hardie and McMillan/Rivera Reports[37]. Informed of their character, he expressed interest and spoke of obtaining a copy of the Hardie Report on his return to Washington from what was a field trip to Manila for AID. Yet three copies of the Hardie Report, including the original Mission draft, sat in an obscure file, forgotten and untouched, in the AID's own Communications and Media Division Resource Library, in the Magsaysay Centre, in Manila.

Michael Korin had worked in Vietnam on the land reform of the early 1970s and had arrived in the Philippines to work on land reform from this Vietnam background[38]. Nevertheless, he did not discover and no-one was able, or found reason, to inform him of the existence and fate of the 1952 MSA reports in the Philippines. What, in any case, might he have learned from them? They were not written in the language of the Dullesian agenda which governed AID discourse on land reform in the Philippines in the 1970s, as it had since 1954, and it seems quite probable that their "relevance" in 1973 would have appeared minimal. All they could offer was a sense of historical shock and dislocation of policy perspectives. Coming from Vietnam in 1973, one might have thought, Korin would have felt the need to seek out some such critical perspective on the land reform debate in the Philippines. It was there, in the Magsaysay Center, on file, between covers, in hundreds of pages of data and argument, but it did not come to Korin's attention. It seems a nice irony that this undiscoverable and muted piece of AID's own institutional history should have been filed out of the way precisely in the Communications and Media Division Resource Library that AID itself kept in Manila in the 1970s.

Chapter Five

Propaganda, Polemic And
Statistics : 1972–1984

*"It seems important that the Congress address [the] incon-
sistency between its mandate to A.I.D. and broader foreign
policy considerations. This inconsistency is particularly relevant to the question of what A.I.D. should do about future
support of the agrarian reform program in the Philippines.
In the past, the U.S. Embassy in Manila has discouraged the
A.I.D. mission from 'getting out in front of the Filipinos'
on land reform. It seems clear that the only interest of the
present Philippine government in land reform is to retain
sufficient illusion of progress to continue its propaganda. If
actual progress is to be resumed, the impetus must come from
a new source, perhaps from foreign aid tied to tough performance standards. If such a fundamental and visible reform as
land transfer is totally dropped from A.I.D. support, it could
well appear that the dominant characteristic of U.S. policy
toward the Philippines is embodied in the status quo and in
the military bases for which we are now negotiating a new
rental agreement."*

— Gerald C. Hickey (1977)

Data on Philippine rural conditions derived from the 1960 and 1971
Censuses of Agriculture and other sources indicate plainly that, in the
years after the passage of President Magsaysay's Agricultural Tenancy
Act in 1954 and Land Reform Act in 1955, down to 1970, rural income

distribution became more inequitable [see Table 13], landlessness and tenancy increased and the average size of small farm holdings decreased, while a disproportionate percentage of agricultural land remained in very few hands. Peasant organization remained weak and ineffective during most of this period, after the effort at radical rebellion made by the Huks from 1946 through til 1957 had been ground down. The remnants of the Communist Party of the Philippines (CPP) and the Huks (HMB), under the leadership of Jesus Lava and Casto Alejandrino after the surrender of Luis Taruc [16 May 1954], decided to attempt a peaceful and parliamentary struggle for socio-economic reform. The Garcia administration, however, outlawed both the CPP and HMB and "other similar organizations" under Republic Act 1700 [June 20 1957] and in the years that followed the CPP was hounded, with Alejandrino being arrested in 1960 and Jesus Lava in May 1964[40]. The threat of radical revolution had, it seemed, been averted without significant social or economic reforms.

Passage of the Agricultural Land Reform Code [Republic Act 3844] in 1963, under President Macapagal, although it came with a rhetorical flourish about completing Magsaysay's "unfinished revolution" and declared tenancy to be "contrary to public policy"[41], made no significant advance on the Land Reform Act of 1955 as far as effectiveness was concerned. Macapagal's code set a nominal retention ceiling of 75 hectares, as compared with the Magsaysay bill's 300, but the legal and practical realities were such that almost no land changed hands. Even had enforcement been rigorous, of course, a retention ceiling of 75 contiguous hectares would have left most tenants completely outside the scope of the program. As Dante Simbulan observed in a major study of Philippine socio-economic elites, completed in 1965, the objective effect of all this conservative agrarian legislation was the proliferation throughout the archipelago in the 1960s of all those pernicious institutional practices which had triggered the Huk rebellion in the 1940s.[42] Plantation agriculture and export crop production flourished, but social ills associated with maldistribution of the fruits of agricultural production deepened and the ground was thus prepared for a recrudescence of radical rebellion, exactly as Hardie and McMillan had predicted in 1952 and 1954[43].

Ferdinand Marcos's election as President in 1965, with promises of no more shortages or importation of rice, reduction of graft and corruption to a minimum, punishment of those who had enriched themselves in office, no persecution of political enemies and faster land reform was not followed by delivery on these promises, any more than the election of Diosdado Macapagal in 1961 on a very similar set of campaign promises

TABLE 13: RURAL INCOME DISTRIBUTION IN THE PHILIPPINES
1956–1971

% Total Rural Income Accruing to	1956	1961	1965	1971
Lowest 20%	7.0	5.9	5.0	4.4
Second 20%	11.1	11.8	9.5	8.9
Third 20%	14.7	13.7	15.3	13.9
Fourth 20%	21.1	21.9	23.0	21.8
Top 20%	46.1	46.9	47.2	51.0
Top 10%	30.1	31.1	30.0	34.4

Source: Gustav Ranis *Sharing in Development: A Program of Employment, Equity and Growth for the Philippines.* I.L.O. 1974 p.10. Figures derived by Ranis from Bureau of Census, Family Income and Expenditure surveys 1956, 1961, 1965, 1971. Table also appears in J. E. Rocamora/C. C. Panganiban *Rural Development Strategies: The Philippine Case.* I.P.C. Quezon City 1975. p.140 and Rene E. Ofreneo *Capitalism in Philippine Agriculture.* Foundation for Nationalist Studies. Quezon City. 1980. p.51.

TABLE 14: AREA HARVESTED IN MAIN CROPS 1961 AND 1971
IN '000 HECTARES

CROP	1961	1971
Palay	3,198	3,113
Maize	2,046	2,892
Sugarcane	232	442
Coconuts	1,200	2,048

had been. While technical programs under the rubric of the "Green Revolution" did result in significant increases of rice production, the access of the mass of rural Filipinos to either productive resources or income did not show a corresponding improvement[44]. As far as land reform was concerned, Marcos so failed to advance on the failures of the Macapagal administration that by 1968 the AID mission in Manila, then headed by Wesley Haraldson, had withdrawn altogether from the program, on the grounds that it was an empty political gimmick without substance or credibility[45]. The extent of frustration with established institutions throughout the country as a whole in the first Marcos administration was not such as to conduce to mass rebellion, but it had begun to reach critical proportions among potential leaders of such a rebellion.

Francisco Sionil Jose, radical novelist and editor of the liberal journal of ideas *Solidarity* perhaps summed up the spreading mood of frustration in a forceful, quixotic open letter to U.S. President-elect Richard Nixon in November 1968:

> "The revolution will come because the twelfth hour is long passed and the compulsions toward change—violent though it may be—can no longer be reversed. Why will it come? Why will no-one be able to stop it? It will come because the oligarchy which controls the political and economic destiny of this country has been grossly irresponsible and has completely cut itself off from the aspirations of the many who are poor. It will come because the pressures from the poor can no longer be accomodated by our fledgling institutions of freedom. It is now time that we must think seriously of supporting a mass revolutionary party built upon class lines, so that the enemies of Philippine nationalism, the oligarchy and its allies, may be banished once and for all ...Is the U.S. interested in developing democratic institutions here? Individual Americans are, but between individual Americans and the sugar lobby and other pressure groups in New York and Washington, the intentions are subjugated by cold business logic. We are actually of some value only to Americans with sugar, mining and some manufacturing interests. And, of course, of great value to those American business groups whose alliances with the Filipino oligarchy go deep and wide. Other than these, Americans just don't care. *You should scrap military aid and devote all assistance to our land reform program*, towards ... making it possible for all tillers of

the soil to own the land they till . . ."[46] [emphasis added]

It was still quite possible to argue in 1968 that "revolution" was not in prospect in the Philippines. Besides, as the Vietnam experience had shown by then, even were a mass rebellion to occur in the Philippines and threaten the state with "revolution", there was no reason to believe that this would induce the United States to press for a dramatic land reform. There had been excellent opportunities to do so in the Philippines under conditions of relative political stability in 1954 and 1963, but the United States had shown no energetic interest in taking such opportunities. Even as, in the course of 1968, the Stanford Research Institute report on rural Vietnam and the agitation of Roy Prosterman and his colleagues began to bring genuine land reform onto Washington's agenda for South Vietnam, amid a full-scale war that was costing the United States three billion dollars per month, land reform had been abandoned in the Philippines as an active concern of the United States. It was in December of that very year that a small group of radical Marxists, having been expelled from the old Communist Party of the Philippines [CPP] for denunciations of the CPP leaders, formed a new party of armed revolution—the Communist Party of the Philippines (Marxist-Leninist) [CPP-ML]—with the idea of making just the revolution of which Sionil Jose had written. The re-election of Ferdinand Marcos as President in 1969, after the expenditure of a staggering fifty million dollars in his campaign[47], began a process of political symbiosis, in which the corruption and maladministration of the Marcos regime fed the efforts of the CPP-ML to organize a movement of armed rural insurrection on Maoist lines.

It was in 1970 that AID again entered the land reform arena in the Philippines. Early in 1970, at the very time when President Thieu, under the influence of the ideas of Roy Prosterman, pushed the land to the tiller bill through the South Vietnamese legislature, interest in the land reform problem in the Philippines seems to have been revitalized, perhaps not altogether by coincidence. In May 1970 AID held a conference devoted specifically to land reform, in its annual spring review conference series. A great many papers were presented at this conference, including numerous country studies and a number of studies of the economic and political aspects of land reform at a comparative and theoretical level[48]. The country paper on the Philippines was authored by Harold Koone, of the AID Mission in the Philippines and Lewis Gleeck of the U.S. Embassy staff[49]. Coincident with the preparation of this study, a review of Philippine land reform was conducted by AID, the Philippine

TABLE 15: BASIC GRAINS TENANCY (1972-75)

Land Use Category (Hectares)	Tenanted Area Hectares	%	Tenant Farmers Number	%	Landowners Number	%
100 & above	410,366	30.55	164,154	15.22	1,524	0.69
50.00 to 99.99	139,030	10.35	69,515	6.44	2,064	0.93
24.00 to 49.99	134,248	10.00	89,499	8.29	4,118	1.86
12.01 to 23.99	189,722	14.12	189,722	17.59	12,022	5.44
7.01 to 12.00	53,804	11.45	170,893	15.84	18,075	8.18
7.00 & below	316,027	23.53	395,034	36.62	182,238	82.90
TOTALS	1,343,217	100.00	1,078,817	100.00	221,041	100.00

Source: J. E. Rocamora/C. C. Panganiban *Rural Development Strategies: The Philippine Case.* I.P.C. 1975. p.151.

National Economic Council [NEC], the National Land Reform Council [NLRC], and the National Food and Agriculture Council [NFAC]. The NLRC was a body that had been formed under the provisions of the 1963 Land Reform Code to co-ordinate the work of the various bureaucracies responsible for rural affairs: the Land Authority, the Agricultural Productivity Commission, the Agricultural Credit Administration, the Land Bank and the Office of Agrarian Counsel.

The conclusion of the review was, not surprisingly, that the national land reform program had achieved very little since 1963. Indeed, it was found that fewer than 3% of the nation's grain growing tenants had even moved from share to leasehold tenancy under the program in those seven years, while a negligible number had become amortizing owners[50]. Given the retention ceiling and the loose framing of the code, of course, this should not have occasioned any surprise. It is instructive to note, however, that these were not the factors that the inquiry found to be the causes of the program's failure. Instead, the problems cited appear to have been simply technical problems of the logistics of implementation:

> "lack of transportation, communication and office equipment, an inefficient administrative structure and insufficient travel and administrative funds."[51].

The initiative coming from this review was one completely consistent with the Dullesian agenda of the late 1950s:

> "It was decided that a one province pilot effort should be undertaken, designed to overcome the problems identified *(sic)* The project would be given broad support and would be charged with determining if and how the national land reform and agricultural production programs could be greatly accelerated."[52]

The one province pilot project so designated was the Nueva Ecija Land Reform Integrated Development Program [NELRIDP], a joint project on the part of the NLRC, NFAC and Nueva Ecija provincial government, with financial and technical assistance from AID and the NEC.

In the perspective of the large claims made in 1956 for the Magsaysay land reform program and in 1963 for the Macapagal land reform program, to say nothing of the more serious proposals of Hardie and McMillan in 1952, the NELRIDP represented an extremely modest approach to the land reform issue in the Philippines. Moreover, it was launched in a province which had already, by 1970, been the scene of almost the only significant share-hold to leasehold transformation of tenancy practices in the country[53]. If one could assume that it marked a beginning, a sort of scientific experiment in the efficient administration of rapid land reform, the NELRIDP pilot project might merit defence on its own terms. However, what it marked, surely, was an uncritical acceptance of the crippling limitations of the existing legislation. This is what was "Dullesian" about it. It was to be followed, in September 1971, by the passage through the Philippine Congress of the revised Code of Agrarian Reform, Republic Act 6389, which, to be sure, once more proclaimed the imminent end of tenancy and exploitation and which was itself to be followed, within a year, by the even more grandiloquent Presidential Decrees 2 and 27, under martial law, declaring sweeping land reform. The NELRIDP itself, however, did not constitute a major initiative. Indeed, in a memorandum to AID/Manila Director Thomas Niblock, dated 2-3 August 1971, marked "For Mission Use Only" and headed "One Year After: Land Reform in Nueva Ecijia", Lewis Gleeck wrote that the NELRIDP was "not taken seriously by Filipinos" who assumed it to be "a ritualistic display"[54]. Nor, as we shall see, did the nominally sweeping Marcos initiatives call forth very much more commitment to vigorous land reform in the Philippines on the part of the United States official Mission than the NELRIDP signified.

Ferdinand Marcos was, in many respects, the nemesis of the political system and style of leadership that had been pioneered by Manuel Quezon in the 1930s. The system had always been riddled with corruption and demagoguery, its democratic characteristics flawed by elite control of the only effective party machines and patronage networks. Marcos, a brilliant and ambiguous figure, rose through the system from the time of his entry into Congress in 1949 as a thirty two year old protege of President Quirino, becoming a shrewd and tough practitioner of its unspoken rules. His relentless ambition was noted before he was first elected President[55]. His use of that office to gain control of enough power and patronage to entrench himself was the distinguishing feature of his rule from 1965 through to the declaration of martial law in September 1972. His espousal of land reform in 1971-72 must be interpreted in terms of his determination to outbid and outmanoeuver all possible rivals for political primacy and not in terms of a sober and responsible philosophy of statemanship. Nevertheless, once he had embarked on a course of making himself a sort of *princeps* and breaking the grip of the old elite on the legislature, political machines and patronage, there was no reason to assume that he would not try to press through some sort of major land reform, as a means to his own ends. He was, for much of his rule, a rather subtle and canny *tyrannos,* but he was surrounded by clients, advisors and henchmen who had no desire to press through with land reform and in the end the sheer corruption of his regime ruined whatever developmental plans his more responsible advisors had been seeking to implement under the shield of authoritarian rule. It is against such considerations as these that one must weigh the land reform rhetoric of 1972 and the discourse among official or semi-official American personnel about land reform in the Philippines in the mid-1970s.

The declaration of martial law by President Marcos, on 22 September 1972, in so far as one can re-establish the intentions and planning behind it, was not a grave measure of state security, but a carefully prepared coup d'etat, to perpetuate the Marcos regime[56]. It was accompanied by a fanfare of propaganda about the "New Society" that would be ushered in, over the opposition of the corrupt old elite and the totalitarian revolutionaries, under the firm, constitutional rule of the self-proclaimed guardian of the commonwealth. On 26 September 1972, four days after the declaration of martial law, President Marcos issued Presidential Decree No. 2 (PD 2), which stressed the "pressing need to accelerate" land reform and "to achieve a dignified existence for the small farmers free from pernicious institutional restraints and practices which have not only retarded the agricultural development of the country, but have also produced widespread discontent and unrest." To this end, PD 2 announced *"the whole country is declared a land reform area"*[57]. Just under a month later, on 21 October 1972, President Marcos issued PD 27, the Emancipation of the Tenants' Decree, the preamble to which announced:

> "Inasmuch as the old concept of landownership by a few has spawned valid and legitimate grievances that gave rise to violent conflict and social tension, the redress of such grievances being one of the fundamental objectives of the New Society, I, Ferdinand E. Marcos, ... do hereby decree and order the emancipation of all tenant farmers as of this October 21 1972. This shall apply to tenant farmers of private agricultural lands primarily devoted to rice and corn under a system of share crop or lease tenancy, whether classified as landed estate or not...In all cases, the landowner may retain an area of not more than seven (7) hectares if such landowner is cultivating such area, or will now cultivate it"[58].

Compared with existing legislation, the retention ceiling had come down markedly. It remained to be seen whether the scope of the program meant what Marcos claimed for it and whether he would be willing or able to take measures for the implementation of his decree which previous administrations had eschewed.

In endeavouring to assess the ostensible scope of the New Society land reform program, one is confronted by severe anomalies in the available data. These anomalies are to some extent resolved by recent studies, drawing on the 1971 and 1980 Censuses of Agriculture, which were not released in full until 1986[59]. There appear to be particular difficulties with data on the extent of tenancy of various types throughout the Philippines for the period from 1960 down to the fall of Marcos. According to Dante Simbulan, writing in 1965, by 1961 50% of Philippine farm operators were tenants[60]. This represented a major increase in tenancy since the time of the Hardie Report and showed that, as Hardie had warned, the institution of tenancy, having reached extremely high levels in Central Luzon by the 1940s, was now proliferating throughout the country unchecked by the ineffectual legislation of the Magsaysay years. Joel Rocamora, writing in 1974, put the figure for tenancy nationwide in 1960 at 46%, which is significantly lower than Simbulan's figure, but within range of it, especially since his lower figure is dated earlier, not later, than Simbulan's. According to the *1960 Census of Agriculture* , however, tenants *of all types* in 1960 numbered 864,538, which the Philippine government's National Economic Development Authority (NEDA) calculated as having represented some 39% of farm operators[61]. Joel Rocamora estimated that by 1971 the tenancy rate must have climbed to 60% and he calculated that, given the expansion of land under cultivation and population growth, this would have given a total for 1971 of some 4,000,000 tenants[62]. Yet NEDA's *1984 Statistical Yearbook*, drawing on the then unpublished *1971 Census of Agriculture*, not only did not indicate any such increase in the level of tenancy or the numbers of tenants, it showed *a dramatic and completely unexplained decrease in both, between 1960 and 1971, to less than 29% of farm operators, or a total of 681,658* tenants of all types.[63]

Rocamora's total number of tenants seems excessive, since, if we take the total Philippine population in 1971 of approximately forty million and allow that 50% of the workforce were engaged in agriculture, then calculate for an average family size of five, it would appear that half the population were tenants or dependants of tenants, which would leave landless and landowning rural populations unaccounted for, even though

it is widely agreed that the number of landless laborers was already substantial by then—and was to increase dramatically in the mart-ial law
years. Fairly clearly, therefore, Rocamora's figure of 4,000, 000 tenants
must be revised downwards, probably by more than half. The NEDA
figures, based on official census data, conversely, are astounding. What
they would suggest is so substantial an increase in the number and percentage of fully-owned farm operations and a decrease in the number
and percentage of tenant-run farm operations during the 1960s, that one
ought to have judged land reform completely unnecessary, in 1971–72,
on the grounds that somehow it was happening spontaneously. It certainly was not happening under the government's land reform program.
Indeed, if NEDA's figures are to be believed, tenancy in the Philippines
was lower in 1971 (i.e. *before* the promulgation of President Marcos's
PD 2 and PD 27) *than at any time since about 1928.*

If these astonishing figures are credited, a computational difficulty
then arises regarding NEDA's own data on the scope and accomplishments of the land reform program of President Marcos's "New Society"
as initiated by PDs 2 and 27 in 1972. NEDA's *1984 Statistical Yearbook*
indicated that a total of of 922,935 tenants benefited from either land
transfer or shift to leasehold under the New Society program between
1972 and 1983. This suggests either that tenancy first increased sharply
after 1971 (by 35%, or from 681,658 to 922,935 tenants) before being,
on the face of it, completely abolished; or that the figure of 922,935
beneficiaries of the New Society program is inflated by a massive overlap between land transfer and leasehold contract beneficiaries, though
no such overlap is indicated in the *1984 Statistical Yearbook*[64]. This
would still leave tenants on non-rice/corn lands unaccounted for, since
they were excluded from the scope of the New Society program from
its inception and numbered several hundred thousand, whereas NEDA's
baseline figure of 681,658 tenants in 1971 was specifically designated as
including tenants of all types. In short, something is pretty clearly awry
with the NEDA data. Even the crudest estimate must *at least double*
NEDA's figure for tenancy as of 1971 and there is good reason to consider
its claims for the achievements of the New Society program enormously
inflated.

Tables 16 and 17 show two independent efforts, by critics of the
New Society land reform, to establish the statistical parameters of the
program. The discrepancies between them may be explained largely
by observing that Kerkvliet accepted quite conservative official data,
which Rocamora and Panganiban had used in 1975, while Rocamora

TABLE 16: BREAKDOWN OF OLT SCOPE, BY J.E. ROCAMORA, 1977

HECTARAGE ANALYSIS

Total Hectares under Cultivation (1974)	10,100,111
Total Rice and Corn lands	6,400,000
Non-Grain Food Crops	920,000
Total Commercial Crop land	2,780,000
Tenanted Rice and Corn lands	3,800,000
DAR (1972) est. Tenanted Rice/Corn lands	1,767,000
DAR (1973) est. Tenanted Rice/Corn lands	1,343,000
DAR (1976) est. Tenanted Rice/Corn lands	1,058,000
Rice/Corn Tenanted lands above 7 has Retention limit	564,000
Rice/Corn Tenanted lands above 1975 Retention limit	464,000
Lands Purchased for Redistribution through land Bank	40,000

TENANCY ANALYSIS

Total Tenants in Philippines**	4,000,000
Total Rice/Corn Tenants	3,000,000
DAR est. Rice/Corn Tenants (1972)	1,078,000
DAR est. Rice/Corn Tenants (1976)	644,000
Eligible Beneficiaries (1976)	230,000
Amortizing Tenants as of 30 June 1976	26,000

** Rocamora and O'Connor commented that the figure "is, of course, a guessti-mate" extrapolated from 1960 Census figures on the assumption that 46% tenancy in 1960 had become at least 60% by 1972 and that 1.3 million hectares of tenanted grain lands had become 3.8 million in the same period, with a corresponding leap from 1.08 million to 4 million tenants. The authors added that since the 1960 Census counted 548,037 tenants on non-grain cropland and since hectarage under such crops has more than doubled in the intervening years while the tenancy rate has increased, a figure of 1 million tenants on these lands would be a conservative estimate. They concluded, "For reasons of its own, the government has not released the results of the 1970 Census. Estimates of the number of tenants must, therefore, remain uncertain. Most students of Philippine agriculture are convinced, however, that government estimates of the number of tenants in the country are much too low."

Source: J.E. Rocamora/David O'Connor "The U.S., Land Reform and Rural Development in the Philippines", in Walden Bello/Severina Rivera (eds) *The Logistics of Repression and Other Essays*. Friends of the Filipino People. San Francisco. 1977. pp.72-74.

TABLE 17: BREAKDOWN OF OLT SCOPE BY B.J. KERKVLIET, 1979

Hectares by Crop:

Rice	3,100,000
Corn	2,400,000
Other	3,500,000

Numbers of landless Peasants by Category:

Rice/Corn Tenants	1,000,000
Other Tenants	280,000
Rural laborers	4,000,000

Operation land Transfer Scope:

Total Peasants		
(heads of Households)	5,280,000	
Minus Rural laborers	4,000,000	
and Non-Rice/Corn Tenants	280,000	
and Tenants on Farms less than 7 has	560,000	
= Tenants Eligible for OlT 1972	440,000	(=8% of Total Peasants)

Source: Benedict J. Kerkvliet, 'Land Reform: Emancipation or Counter-insurgency' in David A. Rosenberg (ed.), *Marcos and Martial law in the Philippines,* Cornell University Press, New York, 1979, pp.129-31.

and O'Connor, in 1977, extrapolated from 1960 data to construct high estimates of their own. Concerning these extrapolations, it must be said that they appear to err on the high side. For example, whereas NEDA reported that, in 1971, 8,493,735 hectares were under cultivation in the Philippines (compared with the 5,726,584 hectares under cultivation according to the *1948 Census of Agriculture* and 7,772,484 hectares under cultivation according to the *1960 Census of Agriculture*), Rocamora and O'Connor gave a figure of 10,100,000 hectares under cultivation by 1974, without explaining the surge in cultivated area in a period when the arable land "frontier" was supposed to have "closed". They allow only 310,000 hectares of their increase under the category "Total Commercial Cropland", which suggests that an additional 1,596,000 hectares were planted to food crops between 1971 and 1974, unless NEDA's figure for 1971 was a gross underestimate. Rocamora and O'Connor stated further that, in 1960, 548,037 tenants were reported as producing crops other than rice and corn, but this figure does not tally with the *1960 Census of Agriculture* and is certainly too high a proportion of the total number of tenants of all types listed there (to be sure, probably an underestimate in itself). In extrapolating a doubling of this figure (of non-rice/corn tenants), based on the nearly 100% increase in hectarage planted to sugar and coconuts between 1960 and 1971, they arrived at a figure of more than 1,000,000 tenants on non-rice/corn lands by 1971; whereas Kerkvliet, in 1979, put the total at 280,000. The vast discrepancy between these two calculations, if one does not summarily dismiss one or the other, is almost certainly to be explained with reference to the category of landless laborers, for which Kerkvliet gives an estimate of 4,000,000, while Rocamora and O'Connor, with their estimated 4,000,000 tenants, give no estimate at all for the landless laborer category. Given these shortcomings in the Rocamora/O'Connor calculations, Kerkvliet's conservative estimates should perhaps be taken as the more reliable data base for reasoning about the scope and achievements of the New Society program[65].

Adding landless laborers and tenants of all types together, Kerkvliet concluded in 1979 that even had the New Society program fulfilled its declared aim of emancipating all tenants on rice and corn lands down to a retention ceiling of 7 hectares, this would have brought benefits to only 8% of the rural poor, or some 440,000 peasants by the official estimates. Now, even going by the official estimates of the Ministry of Agrarian Reform as of 1984 after the declared "completion" of the New Society program—only a very small fraction of the *"targeted"* tenants completed the emancipation process. Assuming Kerkvliet's gross figures to be conservative and therefore perhaps on the low side, and if one uses the "emancipation patent" as the most immediate quantifiable index of land reform under the New Society program, it appears that *no significant land reform occurred at all* under the martial law regime between 1972 and 1979. Drawing on all available official data in 1986, Tadem calculated that the *potential* scope of the program extended to only 6.62% of the total agricultural labor force without land ownership, covering some 13.6% of cultivated land; while in terms of actual accomplishment, the program transferred ownership, signified by the acquisition of an Emancipation Patent, to no more than 14,344 tenants, or 2.27% of the *potential* beneficiaries, covering 15,778 hectares, or a mere 2.2% of the *potential* area of land. While there were other aspects of the land reform program which affected a considerable number of other tenants, it is clear that the bold rhetoric that Marcos used in declaring his land reform in 1972 was not followed by anything like commensurate practical results. Given that he more than once announced that land reform was the "cornerstone" of the "New Society", its *sine qua non*, one is surely justified in observing that even in its own terms the program was a complete failure. The monitoring of it by AID Agriculture staff can be examined in light of these basic statistical facts and in light of the background narrated in this inquiry. Before turning to examine the discourse of AID on the Marcos program, however, it is worth considering some of the better known critiques of that program from outside AID, to establish what sort of point of reference they provide for assessment of AID documents on the subject. I shall consider three such critiques: that by Olson [1974], Rocamora/O'Connor [1977] and Kerkvliet [1979].

The first requirement for an adequate assessment of U.S. involvement in land reform in the Philippines before and since the Hardie Report, I believe, is to come to terms with the seriousness of that report and the meaning of its fate. It is, therefore, somewhat disappointing to find Olson in 1974, in the most sustained critical assessment of U.S. involvement in land reform in both Asia and Latin America up to that time, writing of the Hardie Report:

> "Even Hardie's far-reaching proposal to eliminate tenancy totally was *designed primarily for the protection of U.S. economic interests.* Only coincidentally might his program have offered relief to the Filipino tenant farmer"[66].

Hardie's proposals were, Olson asserted, conceived as a "technique of

TABLE 18: PHILIPPINE 'NEW SOCIETY' AGRARIAN REFORM
ACCOMPLISHMENT
AS OF 31 DECEMBER 1984

		Scope		Accomplishment		Percent
A.	Land Redistribution					
1.	EPs under OIT	427,623	FBs*			
		630,680	EPs	14,344	EPs**	2.27%
		716,520	has.	15,778	has(est)	2.20%
2.	Deeds of sale under	56,302	FBs	12,270	FBS	21.67%
	landed estates program	87,682	has.	19,610	has.	22.37%
		89,220	lots	15,061	deeds	16.88%
3.	Patents under	78,450	FBs	16,998	FBs	21.67%
	resettlement and	565,079	has.	95,117	has.	16.83%
	rehabilitation	216,459	lots	22,393	patents	10.34%
B.	Certificates of	527,667	FBs	248,488	FBs	47.09%
	of Agricultural	562,030	has.	260,465	has.	46.23%
	leasehold (CAl)	872,232	CAls	327,885	CAls	37.59%

* FB - farmer-beneficiary

** As of 31 January 1986

Source: Eduardo C. Tadem, *Grains and Radicalism: The Political Economy of the Rice Industry in the Philippines, 1965-1985.* Third World Studies Centre - UP Diliman, 1986. p. 30

social control"[67] and were intended first and foremost to bolster the
Philippines as an American bastion in Southeast Asia. Curiously, Olson
nevertheless went on to argue that Hardie *misunderstood* the "ultimate political objectives" of the United States government "in stressing
agrarian change"[68]. At the same time, he expressed the belief that
Magsaysay, if not Hardie, was "sincere" in his desire to see agrarian reform in the Philippines, but was deprived of critical United States support from 1954, due to an "*abrupt about face*" by the U.S. as regards such
reform[69]. It was the Davis[Cooper] Report, he averred, which signalized
this "abrupt about face" and he suggests that the change may best be
explained by the defeat of the Huk rebellion and consequent lapse in enthusiasm for agrarian reform among both Philippine elites and American
strategic planners[70]. This is a "more plausible explanation", he asserted,
than that afforded by a conservative shift in U.S. foreign policy with the
transition from the Truman to the Eisenhower administration. Yet he
cast doubt on this claim himself, by observing that Magsaysay was serious about land reform and that there remained in the U.S. Mission after
the departure of Hardie men such as Spruance, Renne and McMillan
who were pro-land reform, but were "gradually recalled from Manila"
in accordance with the new, more conservative policy line[71]. Finally, he
confused the chronology of events, by citing Dulles' 6 May 1954 cable,
without dating it, as if it supported the *Hardie* Report, whereas it indicated Dulles' backing for the recommendations of the *Davis* Report[72].
The least that can be said of all this is that Olson does not appear to
have read the Hardie Report very closely and that he paid insufficient
attention to the evidence that the change of administrations in Washington did have a significant bearing on the "abrupt about face" of the
U.S. government on the land reform question in the Philippines.

Olson's account of the Hardie Report and its fate, because it suppressed or muddled the clear evidence that the Hardie Report represented a definite commitment to genuine land reform in the Philippines,
collapsed the implications of the retreat from that commitment into an
assertion that it had been no more than a rather cynical strategic measure in the first instance. It thus left no room for inquiring more sys-
tematically into the differences among U.S. officials, or the resistance
they faced from Philippine power-brokers when it came to pressing for
land reform. This is all the more notable given Olson's recognition of
the fact that Spruance, Renne and McMillan, as well as Hardie, were
"land reformers" and his belief that they were *recalled* for this reason. Why Olson, an American himself, should have been able to credit

Ramon Magsaysay with sincere interest in land reform while casting aspersions on the intentions of Robert Hardie is difficult to understand, even in ideological terms. The implications, however, are not difficult to understand at all. If even so hard-hitting and thorough a land reform proposal as Hardie's is to be dismissed as no more than a counterinsurgency strategem, then anything short of it must, *a fortiori*, be so dismissed and one is left with nowhere else to turn but the idea of radical revolution. This is virtually spelled out in Olson's conclusion, summing up U.S. involvement in the agrarian question in the Philippines from 1950 to 1973:

> "Thus, for the immediate future, it might be argued that *the less the Philippines land reform programs jeopardize the prevailing internal balance of power* (and there is nothing in Marcos's latest decrees to suggest they would) *the higher the level of U.S. enthusiasm for the programs.* The extent to which these efforts dovetail with the interests of U.S. investors in the Philippines should also engender U.S. support. A dramatic increase in social instability, such as might accompany another Huk threshold, could require U.S. pressure on Manila for a high-risk land redistribution. This would be a last resort. Barring the appearance of such a phenomenon, *one would anticipate U.S. support for carefully controlled measures that ameliorate rural poverty, but do not endanger the status quo.*"[73] [emphasis added].

Olson did not document high levels of U.S. "enthusiasm" for Philippine land reform programs that did not "jeopardize the prevailing internal balance of power". He could have cited Motheral's fulsome comments of May 1956, but he did not and he simply overlooked the evidence that, while U.S. enthusiasm for land reform in the Philippines was rare, when it did occur, it was linked to a clear belief in the need to alter the prevailing internal balance of power in the country. This was especially evident, of course, in the memoranda of Ely, Abbey, Spruance and Acheson in the early 1950s, as well as in the work of Hardie and McMillan, but it was to reappear in the mid-1970s, after the time Olson wrote. Nor was Olson's prediction concerning "another Huk threshold" borne out after 1974. Insurgency gathered momentum after 1975, but U.S. involvement in land reform was terminated in 1978 and when the Marcos regime became less and less stable in the early 1980s, the Reagan administration did *not* start to press for land reform in the Philippines. In short, a more nuanced account of the matter is needed than what Olson provided.

Writing in 1977, at a time when Roy Prosterman had already criti-
cized the New Society land reform for limitations in scope and stagnation
in implementation—criticism to which we shall turn presently—Joel Rocamora and David O'Connor wrote, in a pamphlet titled *The Logistics
Of Repression And Other Essays* :

> "American support of the Marcos regime through military
> grants and sales and through massive loans to cover the
> Philippines' mounting balance of payments deficits is quite
> clear-cut. *American responsibility for the failure of Marcos's
> land reform program is not as well understood.* Criticisms of
> the program by American land reform experts give the *im-
> pression* of serious disagreements with the Marcos regime on
> this issue. Close examination of the program shows, how-
> ever, that it is *basically an American program in conception*
> and that the main goal remains that of defusing agrarian
> unrest."[74] [emphasis added].

The argument here is very similar to the better known arguments by
McCoy and Olson regarding U.S. policy objectives in respect to land reform in the Philippines (and elsewhere) in the 1950s. Indeed, Rocamora
and O'Connor virtually paraphrased McCoy in describing land reform
as *"this most subtle of counterinsurgency instruments."*[75]. Where such
land reform programs fail, the inference seems to be drawn that they
were never intended to succeed—as land reform. Where counterinsurgency also fails, however, the inference is not that it was never intended
to succeed, but that *other factors prevented* it from succeeding. This
reasoning is inconsistent, surely, and to that extent flawed. Quite apart
from consideration of factors that can prevent a land reform from succeeding even where it is "intended" to do so, the line of argument advanced by Rocamora and O'Connor *occludes the entire debate between
land reform advocates and counterinsurgency theorists*, as well as that between land reform advocates and economic/political pragmatists which
actually constitute the history of U.S. policy on land reform in the international arena. This seriously impoverishes a critique of that policy
pursued along such a line.

"None of the land tenure laws of 1955, 1963, 1971 or 1972 has faced
up to the basic issue of land redistribution" Rocamora and O'Connor
observed, while failing to add that this was the direct responsibility of the
Philippine Congress and Executive, rather than something orchestrated
by the U.S. Embassy. They hit hard, quite rightly, at the inadequacies
of these laws, declaring:

"All of them have evaded this issue [of land redistribution]
through a variety of mechanisms. They have [1] excluded
lands planted to export crops and/or untenanted rice and
corn lands; [2] allowed landlords to retain substantial amounts
of their lands and/or provided loopholes for outright evasion
[3] stipulated that the costs be shouldered by already insolvent tenants; and created procedures and administrative
structures which have hindered the implementation of land
reform laws"[76].

There is, however, nothing original in these criticisms and nothing that
Robert Hardie had not already written in 1952 concerning legislation
then on the statute books. Nor do such criticisms differ substantially
from those made by many American and Filipino advocates of land reform between 1954 and 1977. Moreover, in patent contradiction of their
assertion that the Americans were "responsible" for the failure of Marcos's land reform program, Rocamora and O'Connor went on to state:

"For all of Marcos's dramatic pronouncements about land
reform being the cornerstone of the New Society, *many U.S.
officials continue to doubt the seriousness of his intentions*[77].

Now, of course, this simply does not square with their previous argument
and inclusion of this remark, among others, suggests that Rocamora and
0'Connor had not thought through exactly what they were trying to
prove. Having stated that the U.S. designed the New Society program
and was responsible for its failure, it does not seem *pertinent* to then state
that U.S. officials doubted the seriousness of Marcos's intentions. If U.S.
officials had designed and had sufficient influence over implementation
of the New Society land reform that responsibility for its failure could
reasonably be attributed to them, why do doubts about the seriousness
of *Marcos's* intentions enter into the matter? If, on the other hand,
Marcos's intentions were decisive, then how far can one reasonably assign
responsibility for his failures to U.S. officials?

Somehow or other, both logic and evidence appear to suggest that
one must fall back on a different position, which would diminish U.S.
responsibility by casting doubt on the extent of U.S. involvement in and
the seriousness or even the coherence of U.S. intentions regarding land
reform. It is not surprising to find that Rocamora and O'Connor actually
did just this, without, it would seem, perceiving the inconsistencies in
their presentation of the case:

"At one level, one reason for the meager U.S financial commitment to land reform has been that *there is far from a general consensus within the U.S. government on the appropriateness of its present involvement in the program.* Lewis Gleeck, long-time director of U.S.A.I.D. Manila [an error of detail, since Gleeck was *never* A.I.D. director in Manila and the director at that time was Peter Cody], for instance, has proposed the use of carrot and stick psychology, offering Marcos a big financial bonus to bolster his agrarian reform programs only if he will guarantee some results, but threatening withdrawal altogether if he does not produce them. Others view identification with the Marcos reform as a kind of *self-incrimination,* a threat to U.S. credibility, and so propose that U.S. support be low-key for the time being. One well-known American land reform expert, Roy Prosterman, has said outright that the Philippines has virtually given up on its crucial effort to transfer ownership of the land to one million small farmers, once stated to be the cornerstone of Marcos's New Society."[78] [emphasis added].

The scattered evidence here adduced by these authors points to an agitation of *debate* over land reform in the Philippines within American circles in the mid-1970s, which for the first time since 1953 raised the possibility of going beyond what I have called the Dullesian agenda. To press home a critique of U.S. involvement in the failure of land reform under Marcos, one must, I submit, explore this debate and inquire as to why, in the end, the Dullesian agenda was not transcended. In their haste to conclude that the U.S. is to be *blamed* for both the initiation and the failure of land reform in the Philippines, Rocamora and O'Connor, like Olson, became muddled about U.S. debates on the matter and so rendered a less than adequate account of the various positions held by U.S. officials and what stood athwart a serious commitment by the U.S. government to land reform in the Philippines, never mind its successful implementation.

The most careful and consistent account of the Marcos land reform program in the 1970s was provided by Kerkvliet in 1979. However, even Kerkvliet's case seems to me incomplete and subject to qualification on the matter of U.S. policy, land reform and counterinsurgency. Taking off from the suggestion that Marcos's program partook of the old elite paternalism of Quezon, Roxas and Quirino, whose "social justice" programs were intended to "reduce unrest without changing the system"[79], he commented :

> "President Marcos's government has accomplished more land
> reform between 1973 and 1976 than it did in the preceding
> seven years. Its program, however, closely parallels previous
> land reform plans of Philippine governments. These attempts
> brought little improvement for the peasantry; mainly owing
> to four conditions in Philippine politics, conditions that have
> persisted during martial law. First, the purpose of land re-
> form is to protect the regime from rural unrest rather than
> to redistribute substantially wealth and power to villages.
> Second, Filipino elites design and administer the agrarian
> program with scarcely any participation from villages, while
> landlords either resist its implementation or try to manipu-
> late it in order to protect their own interests. Third, largely
> because of the first two conditions, the scope of land reform
> is narrow, only a small fraction of all peasants can potentially
> benefit. Finally, many of those villages who conceivably could
> benefit probably will lose out in the long run. In sum, the
> agrarian reform program in the Philippines seems headed for
> the same fate that has befallen other such programs in sim-
> ilar regimes—a little improvement for a few, but continued
> poverty and oppression for most."[80]

Kerkvliet went on to point out that Marcos was himself a landlord on an
immense scale, having acquired tens of thousands of hectares in Cagayan,
Isabela, Negros Occidental, Davao, Panay and elsewhere even before
1972[81]. Although peasant organization for marches, pickets, protests,
court actions, in defense of tenure change was an indispensable support
to serious land reform, Marcos imprisoned or hounded militant leaders
of the peasant organizations in the 1970s, whether the CPP-oriented
MASAKA or the militants of the Catholic Federation of Free Farmers[82].
Kerkvliet noted that under Marcos numerous tenants were evicted, intimidated, arrested and gaoled, but no landowners were ever arrested for
abuses. DAR/MAR agents, he found, repeatedly caved in to landlords
and settled disputes to the disadvantage of tenants[83].

   The picture drawn by Kerkvliet resembles the devastating report by
Jewett Burr on the South Vietnamese Land to the Tiller program in
An Giang province and the Vietnamese central lowlands between 1970
and 1975. It is all the more significant, then, to stress that Burr was
an AID land reform adviser in Vietnam and worked again for AID in

Washington after writing his PhD on the land to the tiller failures in Vietnam. If Burr was able to take so critical a view of a U.S.-sponsored land reform from within AID during the mid-1970s, AID's own files on the Philippines surely beckon the critic. The most disappointing feature of Kerkvliet's critique of those failures is his rather one-dimensional assessment of the U.S. role in and perspective on them. Like most critics of the U.S. role, since 1946, in the Philippine agrarian question, Kerkvliet anchored his position in reference to the Magsaysay years and the counterinsurgency schemes of Edward Lansdale and Jose Crisol. His account of U.S. policy in respect to land reform in the 1950s was based on an interview with Jose Crisol in 1969, the Davis[Cooper] Report, James Emerson's end of tour report of 1956, Frances Starner's *Magsaysay and the Philippine Peasantry* and Alfred McCoy's 1971 essay "Land Reform as Counterrevolution"[84]. He made no mention of or reference to the Hardie Report or the McMillan/Rivera Report, or the debate surrounding them, and he conflated resettlement and civic action projects— Lansdale's much-touted EDCOR scheme of the early 1950s—with "land reform", observing that Crisol "candidly described the resettlement programs, artesian wells projects and civic action as parts of the psych-war aimed at the soft core of the Huk movement"[85], without differentiating these programs from land reform as such. Muddling the chronology of things in a manner that foreshadowed Montgomery's confused account of these things in 1984, he observed that:

> "Although Magsaysay and some others in the government may have become *more interested later* in land reform as a means to significant changes, most Filipino politicians and U.S. State Department advisors intended to concede *only enough* legislation and funding to *keep rural discontent to a manageable level.*"[86] [emphasis added].

The subordinate clause in the above statement, pivoting on the word "later", is rather confusing. Later than when or than what? Later than the initiation, in 1950, of EDCOR schemes as part of the counterinsurgency campaign against the Huks, at the advice of Edward Lansdale? Later than the 1954 Davis Report? Later than the passage of Magsaysay's legislation in 1955? Kerkvliet did not make this clear and these events were separated by considerable intervals of time, during which an interesting and significant debate had taken place within the U.S. policy bureaucracies in Washington and Manila on land reform in the Philippines as a means to significant change in the country's economy and society.

TABLE 19: NEDA DATA (1975) ON FARM SIZE & AREAS, BY CROP 1960 AND 1970

Crop	No. of Farms (1000s)		Area in Farm (1000s Has)		Average Size of Farm (Has)		% Total Area in Farms of 10 Has+		% Total Area in Farms of 200 Has+	
	1960	1970p	1960	1970p	1960	1970p	1960	1970	1960	1970
All Farms	2,166.2	915.7	7,772.5	3,114.9	3.6	3.4	33	n.a.	8	n.a.
Sugarcane	17.8	14.0	249.4	87.2	14.0	6.2	80	n.a.	43	n.a.
Abaca	36.0	6.8	209.0	33.4	5.8	4.9	49	n.a.	8	n.a.
Coconut	440.3	148.8	1,938.6	734.1	4.4	4.9	38	n.a.	3	n.a.
Palay	1,041.9	407.1	3,112.1	1,037.3	3.0	2.5	20	n.a.	2	n.a.
Corn	378.6	180.3	949.3	516.3	2.5	3.2	20	n.a.	1	n.a.
Tobacco	22.9	2.5	38.4	4.9	1.7	2.0	8	n.a.	0	n.a.
Others	228.5	156.2	1,257.7	641.7	5.6	4.1	n.a.	n.a.	n.a.	n.a.

n.a. = Data not available

p = Preliminary Data obtained from twenty four (24) provinces out of 66

Source: NEDA *Statistical Yearbook 1975* p.141 Table 5:3

TABLE 20: NEDA DATA (1975) ON NUMBER OF AREA OF FARM UNITS
BY TENANCY TYPE 1960 AND 1970

Type of Tenancy	Number of Farms		% of Total		Area in Hectares		% of Total	
	1960	1970p	1960	1970	1960	1970	1960	1970
Cash	3,506	2,205	1.56	0.74	47,008	16,887	2.35	2.06
Fixed amount of Produce	34,145	34,874	3.95	11.76	88,911	89,304	4.45	11.07
Share of Produce	745,426	235,588	86.22	79.39	1,677,857	618,114	83.88	76.66
Cash and Fixed amount of produce	693	n.a.	0.08	n.a.	3,676	n.a.	0.18	n.a.
Cash and Share of Produce	10,847	n.a.	1.25	n.a.	34,083	n.a.	1.70	n.a.
Rent Free	29,816	14,800	3.46	4.99	55,918	49,800	2.80	6.18
Others	30,105	9,265	3.48	3.12	92,748	32,557	4.64	4.0
Total	864,538	296,702	100.00	100.00	2,040,201	806,312	100.00	100.00

Source: NEDA *Statistical Yearbook* 1975 p. 141 Table 5.4

By failing to mention this debate, as well as omitting any discussion of what "significant changes" Magsaysay was "interested in" ["later"], or how U.S. "State Department advisors" regarded such prospective changes, Kerkvliet has flattened the meaning and historiographic usefulness of what occurred in the 1950s and thereby impoverished his critique of U.S. policy over *la longue durée.* His representation of U.S. interest [more precisely, U.S. *lack* of interest] in land reform as a flat and linear policy of counterinsurgency, allowed for no inner tensions or contradictions in U.S. thinking about land reform in the Cold War and the result is to narrow the scope for its critical revision. Instead, the United States as such comes to appear as a mere arsenal of counterinsurgency and any reform proposals emanating from it become the object of suspicion and distrust. The unsatisfactoriness of this conclusion, even if it is implicit and not as explicit as it tends to be in hardline leftist critiques of U.S. foreign policy, is best appreciated if the obverse proposition is posed: that all serious criticism of "*revolutionary*" transformations is more or less "counter-revolutionary". Not the least value of the MSA reports of 1952 is that they provide a point of reference for serious reform proposals not premised on either prior upheaval or a calculus of minimum measures to defuse unrest. By omitting all mention of those ill-fated reports, even in one of the better argued critiques of the New Society land reform, Kerkvliet, the historian of the Huk rebellion, eliminated that point of reference around which a serious *American* interest in land reform in the Philippines might organize itself, in order not to find itself hemmed in and cut off by the narrow discourses of the Dullesian agenda, with its language of inertia, and the mobilization for "revolution", with its gravitation toward Leninism and anti-Americanism. Without such a point of reference, the language of inertia and the mobilization for revolution draw one into a conceptual vicious circle from which, as so much of the Vietnam experience had indicated by 1972, there can seem to be no exit.

Chapter Six

Whistling In The Dark

*"By the fall of 1985, it had become the professionals in the bu-
reaucracies against the ideologues in the White House. From
Abramowitz to Wolfowitz there was agreement that Marcos
would not reform. Bosworth knew it and he was adding that
in much of the country there simply was no government any
more. Armacost knew it, having learned the hard way. Carl
Ford and his staff at the C.I.A. had analyzed the situation
accurately. Over at Defense, Armitage and Admiral Crowe
realized that Marcos couldn't and wouldn't change, and they
were growing increasingly worried about the bases... But just
as these high level American officials couldn't influence Marcos, neither could they reach their superiors in Washington.
Casey, Weinberger, Bush, MacFarlane, even Schultz... clung
to Marcos... because their boss, Ronald Reagan,... refused to
accept the fact that Marcos was as bad as everyone said."*

— *Raymond Bonner (1987)*

Soon after President Marcos declared martial law and announced that
he would make land reform the cornerstone of the New Society he proposed to champion in the Philippines, Roy Prosterman arrived in Manila
to advise his government on the drafting of appropriate legislation.[87] It
was a little over two years since Prosterman had addressed the U.S. Senate Committee on Appropriations, along with Senators Packwood and
Magnusson, on the subject of land reform in Vietnam, and had spoken
in strong terms about the disaster of American unwillingness to push for
a major land reform in South Vietnam in the 1950s. The observations of
Senators Magnusson and Packwood at those hearings, in August 1970,

were to the effect that land reform was, on a world scale, a vital program that the U.S. must support in an active and constructive manner. Prosterman was a personal advisor to Magnusson by then and may be regarded as the source of much of the latter's thinking on these things. According to Eligio Tavanlar, Prosterman's arrival in Manila was accompanied by an offer from Senator Magnusson, Senator Daniel Inouye of Hawaii and Thomas Niblock, the AID director in Manila, to find massive U.S. funding for the land reform that Marcos proposed, but Marcos declined the offer.[88] It would seem that the offer was made unofficially and that Washington backed off from any idea of financing the program or, indeed, appearing to dictate Philippine government policies.[89] However, for the next six years, Roy Prosterman took a keen interest in the New Society land reform program—and quickly became one of its sharpest and most persistent critics.

As early as April 1973, Prosterman informed AID Manila that the 7 hectare retention ceiling that the PD 27 program set for rice and corn landowners was too high and that, if it was adhered to, it would serve to undermine land reform of any thoroughgoing kind. His argument stands out as the most trenchant American position on the subject since the days of Hardie and McMillan, of whose work he shows no sign of having been aware:

> "A seven hectare retention area will give total or substantial exemption to over 90% of the landlords, but will confer benefits on only 25% of the tenants. A variable exemption ranging from about 1.5 to 3.0 hectares and fixed on a province by province basis after the landlord declarations are submitted, will give total or substantial exemption to 66%–75% of the landlords, but will confer benefits on 70% or more of the tenants... Based on the DAR data, one may tentatively estimate rough figures of 350,000 landlords and 1,000,000 tenant households. The across the board seven hectare retention area would affect roughly 25,000 to 30,000 landlords, while giving land to roughly 250,000 tenants; while the variable 1.5 to 3.0 hectare approach here described would substantially affect roughly 90,000 to 120,000 landlords, giving land to roughly 700,000 tenants... a land reform program of sufficient scope to be consistent with President Marcos's statement that reforms to succeed must be radical. Fundamentally, the question is... whether the Philippine landlords will so strongly oppose this standard... that this most fundamen-

tal program of the New Society is destroyed. On one fact we
should all be clear: *it is mathematically inevitable that land
reform will be destroyed if the seven hectare retention area is
preserved.*".[90]

One has only to compare such a statement with the nibbling ambitions
of the NELRIDP or, better, with the fulsome claims of Motheral in
1956, or, at bottom, with the Dullesian agenda of the May 1954 cables,
to appreciate that Prosterman was trying to get accomplished in the
Philippines what he believed should have been attempted in Vietnam in
the 1950s.

Prosterman's data appear to have exaggerated the numbers of both
tenants and landlords who were operating below the 7 hectare retention ceiling. According to a 1975 study drawing on Philippine government statistics dating from December 1973, some 63% of tenants worked
on properties *above* 7 hectares, which is completely incompatible with
Prosterman's belief that 75% of tenants worked on properties *below* 7
hectares. The same statistical source [see Table 15] indicated that 83%
of *landowners* owned properties of 7 hectares or less, but did not differ-
entiate between landowning farm operators, of whom there were many,
and absentee landlords, which suggests that the percentage of landlords
owning 7 hectares or less must have been considerably fewer than the
83% figure and nowhere close to the 90% which Prosterman cited. What
is significant about Prosterman's use of the data is that he erred, if at
all, on the side of *urging a more radical land reform*. The contrast between Prosterman's proposal and the Davis Report, more than twenty
years before, which had explicitly confined its concern to areas of especially high tenancy and to bringing things "under control", deserves to
be emphasised. Not since the Hardie Report had any American advisor
or land reformer laid such forthright proposals on the table. His was
not, however, the dominant voice in American discourse on the matter
and he proved unable, over the years that followed, to effect a substitu-
tion of his proposals for the traditional tinkering and rationalization of
non-reform that I have dubbed the Dullesian agenda.

The New Society land reform had already bottomed out on the sort of
shoals indicated by Prosterman in April 1973 when, in mid-1974, Keith
Sherper arrived in Manila, after having worked in Saigon on the land to
the tiller program, to assume the job as chief land reform advisor in AID's
Agriculture Division in the Philippines. It fell to Lewis Gleeck, already
an Embassy and AID officer of many years experience in Manila and

TABLE 21: NEDA DATA (1984) ON FARM SIZES AND AREAS BY CROP 1960 AND 1971

Crop	No. of Farms (1000s)		Area in Farm (1000s Has)		Average Size of Farm (Has)		% Total Area in 10Has		Farms over 50 Has	
	1960	1970p	1960	1970p	1960	1970	1960	1970	1960	1970
All Farms	2,166.2	2,354.5	7,772.5	8,493.7	3.6	3.6	33	26	12	14
Sugarcane	17.8	27.0	249.4	368.1	14.0	13.6	80	81	71	66
Abaca	36.0	12.5	209.0	64.3	5.8	6.1	49	44	14	9
Coconut	440.3	432.5	1,938.6	2,152.8	4.4	5.0	38	42	8	10
Palay	1,041.9	981.9	3,112.1	2,661.2	3.0	2.7	20	19	5	6
Corn	378.8	514.2	949.3	1,493.9	2.5	2.9	20	22	3	4
Tobacco	20.9	3.9	38.4	7.3	1.7	1.9	8	7	4	0
Poultry & livestock	17.3	38.3	437.3	415.6	25.3	10.8	97	84	91	76
Others	211.2	344.2	838.4	1,330.5	4.0	3.9	36	30	6	13

Source: Drawing on 1960 and 1971 Censuses of Agriculture.

co-author with Harold Koone of the study *Land Reform in the Philippines* for AID's 1970 spring review of land reform, to fill Sherper in on the background to U.S. involvement in the Philippine land reform program over the years.[91] American interest in land reform had been quickened again, Gleeck told Sherper, by overtures to AID's Thomas Niblock from then Land Authority boss Conrado Estrella in 1969[92]; by the 1970 AID spring review conference on land reform [93]; and by Marcos's proclamation of his "New Society" and its "democratic revolution".[94] Gleeck' wrote to Sherper:

> "It was clear from the Washington traffic that the USG [United States Government] wanted to be part of something that *looked like real reform, but didn't want to get sucked into appearing to dictate GOP* [Government of the Philippines] *policies, or into financing the program*".[95] [emphasis added].

Gleeck focused on the organizational confusion of the initial years of the New Society program. From the U.S. side, involvement was modest in scale and ambition, but the constraints on it and the motivational ambivalence behind it must have seemed familiar to Sherper from his experience in South Vietnam.

Gleeck had written to Wolf Ladejinsky a few months before Sherper's arrival, asking the aging land reform proponent to come from his World Bank office in New Delhi to appraise the Philippine program. He apparently described it in very positive terms, for Ladejinsky responded:

> "Thank you for your letter. You sound very optimistic and I hope developments justify you...I cannot make Manila before August...interested in what appears from your letter to be an accomplished fact ..."[96]

That Gleeck actually appreciated how far Marcos's land reform was from "an accomplished fact", as of July 1974, is evident from his report to Sherper that:

> "The atmosphere of the New Society was *(sic)* radical...*DAR thought its day had come and rushed to do the President's bidding without any real plan or system... We were not aware, however, (nor was the President) of the faulty data base for the program*. Although the DAR (and the LA before the DAR) had been doing little but gather data for almost ten

years, the *data were almost totally unreliable*—which is perhaps the most critical indictment that could be drawn up
against the defunct agency. *No-one really knew how many
tenants there actually were*, how much land was involved, or
what the profile of land ownership was! This ignorance has
bedevilled the program ever since."[97] [emphasis added]

Reference has already been made to the data problem, but while one
must heartily agree with Gleeck that the lack of reliable tenure data by
1972 was a critical indictment of the Land Authority and the Department
of Agrarian Reform, what his remarks to Sherper also indicate is that
A.I.D. had made no effort during the decade before 1972 to keep the
tenure problem in clear focus itself. This was underscored by his added
observation that :

"A.I.D. has been badly situated to do anything about this, as
the most conspicuous aspect of our project, *in contrast to all
other mission projects*, is that AID's contribution to the GOP
program is a miniscule portion of the total. In addition, *until
Korin arrived* [as land reform facilitator in October 1973, also
from South Vietnam], *we had no-one intimately familiar with
land transfer* and hence able to check effectively on actual
performance ..."[98] [emphasis added]

The U.S. project to assist the New Society land reform program was, in
short, an attenuated, almost nominal project, with a very weak base of
operations. There is no evidence to substantiate the assertion by its critics that the New Society land reform program was a counterinsurgency
operation designed and monitored by the U.S. government.

Given the history of the Hardie Report and the Davis Report more
than twenty years before, it is significant that Gleeck should have remarked to Sherper in July 1974:

"This is where a new officer in charge should concentrate his
attention: what things have we not been doing that we should
do? What things should be done otherwise, or through other
instruments? What measure of pressure is it appropriate to
aspire to exercise when we provide so little assistance and
where the question remains primarily one of political will?
Also, and this is delicate, should the style of our operation,
which has been buddy-buddy, be revised?"[99]

That the problem was one of political will and that pressure should be exerted to induce the Philippine government to expedite implementation of real land reform were not ideas that had been pronounced in U.S. policy since the time of Ambassador Spruance, Robert Hardie and Robert McMillan. Keith Sherper must have remembered the snarls that these ideas had got tangled in, during the 1960s, in South Vietnam. Lewis Gleeck had not arrived in Manila until 1962 and had served in the NATO area before that, not in Vietnam. He told Sherper, in July 1974, that it was *"critical that an alarm be sounded at the shrinking size in the program."*[100] [emphasis added]. He did not mention insurgency (which was not, in 1974, a major problem), or link land reform to counterinsurgency. His question was whether the New Society program was going to prove to be a real land reform, or another sham of the sort Wesley Haraldson had shrugged off in 1965–66 as unworthy of U.S. interest or support. In an effort to establish this one way or another, Gleeck encouraged a number of land reform investigators to scrutinize the program. Of these, Roy Prosterman was the one who most candidly raised the issues of political will and pressure, in 1975, and, like Robert Hardie, he ran at once into opposition among conservative Filipinos and Americans and became *persona non grata* in Manila. The brouhaha over Prosterman was much less dramatic or substantial than that over Hardie twenty two years earlier, but it recapitulated it in striking ways. The episode threw into relief once more the forces obstructing any U.S. pressure for "rational revolution" in the Philippines.

Prosterman, in March 1975, presented a forthright critique of the failure of the New Society program, which is striking because of his integrated reference to the bureaucratic, financial and political aspects of that failure, the East Asia model of successful, small-holder-oriented reform, and the bitter experience of the U.S. in Vietnam. Noting that, after two years, the program was less than 1% complete, Prosterman commented, in language redolent of the Hardie Report:

> "If President Marcos does not speed up the program—and it takes the man at the top to do that kind of thing—the Philippines may endure a cyclone [typhoon?] of revolution in the future... The Filipinos are, of course, totally free to lie down on any program they want, but I don't think they should enjoy a good press in the U.S. on asserted progress when in fact they have achieved so little ..."[101]

He argued that the much higher rice production per hectare in Taiwan,

South Korea and Japan than in the Philippines was an indication of the
potential benefits of land reform. He added:

> "The Philippines can definitely muster the administrative
> talent and call up the financial resources to do the job, if
> that's really what President Marcos wants."[102]

He was, he wrote, speaking to the sort of "realities not admitted to by
Americans working with Diem on his *make-believe land reform in Vietnam in the late 1950s*". Given the importance of the issue, he concluded:

> "... we should make it totally clear that the ball is in Marcos's
> court. If he flubs it, the Philippines may well become Asia's
> next tragedy. But it will not become America's."[103]

Was this a counterinsurgency plan, on Prosterman's part? Or, to put it
a little differently, was this a counter-revolutionary proposal on Prosterman's part? It might be placed alongside the recommendations of Wolf
Ladejinsky in the late 1940s and 1950s for land reform in Asia, the recommendations of Robert Hardie and Robert McMillan in the Philippines in
the early 1950s, the recommendations of Laurence Hewes in South Vietnam in 1966, as a candid expression of progressive, democratic, and also
anti-totalitarian American thought. None of them succeeded in bringing
about sustained U.S. efforts at "rational revolution", with the possible
exception of Ladejinsky in Japan and Taiwan and the belated and but
partial success of Prosterman in South Vietnam in 1969-70, but this
surely does not erase the stark differences between their aspirations and
those delineated in the stands taken against land reform as such by the
American Council on Japan (1948-50), the Davis Report (1954), or the
Mitchell Report (1966–67). Dismissing them as "counterrevolutionary"
or a calculus of "counterinsurgency" is to miss the point. They were in
a position rather like that of Scipio Aemilianus or Tiberius Gracchus in
the famous land reform debates of late Republican Rome: wanting the
public good and reform, but unwilling in the one case or unable in the
other to find the means to bring about reform short of violent struggle.

   "It is a time for candor", Prosterman stated in a memo to A.I.D.
Manila, a week after the critique of the Marcos land reform just quoted
was published in the *Seattle Post-Intelligencer*. He warned that, if the
scope of the program was not dramatically widened and implementation pushed vigorously, "the entire program—even the portion relating
to lands of over-24 hectare landlords—will be a dead letter by early

1976 at the latest with all of the political and agricultural consequences which that will entail."[104] U.S. officials concerned to preserve smooth relations with the Philippine government were discomforted by Prosterman's public candor. In the July 1974 memo to Keith Sherper, cited above, Lewis Gleeck had written that the A.I.D. mission in Manila had done well by "supplying marginal inputs" and added "*we have stayed out of trouble*".[105] Prosterman's attitude meant trouble and A.I.D. Manila did not want such trouble. The ingrained preference for the uncontroversial "marginal inputs" approach, conformable with the Dullesian agenda down through the NELRIDP project, found expression again and again in opposition to Prosterman's agitation for an all out effort.

Ironically, one of the spokesmen for the "marginal inputs" line, in the course of 1974, was the aging Wolf Ladejinsky, the original advocate of U.S. "export" of land reform to Asia in the 1940s. By then a salaried World Bank representative in India, Ladejinsky was invited to the Philippines by U.S. Ambassador William Sullivan and visited the country in August-September 1974 to assess the Marcos land reform program for the AID mission and for Robert McNamara, of the World Bank. On his return to India, he wrote to McNamara that the program was "not a complete failure, but not a great success story either." There was, in Wolf Ladejinsky's sage opinion, "a perceptible absence of zeal and zest on the highest levels...What has been lacking all along is firm enforcement, which is *sine qua non* in an effort of this kind." Unlike Prosterman, Ladejinsky hesitated to declare that such enforcement was readily possible in the Philippines, even given political will at the top. Nor did he link land reform to the question of insurgency in any direct or dire way. His focus was on the administrative side of the program. "This is" he observed "rather a 'soft' society, inspite of martial law".[106] Significantly, his proposed remedy was to "sweeten" the deal for landlords, by increasing compensation payments. He made no mention of such variables as organization of and for the rural poor. His attention was given, as it had been in Ngo Dinh Diem's South Vietnam after 1956, to a vaguely defined and indulgently viewed process "sweet" for the elites. He simply did not address, in either case, the possible exasperated reaction of the mass of peasants or radical intellectuals to such a process.

Six weeks after his visit to the Philippines, Ladejinsky wrote a letter of encouragement to Secretary of Agrarian Reform Conrado Estrella, urging that the land reform program be pressed through to "completion". He told Estrella:

"I believe that your guidance and the President's support
will see it through for the good of the country. I might add
also, and with no intent of flattery, that you will be carving
out for yourself a lasting place in the history of the agrarian
movement of the Philippines. This, my dear Mr. Estrella, is
a privilege given to very few political leaders and to few administrators. I root for your place among the chosen few."[107]

Sending a copy of this letter to Ambassador Sullivan, Ladejinsky remarked that it would strike Sullivan, no doubt, as "on the flattering
side but, after all, [Estrella] also needs incentives." [108]. Wolf Ladejinsky pursued by flattery and tact the end that Roy Prosterman pursued
by biting, candid criticism: enlightened and more or less equitable land
reform in the Philippines. Neither approach had any discernible success
in moving the Marcos regime in the direction of serious reform. Ladejinsky's approach had failed with Ngo Dinh Diem, in South Vietnam, but
he ended up shutting his eyes to the facts in that case, as the GVN's
Ordinance 57 "land reform" went nowhere in the late 1950s.[109]

In January 1975, Duncan Harkin, an American visiting scholar at
the Agrarian Reform Institute of the University of the Philippines, Los
Baños, completed a paper on land reform in the Philippines in which,
having stated that the productivity case for land reform was weak, he
nevertheless stressed its importance in the transformation of patterns of
effective demand in the national economy and in the sociological transformation of the countryside.[110] The problem, he concluded, was finding
the means to catalyse land reform. That same month, Lewis Gleeck
drafted a memorandum for AID Manila, in which he concluded that the
top technocrats in the Marcos government "put land reform well down
on their list of priorities".[111] He did not add that land reform in the
Philippines was surely at least as far down on the list of priorities of the
White House, the National Security Council or the State Department
in January 1975, though attention was straining toward the approaching denouement of the long U.S. entanglement in South Vietnam, in
which peasant grievances had been so crucial to Viet Cong mobilization and American failure. What he did note, as Embassy and AID
officers had done in Saigon in the mid-1960s, was that "USAID is, of
course, not charged with seeking to influence decisions that are in essence
political."[112] The significance of such a claim is better brought out by
the recollection that Spruance had informed Acheson back in April 1952,
if no such effort was made by the US aid mission in the Philippines then,
in all probability, imperative reforms, among them land reform, simply

would not take place; and, if they did not take place, then, as Robert
Hardie concluded with some bitterness, the whole aid exercise verged on
becoming "a charade and a waste of public funds".

Gleeck's formulation of what AID was [not] charged with doing was
the language of inertia. If the thing did not require doing, then a clear
and cogent study was called for that would redraw the map of Philippine
realities with which AID would work. If, as repeated studies had under-
lined, the thing very much did need doing then some means had to be
conceived to bring it about. The Dullesian agenda, or what Gleeck had,
in his briefing of Keith Sherper, referred to as the "marginal inputs" approach, had not conceived such means. It had operated, for all practical
purposes, as AID had operated in South Vietnam until at least 1970 —
tinkering and eschewing the hard political challenge. Yet in 1970, in the
spring review paper for AID on land reform in the Philippines, Gleeck
had himself as much as pointed to the need for bottom-up pressures from
strong peasant organizations to lever the reluctant elites into change.[113]
The implications of such an observation were, of course, "political" indeed and quite inconsistent with dominant political philosophies in the
United States itself. It was for just this reason and, at bottom, no other,
that John McAlister had told the Senate Foreign Relations Committee in
February 1968 that the United States was unable to sponsor an effective
alternative to the Communist movement in Vietnam and that notions
of the United States having an approach to "revolution" to set against
that of the Communists were something no more than "abstract".

As early as 1959, an American scholar investigating the need for
strong peasant organizations in the Philippines and focusing on the attempt of the Federation of Free Farmers to replace the HMB and CPP
in leadership of the peasants, concluded that:

> "...it is highly questionable that any total reform which
> would reach down deeply into the very foundations of rural
> society can be initiated and pushed through to real comple-
> tion unless the contemporary governing elite is replaced with
> a group genuinely concerned with the public welfare. For
> present Philippine political regimes have not indicated thus
> far that they possess either the administrative integrity or the
> political morality necessary to deliver, as Magsaysay vainly
> promised, 'the substance of democracy to the people'."[114]

When, however, young militants, like Gerardo Bulatao in the FFF,
sought to organize around this idea in the early 1970s, both President

Marcos and FFF supremo Jeremias Montemayor saw their efforts as a
"communist infiltration" which "threatened the integrity" of the FFF.
The descriptions come from a report on Philippine peasant organizations in 1975 for AID, written by Mark Van Steenwyck.[115] The FFF
was purged of these militants by Montemayor in 1973, at the insistence
of Marcos, but nothing was built up to replace the impetus that they
had tried to provide, except the government-controlled peasant organizations, the *Samahang Nayon* which were anything but bottom-up militant
bodies.[116] Yet in 1978 Lewis Gleeck himself was to lament that Marcos
as a land reformer was *"handicapped by the absence of an effective pressure group in the countryside"*, the FFF being lamed because *"nearly
half the opposition had defected to the subversive left and were under
arrest or in hiding."*[117] Thus did AID, over many years, chase its tail in
a vicious circle—impelled toward seeing the need for reforms by recognition of the gross defects of the Philippine social and economic order,
but driven back toward counterinsurgency by fear of radicalism and the
inertia of U.S. foreign policy at the highest levels.

In May 1975 a three man survey team—Jerome T. French of A.I.D.'s
Technical Assistance Bureau, Jonathan Silverstone of A.I.D.'s Bureau
for Program and Policy Co-ordination and John D. Montgomery of Harvard University's John F. Kennedy School of Government—submitted a
report to A.I.D. Manila on the land reform program in the Philippines.
Their report bears the reader, witting or unwitting, firmly around the
vicious circle just described, away from Prosterman's urgency and back
to the policy equivalent of the 1954 "Dullesian agenda". Taken in the
context of the American discourse on rural conditions in the Philippines since 1950, the French/Silverstone/Montgomery Report clearly
followed certain deep circularities in that discourse. After drawing attention to the excessive burden of amortization payments weighing on
ex-tenants and the parlous condition of credit financing [118] the survey
team concluded that, although the program had bogged down, "like
many reform attempts elsewhere", due to technical, bureaucratic and
political difficulties[119], "the gloom is excessive and the disillusionment
premature."[120] The "lack of political will", they added, "may be more
apparent than real".[121]

What, then, of Gleeck's observation of a few months earlier that there
was a lack of political will to land reform among the Marcos regime's
inner circle? The French/Silverstone/Montgomery Report made no mention of such powerful political figures; and, while finding that DAR bureaucrats "appeared much less zealous in Manila, where the decisions

TABLE 22: NEDA DATA (1984) ON NUMBER AND AREA OF FARMS BY TENANCY TYPE 1960 AND 1971

Type of Tenancy	Number of Farms		% Distribution		Area in Hectares		% Distribution	
	1960	1971	1960	1971	1960	1971	1960	1971
Total	2,166,216	2,354,469	100.00	100.00	7,772,484	8,493,735	100.00	100.00
Full Owner	967,725	1,364,990	44.67	57.98	4,135,276	5,345,429	53.18	62.93
Part Owner	310,944	268,665	14.35	11.41	1,139,986	930,841	14.67	10.96
Tenants (All types)	864,528	618,658	39.91	28.95	2,000,201	1,746,455	25.73	20.56
Cash	13,506	5,680	0.62	0.24	47,008	33,688	0.60	0.40
Share	745,426	569,277	34.41	24.18	1,677,857	1,384,732	21.59	16.30
Fixed Share	34,145	49,864	1.88	2.12	83,911	128,302	1.14	1.51
Rent Free	29,816	39,310	1.38	1.67	55,918	133,173	0.72	1.57
Others	41,645	17,527	1.92	0.74	130,507	66,560	1.68	0.78
Manager	2,487	2,458	0.12	0.10	365,309	346,242	4.70	4.08
Other forms of tenure	20,522	36,698	0.95	1.56	133,742	124,768	1.72	1.47

Source: NEDA *Statistical Yearbook* 1975 p.141 Table 5.4

are made, than in the field where the problems are", the authors did
not enlarge on this in their report. Their treatment of the politics of
land reform in the Philippines was superficial even by comparison with
Gleeck's and was certainly bland by comparison with Prosterman's pun-
gent comments of March that year. Yet Gleeck himself was to praise the
French/Silverstone/Montgomery Report, three and a half years later,
writing that it "introduced a welcome realistic note into the discussion
of that frequently oversimplified phenomenon called political will".[122]
To be sure, "political will" is a frequently oversimplified phenomenon —
not least among Cold War conservatives—but it is not easy to see that
French, Silverstone and Montgomery, in May 1975, had introduced any
new or marked realism into U.S. discourse on Philippine agrarian politics
and the "political will" to land reform in Manila. To the contrary, what
stands out painfully from the report is its lapse into the oldest circular
rationalizations of Philippine elite non-reform and U.S. acquiescence in
it.

Prosterman's outburst in March 1975 threatened to open up a critical breach between the U.S. government and the Marcos regime on the
land reform question. French, Silverstone and Montgomery stepped into
the breach and sealed it before the thing got out of hand. " *Political
discourse*", they averred, "*requires hyperbole*, especially perhaps in the
circumstances which existed in the fall of 1972. It may be a sign of practical realism and not lack of political will or commitment, when responsible officials subsequently set their sights lower".[123] This is a truism,
but was it a realistic assessment of Philippine "political discourse" and
the hyperbole of Ferdinand Marcos? Montgomery's muddled account, as
late as 1984, of the history of land reform debate in the Philippines and
of American involvement therein, suggests that he had no clear sense of
Philippine political discourse, with its perennial hyperbole, corruption,
mendacity, inertia and violence, any more than he had a clear sense of
how U.S. policy on land reform in the Philippines had compromised itself over the years to avoid offending the "sensibilities" of [conservative]
Filipinos, as Edward Prentice put it, in January 1953, to the irrita-
tion of Joaquin Elizalde. Certain "foreigners", French, Silverstone and
Montgomery commented, with transparent reference to Prosterman, had
"failed to understand Philippine political discourse".[124] Ironically, it was
they themselves who had done so.

Given their failure to grapple with the realities of agrarian politics
in the Philippines, what might one have expected of these men as regards recommendations for U.S. policy? Their recommendations, in fact,

ran along well-established lines: major increases in the scale of the U.S. aid program would not be realistic; use of such aid as leverage would be "presumptuous"; a useful role could be filled by bringing along the technical, research and administrative staffs of the Philippine rural affairs bureaucracies.[125] One could almost have been reading John Foster Dulles's cable to Ambassador Spruance of 21 May 1954—except that there was, in May 1975, no mention of "marshalling political support for land reform", so that French, Silverstone and Montgomery were in fact espousing no more than that minimalist version of the Dullesian agenda addressed by James P. Emerson in 1956 and Frate Bull in 1958, in their end of tour "progress" reports on land reform in the Philippines.

There was, in the French/Silverstone/Montgomery Report, no serious attempt to reckon with the fact that two decades of the sort of aid being recommended once more had not brought about meaningful land reform in the Philippines, or built strong technical, research and administrative agencies with a cohesive, positive approach to the land reform problem. The crippling failure of the Land Authority/Department of Agrarian Reform or other bodies to keep clear and incisive data on land tenure between 1954 and 1974 went unmentioned. The actual disposition of political forces was not examined, nor was any recommendation made in the report that it be examined. The history of Philippine land reform legislation was not seriously assessed. The record of Ferdinand Marcos as both politician and land reformer was passed over without comment. The corruption of his regime was not listed as a factor to be taken into account. The sole concession to historical perspective came in the form of a recommendation to look straight ahead without blinking, moving steadily along what these policy analysts appear to have considered a long, shallow curve of "progress", but which, I submit, was the wide curve of the old vicious circle:

> "since the friar land reform in 1903, the United States has not consistently supported agrarian reform in the Philippines. There might be some value if we were to show a more steady, enlightened interest and support, avoiding either over-promoting or completely rejecting the Philippine Government's efforts. The latter, if premised on the notion that the program is failing, may help to ensure just that effect, something which most critics presumably do not want".[126]

This superficially reasonable recommendation invites recollection of James Price Gittinger's 1961 essay on land reform in U.S. foreign policy,

in which he had remarked that such policy in the Philippine case, after
the departure of Robert Hardie, had been infused with "a marked note
of caution" and that Frate Bull, in 1958, assessing the [complete lack of]
"progress" under that policy of "caution" had nothing to recommend
but *"more of the same"*.[127], an "irresolution", Gittinger had warned,
which would entail serious future costs. It cannot be said that anything had occurred between 1961 and 1975 to indicate that Bull, rather
than Gittinger, had best understood the nature of the challenge in the
Philippines. The poverty of the French/Silverstone/Montgomery Report
consisted in its failure even to ponder things in this sort of perspective.

The problems in rendering effective support to land reform in such
countries as the Philippines ought not be underestimated out of impa-
tience with conservative policies which fail to bring such effective support
to bear. The fundamental problem, however, is clearly the lack of "political will" among ruling elites in such countries to implement a land reform
susceptible of being supported in the first instance and their resistance to
critical studies of implementation processes where they do initiate a land
reform. Where such will is lacking or is ambiguous, the external "support" agent must labor to keep his own will and relation to the problem
as clear and well-informed as possible, or else forfeit all effective involvement in the matter. Well before 1975, A.I.D. and the U.S. government
had forfeited their hand in the matter of land reform in the Philippines,
but neither understanding nor admission of this were in evidence at that
date. One can trace a line of analytic integrity from Hardie, Spruance
and MacMillan through Gittinger to Prosterman, but this line diverges
more and more from A.I.D. institutional orientation and U.S. official
policy between 1953 and 1975. Richard Hough a veteran of the land to
the tiller program in Vietnam described AID in 1985 as "a highly technical, introverted, resource-transferring institution and heaven help you
if you have to deal with anything political or controversial".[128] Michael
Korin, another such veteran, before he became AID's leading land reform man in Manila between October 1973 and October 1977, presented
the obverse side, as it were, of AID's self-image, in declaring that this
is not so. AID is, rather, an institution which "has to accept the realities of the world and the way business is done" in countries such as the
Philippines.[129]

There is, in this light, a certain poignancy to Lewis Gleeck's 3 September 1975 memorandum to Keith Sherper, entitled *Misinformation on
Land Reform,* in which the veteran AID hand who, only two months
before, had written that AID was not mandated to seek to influence

"decisions that are in essence political", now contested just such a viewpoint coming from others:

> "I must challenge head-on a viewpoint popular in our own agency and among our Embassy colleagues, which passes for realism and sophistication: [that] we must consider the problem of political will out of bounds. . . If the GOP falters, that's their problem . . . We mustn't substitute our determination for theirs, the argument runs. And, above all, we mustn't get out in front. Horrors, what if the program failed? How would we look? That argument, I have taken the liberty of saying to the Ambassador, where it doesn't amount to knocking down a straw man, is poppycock. *The United States Government, and we as Americans, will be far better off if the record shows [that] we were, where necessary, a little in front, urging or encouraging the GOP to take the steps necessary* to give substance to its claims that it seeks to do more for those who have less. Can you imagine our opponents in Moscow [or] Peking. . . instructing their representatives not to exert such influence as they possess, let alone might acquire? Have we forgotten, or do we now in fact not believe, that we are the good guys?"[130]

Almost anybody looks like a "good guy" compared with Stalin or Pol Pot, but what was Gleeck really trying to say here? Like the Americans in Burdick and Lederer's *The Ugly American* (1958), Gleeck and those around him may have seen themselves as building "Freedom Road", in the Philippines of President Marcos, if not in the fictional Sarkan; but from the point of view of Philippine nationalists and radicals, they were "ugly Americans" supporting a dictator with abundant arms and money. What "we" did he have in mind as constituting the "good guys"? Henry Kissinger, then U.S. Secretary of State? Regardless of whether one considers Kissinger as one of the "good guys"—and Gleeck is a professed admirer of Kissinger—he had no interest in the Philippines, mentioning it not once in the 2,700 pages of his memoirs (which Gleeck described in 1985 as a masterpiece of diplomatic history and literature[131]), much less in land reform for such a country. Philip Habib, then Assistant Secretary of State for East Asian and Pacific Affairs? Habib has a formidable reputation as a diplomat, but he had shown a distinct hostility to land reform in South Vietnam as Political Counsellor in the Embassy there in the mid-1960s, and the cautious Michael Korin has described him as being "cautiously supportive" in 1976-77 of what was itself a cautious and attenuated land reform commitment by the United States in the Philippines[132] The U.S. Department of Agriculture, by the mid-1970's, was even more agribusiness-oriented than it had been twenty years earlier, when Secretary Ezra Benson had attacked Wolf Ladejinsky as a "socialist" because of his land reform work in Japan, and thus not likely to assume the role of a land reform lobby against landed interests in the Philippines.

As for the U.S. Congress, Gleeck was not even sure that it was, after the Vietnam War, a responsible body, as far as foreign policy was concerned. He regretted its 1974 termination of AID's "public safety" police-training program, in the Philippines as elsewhere, ascribing this to "an ideological tantrum on the part of the United States Congress".[133] Gleeck begins to appear as a Diogenes, bearing his lantern in the morning, looking for a "good guy" in the market-place. As he wrote this anything but cynical reflection in September 1975, the Pol Pot catastrophe was smiting Cambodia, and American power, defeated in Indochina, was entering its greatest crisis since the Second World War. There was, perhaps, a need among Americans like Gleeck to believe themselves to be the "good guys". Yet the dilemmas and divisions that had led Americans with similar self-images to frustration and failure in Vietnam had not even begun to be resolved. There was no exit from the old vicious circle in the direction indicated by French, Silverstone and Montgomery. And Gleeck, writing to his colleagues about "we, the good guys" was, if not bearing his lantern in the morning, simply whistling in the dark.

Not only was land reform in the Philippines not a major concern of the U.S. government in the mid-1970s, but the A.I.D. mission in Manila itself appears to have had no clear sense, under Directors Garnett Zimmerly and Peter Cody, of what it was trying to accomplish, as far as land reform was concerned. Jewett M. Burr, having, in 1976, completed his doctoral dissertation on the land reform in South Vietnam, with its stinging description of corruption, inertia and flawed policy, was, by early 1977, working for AID Washington on the Philippines. Given the observations he had made on the "schizophrenic" policy of the U.S. and the Thieu regime in South Vietnam in the early 1970s, it is of considerable interest to find him cabling Korin, who had worked with him in Vietnam[134], at that late stage in U.S. involvement in land reform in the Philippines, and stating:

> "I'm asking you to think in terms of a mission strategy...for what is needed is a mission consensus ...".[135]

The disarray on land reform in the Philippines to which this cable spoke led A.I.D., in late 1977, to convene a major conference on the matter in the RAND Corporation's Washington D.C. offices, attended by Keith Sherper, Peter Cody and Roy Prosterman, among others, though Korin was not there, having been reassigned to Indonesia a couple of months before.[136] The report that issued from that conference, written by Gerald C. Hickey, a veteran of many years rural work in South Vietnam, especially among the much-abused peoples of the Central Highlands, and AID's John Wilkinson, was to precipitate termination of U.S. involvement in the New Society land reform program, at the peremptory insistence of President Marcos, under circumstances recalling those of December 1952 and early 1953, when the Hardie and McMillan/Rivera Reports had been released to the public and had roused the ire of Philippine conservatives. The episode takes us for a heady spin around the vicious circle and anyone concerned with land reform under the Aquino regime and a prospective U. S. role in it, would do well to reflect on it.

The Hickey Report, sometimes more vaguely referred to as the Rand Report, did not emerge direct from the December 1977 conference in Washington D.C. It did not get into circulation until early 1978 and never became a front-page newspaper story or public debating point, as the Hardie Report had done. Cody and Sherper, in particular, as ranking members of the AID Manila mission, do not seem to have expected that it would be phrased the way that it was, or that it would be disseminated outside the AID/RAND circle. They were furious when they discovered that a copy had been presented to a Philippine official in Washington D.C. with a challenge to address its hard-hitting findings. Hickey, for his part, found the attitude of Sherper and Cody overbearing and came to see them as "cabalistic, supercilious super-bureaucrats".[137] The Hickey Report once more reiterated the sort of perspective on the rural Philippines which Prosterman had spoken for in 1975 and which had been so forcefully articulated in the Hardie and McMillan/Rivera Reports of 1952. The counter-views expressed, for the most part in internal memoranda, by AID Mission director Cody take us right around the vicious circle that was entailed in the Dullesian agenda and had become the well-worn path of AID land reform policies in the Philippines since 1954.

Cody's views were spelled out in a memorandum he wrote for interim Ambassador David Newsom in January 1978. In this memorandum, he freely described the New Society land reform program as having reached an "impasse" which, though he avoided making this inference, pointed directly to "political will" and the organization of peasants as the crucial variables in the equation. Cody posed questions without offering any answers:

> "...under certain conditions, decentralization and participation could make land reform a component of a more meaningful social process among the bureaucracies. But what are these conditions? And how can the Philippines move toward the position where these conditions obtain? *Possibly this issue has taken DAR to its present impasse.* After all, what mandate does DAR have and require *to change the power structure in the rural areas, so that the forces of reaction can be made to yield to the forces of change?*"[138] [emphasis added].

The lack of any answer on Cody's part to these questions is indicative of the fact that the Dullesian agenda was every bit as much at an impasse by 1978 as was DAR. Serious attempts to answer such questions would at once have threatened to derail that agenda. Cody clung to the rails and his summary of the history of and rationale for U.S. program support for land reform in the Philippines over the years, as he presented it to Newsom, exhibits a resolute avoidance of "subversive" thoughts:

> "The extremely low level of A.I.D.'s support and its restriction to highly technical areas conforms closely to precedents set by past USG policy. On both sides this has been a reflection of practical realism, but never a sign of lack of political commitment. What the USG could not deliver over an extremely short period under an authoritarianism, it has delivered in the Philippines over a protracted period in the areas of administrative machinery, land surveys and records and, to a much, much lesser extent, in the form of strengthening local organizations".[139]

The only portion of this summary that is tenable is the sentence that begins it.

The assertion that there had never been a "sign" of lack of political commitment to land reform on the part of either the U.S. government or that of the Philippines since 1946 or 1954, or whenever Cody was dating his long view from, is risible. The reference to "authoritarianism" is confused and contradictory. Cody's wording implies that "authoritarianism" is the way to get land reform done "over an extremely short period", but does not explain why the authoritarianism of Marcos had not got it done in more than five years; and the proposition stands in contradiction with his earlier call for "decentralization and participation" in land reform. Having admitted that land reform was at an impasse, he nevertheless wanted to claim that the U.S. *had delivered* "over a protracted period" (the duration of which he left undisclosed) what it would have delivered "over an extremely short period under an authoritarianism", namely administrative machinery, land surveys and records and the strengthening of local organizations. Whence, then, the administrative paralysis, the hopeless confusion over land tenure data and the lameness of peasant organizations such as the FFF that were so evident by 1978 and had been so not later than 1974?

Writing up their report on the December 1977 conference, even as Cody drafted his memorandum to Newsom, Hickey and Wilkinson were much more forthright than Cody as to the results and prospects of the Marcos land reform program and the role of U.S. policy therein. In their preface to the report, the two men stated that the RAND seminar's point of departure had been the question posed at an April 1975 SEADAG conference on land reform at Baguio: "To what extent can a balanced and moderate program succeed in a nation marked by severe social, political and economic inequalities?". Concern was expressed at the RAND conference, they reported, over the bogging down of the land reform program of the Philippine government during 1976-77 and the seminar had pondered the social, economic, environmental and political contexts of land redistribution, Philippine program options and U.S. policy options. In the body of the report Hickey and Wilkinson did not mince their words and, fairly predictably, the reaction of Malacanang, DAR and AID Manila officials caught in the crossfire was to take exception to their "intemperate and insulting language".

In the light of decades of history and with clear recollection of the fate of the Hardie and McMillan/Rivera Reports of 1952, the Hickey Report makes fascinating reading. All the problems stringently addressed by the 1952 MSA reports were found by Hickey and Wilkinson to have worsened in magnitude and complexity in the intervening generation. In particular, they drew attention to the grave population pressure on the environment in an unreconstructed economy; tenure insecurity and poverty themselves exacerbating deforestation, soil depletion and waste of human and natural resources, with "implications staggering even in the near future" .[140] Even more explicitly than Hardie or McMillan, Hickey and Wilkinson identified the fundamental problem as "lack of

TABLE 23: NEDA DATA (1984) OPERATIONS LAND TRANSFER AND LEASEHOLD
ADMINISTRATIVE BY REGION.

Region	Operation Land Transfer		CLITs Issued/Printed	Leasehold Operation		Number of Leasehold contracts
	Number of Tenant Recipients	Area (Has)		Number of Tenants Involved	Area (Has)	
1	32,594	36,885	64,674	94,747	82,506	108,801
2	46,006	82,384	72,927	39,201	50,727	63,661
3	115,588	249,728	173,105	61,886	100,128	78,790
4	25,717	39,840	35,343	55,791	66,675	75,512
5	51,352	72,308	72,308	35,391	28,701	48,225
6	44,224	63,525	61,940	67,625	73,296	71,973
7	22,310	23,410	85,720	29,167	14,430	36,606
8	21,350	29,014	33,288	38,592	31,579	49,465
9	10,324	15,617	16,274	9,430	11,493	9,430
10	21,800	40,709	30,521	21,921	23,738	23,838
11	18,694	39,126	24,561	23,253	33,992	29,305
12	21,216	54,647	24,384	15,232	20,465	15,232
Total	430,679	739,493	644,415	492,236	540,647	610,838

Source: NEDA *Statistical Yearbook 1984* pp 322-324. Figures declared valid as of 31 October 1983.

political power in the hands of the rural poor".[141] They stressed the need for comprehensive and integrated agrarian reforms, embracing not only rice and corn tenurial practices, but environmental considerations, population dynamics, production and marketing infrastructure, rural-urban migration, social and corporate organizations, timber and water resources, fisher people's rights, the status and structure of export crop production (sugar, coconuts, pineapples, bananas) and landless laborers' employment and working conditions.[142] They also took an overdue stand on the matter of political mobilization, democratic organization and the anomalies of "authoritarianism" as a path to reforms. Emancipation, they stated, is supposed to reinforce the freedom of peasant organizations to defend peasant interests, but martial law had circumscribed this freedom. The Marcos regime's New Society Movement and *Samahang Nayon*, they wrote, were merely devices for government control and manipulation, which made *barrio* council elections farcical. Genuine peasant organizations that "do emerge because they focus on issues that galvanize the villagers, tend to be regarded by the government and the military as subverse and dangerous".[143] They went on:

> "If genuine grass-roots planning is fostered by the Philippine government and AID, then both the Philippine and U.S. governments will have to face the issue of how they should view such emerging organizations as they demonstrate increasing militancy. It is hoped that American apprehension about Communist infiltration in the Philippines will not lead to opposition to any legitimate local protest".[144]

The long record of American assistance to the Philippine elites in suppressing just such vigorous or militant protests, down to the Van Steenwyck analysis of the FFF militants as "subverse and dangerous" in 1975, could provide little reassurance that the "good guys" would take the course urged by Hickey and Wilkinson.

Hickey and Wilkinson questioned established U.S. foreign policy priorities and indicted the results of decades of balance of power fixations and "trickle-down development". The historian of these matters rubs his eyes from a sense of *déja vu*, so closely does the final paragraph of the Hickey Report resemble the buried and forgotten words of Robert Hardie a generation earlier, before the Vietnam War and before Ferdinand Marcos:

> "In the hope that the Philippine government can be encouraged to continue the reforms it began, AID should of-

fer support to the agrarian reform program, tied to tough
performance standards. If aid on such terms is refused, as
well it might be, then at least the record will show that we
tried...The U.S. should indicate nicely but firmly that it
knows the facts. *The U.S. should also indicate that it would
be willing, as it was not in 1972-73, to support a genuine
land transfer program...It should be noted that rental control laws in the Philippines do not work now and never have
worked.* The Filipinos must stop deluding themselves about
land reform—it has not happened. It is desperately needed
and will be more so the longer they wait. The U.S. must
firmly eschew joining them in such self-delusion. The New
People's Army has twice the strength now that it had when
martial law was declared in September 1972. Because of
the U.S. economic and political support of the Marcos government, U.S. military bases could be subject to guerrilla
attacks...This might require a 'protective response', leading
to a situation where the U.S. could become steadily enmeshed
in helping the Marcos government's struggle against the New
People's Army. *All of the ingredients for the making of a
quagmire are clearly present.* The risks must be discussed at
the highest level and the option—the only one that would
make any sense if the base agreements are to be renewed—of
conditioning payments and/or of carrying out the land reform must be explored. It seems to make no sense at all to
say that this is strictly 'military aid' for military bases and
that economic aid or socio-economic changes play no role"[146]
[emphasis added].

AID Manila, however, experienced the Hickey Report as "a bomb with a
delayed action fuse" which "blew the whole enterprise sky high", which
is to say, it jolted the policy preference of the Cody-led mission off the
rails. When the report was shown to President Marcos, he curtly suggested that AID withdraw from a program it had stigmatized as a failure.
Dismayed by this turn of events, Sherper and Cody moved quickly to
assure the Philippine government that, in the words of Lewis Gleeck:

> "...the report had no official character and...the United States
> entertained no views on Philippine land reform which could
> be reasonably regarded as offensive".[147]

This was virtually the epitaph on an era of U.S. involvement in land reform in the Philippines and a quite appropriate one, given its history; for the Marcos regime was not mollified by Cody's abject repudiation of the Hickey Report and was, in any case, preparing to announce the "completion" of the New Society's land reform program.

AID, of course, remained on in the Philippines, for land reform had not been an important part of its *raison d'être* there. All involvement in land reform, however, was terminated in 1978 and not renewed while Marcos remained in power. The Hickey Report having been repudiated as having no official character, one cannot say that the exercise ended with a bang. It ended with a whimper and it left behind it rural problems and an insurgency, with a contingent but potent nexus, that neither the Philippine government nor the U.S. government had come to terms with in all the years that separated the Hardie Report from the Hickey Report. As the Marcos regime entered its terminal crisis, in mid-February 1986, Roy Prosterman once more trumpeted his belief in the urgent need for a major land reform in the Philippines:

> "Having made eight extended visits to the Philippines between 1972 and 1975 at the invitation of the Marcos government, as an unpaid independent adviser on land reform, I am aware of how fundamental the problem is and how little has been done to solve it...Ultimately, a freely elected government may succeed to power, but if such a regime fails to carry out land reform—and diligence is far from assured given the pre-1972 record—it could well collapse, Kerensky-like before the peasant revolutionaries. Only land and not ballots alone will assuage the rural grievances; true democracy in the Philippines requires both".[148]

A matter of two weeks later, Marcos toppled from power and the freely elected government of Corazon Aquino assumed office.

The doubts that Prosterman had expressed as to the probable diligence of the Aquino Administration in the area of land reform appear to have been warranted. The explanation is not far to seek. As one American observer expressed it, writing in 1986, the country's "very fundamental agrarian problems" were so deep and so serious as to be more than ever caught in the "strongest and most complex political and economic cross-currents":

> "No other issue so directly tests the nature of the February revolution, no time has appeared better for a serious commitment to agrarian reform. Or has the problem become too

serious for this kind of government to make and mobilize a
broad commitment? That is the opportunity and the irony.
Which will it be?".[149]

Wasted opportunities and ironies had marked American policies in the
Philippines for decades by 1986; and the probable stance of the United
States as far as land reform and rural strife in the Philippines were
concerned had, by the mid-1980s, been made rather clear, in a tragic
quagmire on the far side of the Pacific—El Salvador. In that strife-torn
and much-abused country, the Reagan Administration had begun by re-
moving an Ambassador who believed in land reform and had proceeded
to increase military counterinsurgency aid to the dominant, repressive
Salvadoran "security" forces by 7,500% between 1981 and 1984. Having
supported President Marcos up to the last possible moment, the White
House then passed its support to Mrs Aquino, as the symbol of political
legitimacy in the Philippines. However, throughout 1986 and 1987, as
the land reform issue was debated in the Philippines and the new Philippine Congress strangled efforts at genuine land reform, the AID mission
in Manila remained aloof from the matter and the weight of U.S. policy
continued to lend support to conservative forces in the Philippines. In
the end, one must conclude, it is not only Philippine land reformers who
are caught in the strongest and most complex political and economic
cross-currents. Any Americans with a serious interest in the Philippines
are likewise caught in such currents—on both sides of the Pacific.

Conclusion

*" 'I did that', says my memory. 'I cannot have done that',
says my pride, and remains adamant. Finally, memory yields. "*

— Nietzsche *Beyond Good and Evil.*

There is no reason to assume that land reform of any significant magnitude will occur in the Philippines under the Aquino Administration. Nor, one must insist, is it at all obvious that the result will be the triumph of the New People's Army by the turn of the century. The histories of such Latin American countries as Peru, Bolivia, Colombia, Brazil are probably better parallels to what can be expected in the Philippines in the foreseeable future than are the histories of Vietnam or Cuba or Nicaragua. Moreover, even were the New People's Army to win state power in the Philippines, the history of radical revolutions in the twentieth century suggests that the consequences for the Philippine people are as likely to be disastrous as liberating.

It is important to reflect on the implications of these judgements—for they are judgements, not "facts". Since Robert Hardie did his work, the population of the Philippines has trebled: from around 21 million to 63 million. The land "frontier" has, for all practical purposes, long since been "closed". The ecological crisis of human demographic pressure on the natural environment, endemic throughout the world in the 1980's, is increasingly acute in the Philippines. Yet long-established structures of exploitation and maladministration remain fundamentally unchanged and economic growth continues to be measured substantially in the agro-export fortunes of a narrow elite. If the combined forces of social disintegration, economic instability and political delegitimation bring down the old order in the country, those who seize the reins of state power will be faced with awesome problems that have no obvious solutions. That which flourished under the old order will, in the nature of the case, be in a state of dissolution; the economic and political, military and judicial elites of the old order will be the avowed enemies of the new. Those external forces, chiefly in the United States and Japan, with the financial resources to succour the new regime will see it as a confiscating and violent enemy and as economically insolvent. As in so many other revolutions, the fate of democratic intellectuals, economic and technical specialists and the masses themselves in the Philippines is likely to be grim under such circumstances.

Where does recollection of the Hardie Report belong in such sombre prognoses? It certainly is long since outdated as an analysis of rural conditions in the Philippines, or as a prescription for improving them. Economic and administrative specialists assigned to deal with current conditions may regard it as an irrelevant piece of "ancient history". I would argue, however, that it is among the most "relevant" pieces of "ancient history" available to those engaged in analysing and working to improve the grave maladies of Philippine rural society. Above all, it is a document vital to getting American involvement in Philippine rural affairs, over the long haul, into clear perspective. It enables one to anchor a critique of conservative policies in something other than the rather worn ideological clichés of Marxism-Leninism. By its biting and sweeping character, it places in question not only the corruption and exploitation characteristic of the renascent old order in the Philippines, but also the tinkering and politically neutered prescriptions of Philippine, American and other foreign "technocrats" over three decades and more. At a time when new momentum in rural programs is desperately needed in the Philippines—not for the sake of American interests, not for the sake of the ruling elites, but for the sake of the mass of malnourished and ill-treated Filipinos—it seems to me that the Hardie Report and the debate which it provoked might contribute freshness and pungency to a discourse that has become stale and sclerotic.

To express such a thought is, clearly, to take something other than a "value-neutral" stand in the matter. While this involves no difficulties for a Marxist, it gives pause to a social "scientist" whose approach to "knowledge" is more Weberian than Marxist. In a recent, provocative paper entitled "Demographic and Cultural Constraints on the Comprehensive Agrarian Reform Program", American scholars Ross Eshleman and Chester Hunt have argued that a land reform in the Philippines which seeks to abolish tenancy and create the maximum possible number of family-size farms will be attempting to make water flow uphill. They caution, "if disastrous effects are to be avoided, it will be necessary to use the pragmatic criterion of what is likely to work, rather than the ideological test of which policies harmonize best with left-wing slogans." Such arguments must be taken seriously. It is of no more use to the putative beneficiaries of land reform to make a dogma out of the Hardie Report than it is to press upon them the dogmas of the left-wing ideologues. Pragmatic and practical policies are required whoever is in power, if real problems are to be solved. The history of the Hardie Report is offered here, therefore, not by way of saying "Go ye now and do likewise!". Rather, it is offered as a provocation to critical thought about the postures of Philippine and American decision-makers and policy analysts in the long land reform debate.

It is precisely in a reading of such contemporary policy papers as that by Eshleman and Hunt that this history enlivens the understanding. They make no reference to the Hardie Report, the McMillan/Rivera Report, the Sorongon Report, or the Davis Report in their paper; their summary of the land reform debate in the Philippines leaps from the friar-lands purchase of 1903 to the paternal programs of the 1930's and then the Marcos program of the 1970's. Yet their analysis and prescription bear a striking resemblance to that offered in the Davis Report of 1954 and, in particular, their insistence on the need for both tenancy and "agrobusiness" recall the emphasis in the Davis Report on allowing "sufficient flexibility" in the Philippine rural sector to encourage free-market development. Their case is better put than that of the Davis committee in 1954, but it is also easier for them to put it, given the appalling problems confronting serious land reform in the Philippines by 1989. The case put by the Hardie Report was, of course, not one for either inflexibility or an unfree market; it was an insistence that the problem had to be tackled at its root and nationwide if anything was to be accomplished. While Eshleman and Hunt may be correct that a land reform along the lines envisioned by Hardie can no longer solve the problems the Philippines faces, the point need not be conceded quite so readily as they appear to believe and their own rhetoric goes far to indicating where their argument may come to grief.

The Philippines, these scholars aver, has committed itself to following the development pattern of Taiwan and South Korea and, to that end, will press for rural industrialization. Yet they do not so much as note in passing that both Taiwan and South Korea began this pattern of development with substantial land reforms of the kind Eshleman and Hunt now discountenance for the Philippines. Further, they deprecate the wisdom of government management of farm production or credit facilities, insisting that the "free market"—unreconstructed and semi-feudal though it may be—will handle these things better than public servants. They may be correct. It would be dogmatic indeed to insist otherwise. Yet they then prescribe a stern population control policy for the Philippines modelled on that of the People's Republic of China "with the use of every method of preventing births along with rewards for small families and penalties for large ones." Why such presumption and interference in population policy coupled with such a defence of what amounts to *laissez faire* in land tenure policies? Dare one suggest that Eshleman and Hunt here let slip an ideological bias, or a "hidden agenda"? The contradiction in their development philosophy does not damn them, but it does, I submit, indicate that the sorts of reformist perspectives open in the Hardie Report and the sorts of conservative reaction that that Report brought forth, remain of enlivening pertinence in the current debate over Philippine agriculture and politics. This study will more than serve its purpose if it reminds participants in this debate of the hollowness, bad faith and weak institutional memory that tend to afflict conservative policy analysts confronted by the notion of radical socio-economic change.

Part One : Endnotes

1. Teodoro Agoncillo and Milagros C. Guerrero, *History of the Filipino People*, 5th edition, University of the Philippines Press, Quezon City, 1977, pp. 117–137.

2. John N. Schumacher S.J., *Revolutionary Clergy: The Filipino Clergy and the Nationalist Movement, 1850–1903*, Ateneo de Manila University Press, Quezon City, 1981, pp. 13–32, 87–123.

3. David Sturtevant, *Philippine Social Structure and Its Relation to Agrarian Unrest*, Unpublished Ph.D. dissertation, Stanford University, 1958. See also his *Popular Uprisings In the Philippines, 1840–1940*, Cornell University Press, Ithaca, 1976.

4. Francisco Nemenzo, Jr., "The Millenarian-Populist Aspects of Filipino Marxism," in Randolf S. David (ed.), *Marxism In The Philippines*, Third World Studies Center, University of the Philippines, Diliman. Quezon City, 1984, pp. 1–13. See also James S. Allen, *The Radical Left on the Eve of War: A Political Memoir.* Foundation for Nationalist Studies, Quezon City, 1985.

5. Alfred Thayer Mahan, doyen of American sea-power theorists, called for acquisition of naval bases in the Pacific to secure U.S. lines to the Orient and the South Seas. For the bearing of his ideas on U.S. conquest of the Philippines, see Stuart C. Miller, *Benevolent Assimilation: The American Conquest of the Philippines*, Yale University Press, New Haven, 1982, pp. 7–8. See also James C. Thomson Jr., Peter W. Stanley and J.C. Perry, *Sentimental Imperialists*, Harper & Row, New York, 1981, pp. 110–115.

6. Marshall S. McLennan, "Changing Human Ecology on the Central Luzon Plain, 1705– 1939," in Alfred W. McCoy and Ed. C. de Jesus (eds.), *Philippine Social History: Global Trade and Local Transformations*, Asian Studies Association of Australia, George Allen & Unwin, Sydney, 1984, pp. 57–90.

7. Dennis M. Roth, "Church Lands in the Agrarian History of the Tagalog Region," in Alfred W. McCoy and Ed. C. de Jesus (eds.), op. cit.

8. Dean Worcester and John Ralston Hayden, *The Philippines: Past and Present*, Macmillan, New York, 1930, p. 254.

9. ibid., p. 668.

10. ibid. p. 208.

11. pp. 197, 201–02, 205–06, 661, 673–74.

12. Glenn A. May, *America In The Philippines: The Shaping of Colonial Policy, 1898–1913*, Unpublished Ph.D. dissertation, Yale University, New Haven, 1975, pp. 319–20.

13. ibid. pp. 321–22.

14. Peter W. Stanley, *A Nation In The Making: The Philippines And the United States, 1899–1921*, Harvard University Press, Cambridge, Mass., 1974, pp. 251, 259, 265–66, 268–78. See also Lewis E. Gleeck Jr., *The American Governors-General and High Commissioners in the Philippines: Proconsuls, Nation-Builders and Politicians*. New Day, Quezon City, 1986, pp. 134–193.

15. ibid., p. 270.

16. George E. Taylor, *The Philippines And the United States: Problems of Partnership*, Praeger, New York, 1964, pp. 80, 144–45.

17. A.V.H. Hartendorp, "The Tayug Colorums" (*Philippine Magazine*, Vol. xxvii, 1931) and "The Sakdal Protest" (*Philippine Magazine*, Vol. xxxiii, 1935) are examples. See also Joseph R. Hayden's report in the *Christian Science Monitor* 12 Sept. 1931. According to David Sturtevant, Governor Frank Murphy even observed, in 1935, that the Sakdals might emerge as a genuine opposition party, to the benefit of Philippine democracy. This did not happen and the Americans do not appear to have made any effort to help it come about. See Sturtevant, 1958, op. cit., p. 169, n27.

18. Peter W. Stanley, op. cit., p. 271.

19. Thomson, Stanley and Perry, op. cit., pp. 270–71.

20. Sturtevant, 1958, op. cit., p. 208; and Benedict J. Kerkvliet, *The Huk Rebellion: A Study of Peasant Revolt in the Philippines*, University of California Press, Berkeley, 1982, pp. 17, 23. See also Brian Fegan, "The Social History of a Central Luzon Barrio," and Marshall S. McLennan, "Changing Human Ecology on the Central Luzon Plain: Nueva Ecija 1705–1939" in Alfred W. McCoy and Ed C. de Jesus (eds.), op. cit., pp. 91–130, 57–90, respectively.

21. Kerkvliet op. cit. pp. 17–25.

22. *New York Times* 5 May 1935.

23. Brian Fegan loc. cit. p. 107. See also Sturtevant 1958 op. cit. pp. 164–65, 171–73, 196–98.

24. Kerkvliet op. cit. pp. 143–50. See also Luis Taruc *Born Of The People* Greenwood Press 1975 pp. 212–77 and Hernando Abaya *Betrayal In The Philippines* New York 1946 pp. 134–50, 206–23, 250–54.

H. Scaff *The Philippine Answer To Communism.* Stanford University Press 1955 is a text representative of official American reaction to the Huk Rebellion. See also Edward G. Lansdale, *In the Midst of Wars* . Harper & Row New York 1972, pp. 8–10. Lansdale, an advertising man in San Francisco until enlisted in Army Intelligence in 1941, finished the Second World War an Army Major and Chief of the Intelligence Division of the Armed Forces (G–2) for the Western Pacific. He worked in Manila from the end of the war until 1948. He then returned to the U.S. to teach at the Air Force's Strategic Intelligence School, in Denver, Colorado. In 1949, he went to Washington D.C. to work as a Cold War policy analyst. Then, in August 1950, he was sent back to Manila by the National Security Council to help in the struggle against the Huks. He developed psychological warfare tactics based on his knowledge of American experiences in the Greek Civil War a few years earlier (ibid. pp. 4–14).

Stephen R. Shalom, in an extensively documented account of this period, has argued that the State Department and JUSMAG/Manila at no point encouraged President Elpidio Quirino to negotiate with the Huks, resolving that, although there was virtually no evidence of external support for the rebels, the case should be described and treated as a case of "Communist aggression". *The United States and the Philippines: A Study In Neo-Colonialism.* New Day Publishers, Quezon City 1986, pp. 1–32, 74, 215–16.

The U.S. counterinsurgency campaign in the Philippines generated a number of studies that merit the consideration of the historian. See, in particular, A. H. Peterson, G. C. Reinhardt, E. E. Conger (eds) *Symposium On the Role of Airpower in Counterinsurgency and Unconventional Warfare: The Huk Campaign.* RM-3652. RAND Corp. Santa Monica, CA. June 1963; Napoleon Valeriano/Charles R. Bohannan *Counter-Guerrilla Operations: The Philippine Experience.* Praeger New York 1962; Louis F. Felder *Socio-economic Aspects of Counterinsurgency: A Case Study—Philippines.* Industrial College of the Armed Forces (ICAF) Washington D.C. 1963; J. N. Tinio *The Huk Rebellion: A Case Study In the Social Dynamics of Insurrection.* ICAF. Washington D.C. 1964; Jose M. Crisol *The Red Lie.* Manila 1954; Uldarico S. Baclagon *Lessons From the Huk Campaign in the Philippines.* Manila 1960; F. H. Barton *Salient Operational Aspects of Paramilitary Operations in Three Asian Areas.* Washington D.C. Operations Research Office Technical Memorandum CRO.T 228 1954.

Edward Lansdale (op. cit. p. 19), writing in 1971, declared his shock on discovering, in 1950, that "curiously enough, Philippine and Amer-

ican officials barely mentioned the political and social factors in briefing me. They dwelt almost exclusively on the military situation. It
was as though military affairs were the sole tangible factor they could
grasp." On a trip outside Manila, in late 1950, he began, he wrote more
than twenty years later, to get a sense of the outrage in the countryside
against the corruption and thuggery of the Quirino Administration. He
was, he wrote, appalled at the mounting polarization between two power
groups he saw as unregenerate reactionaries and unreconstructed stal-
inists. "Surely" he exclaimed, looking back, "the principles I believed
in, the rights of man as a free individual, lay in between such harshly
jumbled political and social terrain." (ibid. pp. 28-9). Certainly they
did, of course, but Lansdale's work did not in any clear sense show how
those principles might triumph in such terrain.

25. Sturtevant 1958 op. cit. p. 7.

26. Samuel p. Hayes, *The Beginning of American Aid to Southeast Asia:
The Griffin Mission Of 1950*. Lexington, MA. 1971. Hayes, an economist,
was himself a member of the Griffin Mission.

27. Michael Schaller *The American Occupation of Japan: Origins of the
Cold War In Asia*. Oxford University Press. 1985. pp. 223–24.

28. ibid. pp. 225–27.

29. David Omer Drury Wurfel *The Bell Report And After: A Study of the
Political Problems of Social Reform Stimulated By Foreign Aid*. PhD.
Cornell University 1960, pp. 119–21.

30. President Quirino had, in March 1950, set up a Philippine Economic
Survey Mission, headed by Jose Yulo, but the idea of a commission of
inquiry into Philippine public and economic affairs dated back to January 1950, when Quirino had visited the U.S. looking for aid. In Wurfel's
words, "The economic discussions with U.S. officials which took place
at this time resulted in a simultaneous announcement from Washington
and Manila on February 11 ... to the effect that a high level commission
would be created shortly to advise on the establishment of a sound and
well-balanced economy in the Philippines. President Truman later gave
President Quirino full credit for the plan. The *Manila Bulletin* credited
Ambassador Cowen with major responsibility." ibid. p. 120.

31. ibid. p. 121.

32. ibid. pp. 122–25. August L. Strand, President of Oregon State College
"headed the Agricultural Survey undertaken by the Mission". Vincent
Checchi, "at that time chief of the Far Eastern Trade Policy branch of
ECA and soon to become ECA mission chief for the Philippines" was a
prominent member of the Bell Mission.

33. ibid. p. 134. Quirino immediately began a campaign to evade such
reforms, partly by baldly asserting that they had already taken place.

When Bell Mission spokesman, Edward Bernstein, described the Quirino Administration as corrupt and inefficient, in an address in New York prominently reported in the *Washington Post,* Quirino released an unsigned statement from Malacanang, angrily denouncing such allegations and charging, in turn, that that the United States led the world in racketeering, graft and corruption, but disowned the statement before signing the Quirino-Foster Agreement on 14 November 1950.

Ambassador Cowen was careful to declare, in July 1950, on the arrival of the Bell Mission: "When the Mission completes its survey, its report will indicate what can be done and how the U.S. can most fruitfully assist in the doing ... But the Philippine Republic will be under no compulsion other than its own self-interest to accept such plan or assistance."

34. Office Memo. State Dept. 13 October 1950. From: PSA Shohan. To: FE Rusk, Merchant. Subject: Land Reform in South East Asia. U.S. National Archives Diplomatic Branch. Philippines 1950–54 Decimal File Box 5710—*henceforth referred to as DFB 5710.*

35. Robert S. Hardie *Philippine Land Tenure Reform: Analysis And Recommendations.* MSA Manila 1952. 291 pp. Appendix F pp. 1–2. This document will henceforth be referred to as the *Hardie Report.*

36. Restricted Cable to State Dept./Foreign Agriculture. From: Merrill W. Abbey, Manila 874 20 Dec. 1950. Ref: 40021. Subject: *Land Settlement and Development Corporation.* DFB 5710.

37. Telegram. Restricted. Rec'd 15 Feb. 1951. From: Manila. To: Secretary of State. No. 2412. DFB 5710.

38. Restricted Cable No. 166. To: Officer-In-Charge, American Mission Manila. 9 March 1951. From: State Dept./Foreign Agriculture. DFB 5710.

39. Restricted Cable to State Dept. From: Merrill W. Abbey. Subject: Land Settlement. Manila 1419. 3 April 1951. Ref: 400221 DFB 5710.

40. Confidential Cable No. 34 9 July 1951. Merrill W. Abbey to State Dept. Ref: Dept. AS77 15 June 1951 DFB 5710.

41. Unclassified Cable No. 133. Merrill W. Abbey to State Dept. 24 July 1951 DFB 5710.

42. Richard T. Ely "An American Land Policy" in E. M. Friedman (ed) *America And The New Era.* Dutton New York 1929 p. 149.

43. Richard T. Ely memo. to Leonard Tyson March 1951. DFB 5710.

44. U.S. Dept. Agriculture, Office of Foreign Agricultural Relations (OFAR) 6 March 1951. From: Wilhelm Anderson, Head Far Eastern Division OFAR. To: Leonard Tyson, Edward Fried, Dudley Kirk (State), Robert Coote (Interior), Raymond H. Davis (ECA), Marshall Harris

(BAE/USDA). Subject: *Land Reform in the Philippines.* Attachment: Draft of report on land reform in the Philippines, summary and recommendations by Mr. Ferber 5 March 1951. DFB 5710.

45. Immortalized by John Steinbeck in *The Grapes of Wrath* in the form of the benign Weedpatch Camp, detested by the "Bank of the West"-dominated "Farmers' Association" as a seed-bed of "Communism".

46. Robert S. Hardie, letter to the author 20 April 1986.

47. Laurence I. Hewes Jr., *Japan: Land and Men.* Iowa State College Press 1955 p. 68. Strangely, Alfred McCoy, in 1971, (op. cit. pp. 28, 47 n76) gave this book and page as a reference for his statement that, in 1950–51, Edward Lansdale urged Magsaysay "to adopt an immediate program of rural reform to erode peasant support for the Huks." Like Gary Olson, in 1974, McCoy appears to have conflated EDCOR and psych-war with land reform, which was a different undertaking and one with which Lansdale himself does not seem to have been directly connected. In any case, neither at p. 68 nor at any other point in his book, did Hewes make any reference to Lansdale or land reform in the Philippines.

48. Robert S. Hardie, letter to the author 20 April 1986.

49. Robert S. Hardie, letter to the author 22 Feb. 1987.

50. ibid.

51. Merrill W. Abbey, letter to Ambassador Myron M. Cowen, dated Manila 27 November 1951. DFB 5710.

52. U.S. Dept. Agriculture OFAR. From: Wilhelm Anderson. To: Leonard Tyson, PSA. 22 Jan. 1952. DFB 5710.

53. Confidential Cable. From: Secretary of State, Dean Acheson. To: American Embassy, Manila. 3 April 1952. DFB 5710.

54. Ambassador Raymond A. Spruance to Secretary of State Dean Acheson. Telegram 2542 9 April 1952. DFB 5710.

55. Confidential Cable. Dean Acheson to AmEmb. Manila 18 April 1952. DFB 5710.

56. Wurfel 1960 op. cit. p. 508.

57. Frances Lucille Starner *Magsaysay And the Philippine Peasantry*. Stanford University Press 1961 p. 120.

58. Gary L. Olson *U.S. Foreign Policy and the Third World Peasant: Land Reform In Asia And Latin America.* Praeger 1974 pp. 80–81. The figures are actually drawn from Frate Bull *Land Reform In The Philippines 1950–58*. ICA Manila 1958 p. 18.

59. Alfred W. McCoy "Land Reform As Counterrevolution: U.S. Foreign Policy and the Tenant Farmers of Asia." *Bulletin of Concerned Asian Scholars.* Winter-Spring 1971 Vol. 3. No. 1. p. 28.

60. John Locke *Two Treatises Of Government*. Mentor New York 1965. Second Treatise: An Essay Concerning the True Original Extent and End of Civil Government. Ch. xiii:158. pp. 419–20. Hardie Report Appendix K pp. 11, 15–16.

61. Hardie Report p. 1.

62. ibid. Summary Statement p. v.

63. ibid. pp. v–vi.

64. ibid. p. vi.

65. ibid. p. vii.

66. ibid. p. 5.

67. ibid. p. 3.

68. ibid. pp. vi, 9–10.

69. ibid. p. 7.

70. ibid. p. 7.

71. ibid. p. 8.

72. ibid. pp. 8–9.

73. ibid. pp. 10–11.

74. ibid. pp. 11–12.

75. ibid. p. 20.

76. ibid. pp. 20–21.

77. ibid. p. 21.

78. ibid. pp. 21–22.

79. ibid. p. 24.

80. ibid. p. 25.

81. ibid. pp. 29 n10, 30 n12.

82. Robert S. Hardie "On My Relations With Philippine Land Reform." 7 pp. Attachment to letter to the author 22 Feb. 1987. p. 2. Henceforth referred to as the *Hardie Statement* .

83. Daniel M. Braddock, AmEmb. Manila, to State Dept.Desp. 740, 12 Jan. 1953. DFB 5710.

84. Thomas B. Buell *The Quiet Warrior: A Biography of Admiral Raymond A. Spruance*. Little, Brown & Co. Boston. 1st edition 1974. p. 404.

85. Lewis E. Gleeck Jr., letter to the author 17 April 1986.

86. Frances L. Starner *Magsaysay And The Philippine Peasantry*. Stanford University Press 1961 p. 268 n52.

87. *Daily Bulletin,* Manila, 55th anniversary edition, 28 March 1955. Section 1. p. 3: "The Quiet Ambassador Interviewed."

88. Buell op. cit. pp. 403–04.

89. *Hardie Statement* p. 4.

90. ibid. pp. 5–6.

91. Ambassador Raymond A. Spruance to Secretary of State Dean Acheson. 7 Jan. 1953 1998. DFB 5710.

92. Spruance to Acheson 18 Dec. 1952 1776. DFB 5710.

93. Spruance to Acheson 18 Dec. 1952 1779. DFB 5710.

94. Spruance to Acheson 20 Dec. 1952 1816. DFB 5710.

95. Spruance to Acheson 20 Dec. 1952 1832. DFB 5710.

96. *Philippines Free Press* 3 Jan. 1953 p. 10.

97. *Philippines Free Press* 10 Jan. 1953 p. 2.

98. *Manila Times* 5 Jan. 1953 p. 1.

99. *Manila Times* 6 Jan. 1953 p. 1.

100. *Manila Times* 10 Jan. 1953.

101. *Philippines Free Press* 10 Jan. 1953.

102. Spruance to Acheson 6 Jan. 1953 1970. DFB 5710.

103. Office Memorandum, State Dept. PSA: Shaw to Day 27 Jan. 1953 re. Manila Despatch 734 9 Jan. 1953. DFB 5710.

104. Despatch 734: Daniel M. Braddock, AmEmb. Manila, to State Dept. 9 Jan. 1953. DFB 5710.

105. *Manila Bulletin* 25 Dec. 1952 p. 1.

106. *Manila Times* 3 Jan. 1953 p. 9.

107. *Philippines Free Press* 24 Jan. 1953.

108. *Philippines Free Press* 10 Jan. 1953.

109. *Manila Bulletin* 25 Dec. 1952 p. 1. Antonio C. Alano "Solons React to Hardie Report."

110. *Manila Times* 7 Jan. 1953 p. 1: "Yulo Backs Rivera-McMillan Report As Perez Stands Pat."

111. *Manila Bulletin* 27 Dec. 1952 p. 1: "CUFA Wants To See MSA Report."

112. *Daily Mirror,* Manila, 3 Jan. 1953 p. 1: "Red Rap On Hardie Repelled: Dalisay Clears Land Expert of Commie Leanings At Hearing."

113. *Manila Times* 16 April 1953.

114. Despatch 734. Daniel M. Braddock, AmEmb. Manila, to State Dept. 9 Jan. 1953. DFB 5710. Use of the phrase *"large landed estates "* by Braddock in this context is jarring, given Hardie's pointed repudiation of the notion that the land reform needed in the Philippines consisted simply in attacking big properties because they were big. See the *Hardie Report* pp. 10–11.

115. *Philippines Free Press* 17 Jan. 1953 p. 4.

116. *Christian Science Monitor* 11 April 1953.

117. *Philippines Free Press* 17 December 1952 p. 4.

118. *U.S. Congressional Record.* Vol. 99. 1953 Pt. 8. pp. 11099–11100.

119. Robert S. Hardie, letter to the author 22 Feb. 1987.

120. Gary L. Olson op. cit. p. 98 n44.

121. Interview with John L. Cooper, Washington D.C. 5 Dec. 1984.

122. Robert S. Hardie, letter to the author 20 April 1986.

123. Robert S. Hardie, letter to the author 22 Feb. 1987.

124. *Hardie Statement* pp. 6–7.

125. H. H. Scullard "Scipio Aemilianus and Roman Politics." *Journal of Roman Studies.* Vol. L. 1960. p. 65.

126. Theodor Mommsen *The History of Rome.* E. P. Dutton & Co. New York 1911. Vol. III. Ch. iii: "The Revolution."
Mommsen, in fact, believed that the Sempronian Agrarian Law of 133 B.C., the land reform of Tiberius Gracchus, really did achieve so considerable a redistribution of public lands as to create some 75,000 new freehold peasant farmers. Census figures between 132 and 125 B.C. showed an increase in the number of registered citizens from 319,000 to 395,000, and Mommsen commented that this was *"beyond all doubt solely in consequence* of what the allotment commission did for the Roman burgesses." (op. cit. p. 96). Gaius Gracchus, he added, strengthened the commission "only to save the principle", not to extend land reform, "because the domain land intended for redistribution by his brother was *already in substance distributed."* (ibid. p. 103) [emphasis added].
More recent scholarship, David Stockton has noted, casts doubt on these conclusions of Mommsen's. Hugh Scullard could still comment in 1959 that the census figures *"almost certainly* reflect the increase of land settlement" (*From the Gracchi to Nero.* 5th edition. Methuen London 1982 p. 30), but Stockton, in 1979, drew attention to the fact that the census data do not provide a reliable basis for an inference of this kind. He described the inference as *"prima facie* ... tempting", but commented that it rests on the assumption that the census "recorded not

the total number of male citizens, but only the number of *adsidui,* viz.
those who were registered as possessed of at least the minimum property
needed to qualify for legionary service." He observed that, on the one
hand, Beloch, Fraccaro, Frank and Brunt have established convincingly
that the census figures were *not* confined to *adsidui* but did record "all
male citizens of every class and category"; and that, on the other hand,
the *adsiduus* qualification may have been lowered anyway about 130
B.C., "in response to the legionary manpower shortage." (*The Gracchi.*
Clarendon Press Oxford 1979 pp. 49–50), so that Mommsen's inference
may very well be erroneous.

Gaius Gracchus attempted much more than land reform, of course. He
clearly aimed at the overthrow of the oligarchic establishment and its
replacement with a principate. Mommsen's learned commentary on the
ambitions, downfall and political legacy of Gaius Gracchus shows quite
clearly his concerns as a German national liberal, writing in the years
after 1848, and anticipates, in many ways, Max Weber's remarks on the
politics of Bismarck, in *Economy And Society.* It remains of considerable
pertinence to the debate on the politics of Lenin and Mao and other
modern radical revolutionaries:

"Now the Sempronian Constitution shows very clearly to everyone who
is able and willing to see that Gaius Gracchus did not at all, as many
good natured people in ancient and modern times have supposed, wish
to place the Roman republic on new democratic bases, but that, on
the contrary, he wished to abolish it and to introduce in its stead a
Tyrannis—that is, in modern language, a monarchy not of the feudal or
theocratic, but of the Napoleonic absolute type ... *an unlimited tribune-
ship of the people for life.* In fact, if Gracchus, as his words and still more
his works plainly testify, aimed at the overthrow of the government of
the senate, *what other political organization but the Tyrannis remained
possible,* after overthrowing the aristocratic government, in a commonwealth which had outgrown collective assemblies and had no knowledge
of parliamentary government? ..." (ibid. pp. 112–13) [emphasis added].
What Gaius Gracchus lacked, in order to achieve this end, was gradually
acquired by Marius, Sulla, Pompey, and finally used by Caesar and his
heirs to overthrow the patrician government of the senate and with it
the republic.

127. Niccolo Macchiavelli *The Prince.* Penguin 1975 Ch. vi. p. 52: "...all
    armed prophets have conquered and unarmed prophets have come to
    grief."
    Isaac Deutscher *The Prophet Armed: Trotsky 1879–1921.* Oxford Uni-
    versity Press 1976. p. xii.

Part Two: Endnotes

1. Interview with Albert Ravenholt. Magsaysay Center, Manila. 24 November 1987. Raymond Johnson was MSA/FOA/ICA Agriculture Division chief in Manila from August 1952 until July 1955. His opposition to Hardie's recommendations would seem to have been recorded by David Wurfel, in 1960, in the latter's claim that Hardie found himself involved in a "heated debate" within the U.S. Mission, against opponents "from Dr. Renne at the top down to the Chief of the Agriculture Division and including at least one of Hardie's fellow technicians in the Agriculture Division." See Wurfel *The Bell Report And After: A Study of the Political Problems of Social Reform Stimulated By Foreign Aid* (PhD. Cornell University 1960) p. 509. Since Wurfel claimed that the "heated debate" erupted almost as soon as Hardie circulated his proposal within the Mission, and since Johnson did not replace Edward Bell as chief of the Agriculture Division until almost the time of the submission of the Hardie Report to Malacañang (August:September 1952), it is possible that the man Wurfel was referring to was actually Bell rather than Johnson. If this was the case, the "fellow technician" referred to might, ironically, have been Johnson himself, since he was Agriculture Production Advisor from January to August 1952, before taking over from Bell. Unfortunately, Wurfel did not name most of the parties to the "heated debate". Nor did he cite interviews with any of the participants, except Robert Hardie himself. Nor did he indicate the precise nature of the issues in the "heated debate". Yet so far as the present author has been able to ascertain, the available historical records do not carry any traces of such a "heated debate" and Robert Hardie himself wrote in 1986 that he had had no significant differences with Dr. Renne or other members of the Mission during 1951–52. (Robert S. Hardie, letter to the author 20 April 1986).

2. Starner 1961 op. cit. pp. 137–38: "Surprisingly, this change in the American position on agrarian reform received little or no public acknowledgement. As late as 1955, the Manila press seemed totally unaware that the United States mission had reversed the stand on land reform which was enunciated in the Hardie Report; even in Congress it was not gener-

ally recognized that the Hardie recommendations no longer represented
the official attitude of the United States ... This is documented to some
extent in Senate records on the debate on Senate Bill 90 ..."
The articles by Teodoro Locsin in the *Philippines Free Press*, between
April and August 1955, are an interesting illustration of Starner's observation here concerning the Manila press. Under the heading "The
President's Bill [House Bill 2557, the Land Reform Act]: Nationalism
As Nonsense", on 23 April 1955, Locsin wrote: "Nothing remotely re-
sembling land reform has, so far, been accomplished in the Philippines
and there is very little that the United States can do about it."

3. Olson 1974 op. cit. pp. 85–86; Starner op. cit. pp. 138–39.

4. Joseph L. Dougherty, Agricultural Attache, to State Department. Despatch
   No. 741. 8 Jan. 1954. In Philippines Decimal File 1950–54 Box 5710.
   National Archives. Washington D.C. (DFB 5710).

5. State Dept. cable to AmEmb. Manila 1858 26 Jan. 1954 re. Emb.
   Despatch No. 741. Cleared FOA: Burness PSA: James D. Bell, Leonard
   Tyson. Transmission and Classification: PSA: Philip W. Bonsal. DFB
   5710.

6. Frate Bull *Philippine Land Reform 1950–1958*. ICA Manila 1958 p. 20.

7. Embassy-USOM Land Tenure Committee (Raymond E. Davis, Herbert
   K. May, Daniel M. Braddock, John L. Cooper, Robert T. McMillan),
   Memorandum to Ambassador Raymond A. Spruance and Director Harry
   A. Brenn, 19 March 1954: "Report Concerning Land Tenure Policy",
   in transmission of *The Philippine Agricultural Land Tenure Study* [the
   Davis Report]. USOM/FOA Manila March 1954, pp. 12-13:

   > "Senate Bill 90 ... should not be supported in its present
   > form, because it seeks to solve the tenant problem solely
   > by a sweeping nationwide transfer of titles to tenants. This
   > is not considered practical ... Such a program would bring
   > about extreme financial difficulties for the economy, have lit-
   > tle chance of Congressional approval, and involve more com-
   > plicated administrative problems than can feasibly be dealt
   > with successfully in the Philippines ... "

   In the body of the *Davis Report* itself, at p. 30, the authors stated: "It
   is not feasible to make tenants the owners of the land they till through
   a nationwide land transfer program ..."

8. Embassy/USOM Land Tenure Committee Memorandum to Ambassador
   Raymond. A. Spruance and FOA Director Harry A. Brenn *Report Concerning Philippine Land Tenure Policy*. 19 March 1954 p. 2.

9. Interview with John L. Cooper, Washington D.C. 5 Dec. 1984.

10. Teodoro Locsin observed drily, in April 1955: "Congress is mainly composed of landlords and their lawyers; to expect land reform from it would be to expect blood from a turnip, water from a stone." *Philippines Free Press* 23 April 1955 p. 2. Indeed, he commented bitterly:

> " ...even if both House and Senate were to approve [the Land Reform Act] there is no indication that it would be implemented. The chances are that it would be one more of those dead laws that clutter up our statute books. Congress may pay lip service to land reform; that is the popular, the 'political' thing to do these days; Congress is not expected to take it seriously." *Philippines Free Press* 9 April 1955 p. 4.

When the Land Reform Act was finally legislated, he described it as "a futile, mutilated, queer piece of legislation". *Philippines Free Press* 16 July 1955 p. 2: "Congressmen Mutilate President Magsaysay's Land Reform Bill".

The enduring realities of Philippine politics may be grasped by the simple observation that almost exactly the same phrasing as that used by Locsin in 1955, in reference to the Magsaysay Land Reform Act, was used, with every justification, by commentators, including the aged Locsin himself, in 1987–88, in reference to the Aquino land reform legislation.

11. *Davis Report* p. 21: "It has become increasingly clear that effective measures to improve land tenure conditions would destroy the major social issue which the Huk leaders have been exploiting as an excuse for the dissident activites." The report went on to quote Huk leader Luis Taruc, from an interview with Benigno Aquino, published in the *Manila Bulletin* on 16 Feb. 1954:

> "The Pampanga rebel leader reiterated his belief that his movement is a just and a valid cause. He said that he would neither compromise nor surrender, if the reforms he and his followers have been demanding since they took up arms are not granted by the government. His foremost demand has not changed. It is still the complete revamp of the country's tenancy laws 'to afford the masses of our people the chance to live decently' or at least a liberal and humane application of present tenancy laws."

12. *Davis Report* p. 34.

13. *Davis Report* p. 38.

14. McCoy "Land Reform as Counterrevolution: U.S. Foreign Policy and the Tenant Farmers of Asia." *Bulletin of Concerned Asian Scholars.* Winter-Spring 1971. Vol. 3. No. 1. p. 29. Gary L. Olson *U.S. Foreign*

Policy and the Third World Peasant: Land Reform in Asia and Latin America. Praeger, New York 1974. pp. 84–85.

15. John Foster Dulles, Secretary of State, to AmEmb. Manila 2865 6 May 1954. DFB 5710.

16. *Hardie Report* p. vii.

17. John Foster Dulles, Secretary of State, to AmEmb. Manila A–484 21 May 1954. DFB 5710.

18. The phrase is Olson's 1974 p. 87. "U.S. interest in land reform" Olson wrote "was confined within narrow strategic parameters. If stability could be achieved without risking the oligarchy's position, land reform would be avoided altogether." p. 86.

19. Dulles 21 May 1954, as in n144.

20. Emmanuel Pelaez, Philippines *Congressional Record* 3rd Congress, 1st Session p. 1350. Quoted by Starner op. cit. pp. 138–39.

21. *Davis Report* p. 30.

22. During Congressional debates, ceilings of 500 hectares for riceland and 1,024 hectares for other crops were suggested. *Philippines Free Press* 16 July 1955 p. 69. The final ceilings were 300 hectares for individual owners and 600 for corporations. *Philippines Free Press* 6 August 1955 p. 5: "Land Reform Bill Doomed".

23. Edward R. Kiunisala *The Quiet Revolution: Land Reform In the Philippines.* Newstime Publications, Quezon City, 1985. pp. 85–86.

24. Joseph R. Motheral "Land Tenure in the Philippines." *Journal of Farm Economics* Vol. 38 No. 2. May 1956 p. 474.

25. *Philippines Free Press* 16 July 1955 p. 69: "The measure as changed by the House is shot through and through with loopholes which will enable the landlords — with the aid of clever lawyers —to defeat its purpose." As Leon O. Ty observed, the original bill had stipulated that lands in excess of 144 hectares were to be expropriated where there was evidence of marked agrarian unrest; but, in the final version, the law read, 300/600 hectares and where there was "justified" agrarian unrest. Manuel Cases, (LP La Union) called this piece of legislation the "Landlord Tenure Bill ... because it is more favorable to the landlords than to the tenants". None of this prevented House Speaker Eugenio Perez from describing the bill as "dangerous", on the grounds that it "would drastically alter our age-old system of land tenure" and result in "deprivation of private property." *Philippine Free Press* 6 August 1955 p. 5.

26. Arturo P. Sorongon *A Special Study of Landed Estates in the Philippines: Analysis and Findings.* USOM/ICA Manila 22 August 1955.

27. ibid. pp. 2–6.

28. James P. Emerson Land Reform Progress In the Philippines 1951–1955. ICA Manila 1956 p. 6.

29. Robert T. McMillan/Generoso Rivera *The Rural Philippines.* MSA/ PHILCUSA Office of Information Manila Oct. 1952. p. 86. This study will henceforth be referred to in the present study as the *McMillan/Rivera Report.* This study was a sociological survey of thirteen selected, widely separated rural *barrios,* out of the estimated 17,403 such *barrios* in the Philippines. It was conducted between 15 December 1951 and 1 March 1952. It involved interviews with 3,479 heads of households. It compiled a great deal of fascinating data on social and physical conditions in these sample *barrios.* This data was tabulated in the report at pp. 17–114. Its authors acknowledged the assistance of Arthur F. Raper, Amando M. Dalisay, James P. Emerson, Mark B. Williamson and some 200 Filipino staff.

30. Robert T. McMillan "Land Tenure in the Philippines." *Rural Sociology* Vol. 20. No. 1. March 1955. pp. 25–33. Quote from pp. 31–32.

31. ibid. p. 32.

32. Emerson 1955 op. cit. p. 14.

33. Frate Bull *Philippine Land Reform 1950–1958.* ICA Manila 1958 p. 20.

34. John D. Montgomery (ed.) *International Dimensions of Land Reform.* Westview Press, Boulder, Colorado 1984. p. 118. Montgomery's essay in this volume, "United States International Advocacy of Land Reform" runs pp. 115–148.

35. John Melby, letter to the author, 31 March 1987.

36. Edward Lansdale, letter to the author, 19 September 1986.

37. Interview with Michael Korin, Magsaysay Center, Manila, 15 December 1987.

38. ibid.

39. Alfredo B. Saulo *Communism In The Philippines: An Introduction.* Ateneo de Manila University Press, Manila, 1969. pp. 70–71.

40. Kiunisala 1985 op. cit. pp. 89–97.

41. Dante Cantos Simbulan *A Study of the Socio-Economic Elite in Philippine Politics and Government 1946–1965.* Unpublished PhD dissertation, Australian National University, Canberra 1965 p. 328.

42. Rene E. Ofreneo *Capitalism In Philippine Agriculture.* Foundation for Nationalist Studies, Quezon City, 1980, pp. 31–131.

43. For a summary of the evidence and useful bibliography, see Rehman Sobhan *Rural Poverty And Agrarian Reform in the Philippines.* FAO, Rome, 1983, esp. pp. 7–39. Also, Eduardo C. Tadem *Grains and Radicalism: The Political Economy of the Rice Industry in the Philippines 1965–1985.* Third World Studies Center, University of the Philippines, Quezon City, September 1986. Simbulan 1965 remains an indispensable guide to the sociology of power and the frustration of reform in the Philippines.

44. Lewis E. Gleeck Jr. "Twenty Five Years of USAID in the Philippines." *Bulletin of the American Historical Collection.* Manila Vol. V No. 2 April 1977 pp. 46–68. Fred Poole/Max Vanzi *Revolution In the Philippines: The United States In A Hall of Cracked Mirrors.* McGraw-Hill, New York, 1984, p. 24.

45. Francisco Sionil Jose "The Progressive View: Dear Mr. Nixon." *Solidarity* Vol. 3 No. 11. November 1968 pp. 1–2, 75–78. See also Jose W. Diokno "The Issue With Americans." *Solidarity* Vol. 3 No. 10 Oct. 1968 pp. 11–19 and Jean Grossholtz "The Myths About Malacanang: The Bulwarks of Inequality." *Solidarity* Vol. 1 No. 2 April-June 1966 pp. 3–8.

46. Raymond Bonner *Waltzing With A Dictator: The United States and the Marcoses.* Ken Inc. Quezon City 1987. Lewis E. Gleeck Jr. *President Marcos and the Philippine Political Culture,* Loyal Printing Inc., Manila, 1987. p. 77 supplied no figures, but remarked of the 1969 Presidential campaign: "The accompanying outpouring of public funds which preceded and accompanied [sic] the election provoked a *peso* crisis and the government ran short of funds for its regular expenses."

47. In particular, see Princeton N. Lyman/Jerome T. French *Political Results of Land Reform;* Harold E. Voelkner *A Dynamic Model For Land Reform: Analysis and Public Policy Formulation;* Edgar Owens *Factors In Carrying Out Land Reform: Farm Organization and Peasant Participation.* These and other country studies and analytic papers presented at the 1970 Spring Review Conference contained a great deal that was both lucid and positive, but their impact on policy seems to have been negligible. AID veteran Richard Hough remarked of this matter, in 1985: "AID as an institution has never taken agrarian reform as a serious instrument of development ... There is a major conflict over whether land reform actually works in economic terms ... The 1970 Spring Review papers were filing cabinet studies that never had a positive policy impact ... The inactivity of AID and its non-acceptance of land reform were based on premises debunked in the Spring Review." Interview with Richard Hough, Washington D.C., 8 Feb. 1985.

48. Harold E. Koone/Lewis E. Gleeck Jr. *Land Reform In the Philippines.* AID Spring Review of Land Reform. June 1970 2nd Edition Vol. IV.

49. Basilio N. de los Reyes "Can Land Reform Succeed?" in Frank Lynch SJ (ed) *View From the Paddy: Empirical Studies of Philippine Rice Farming and Tenancy. Philippine Sociological Review* Vol. 20. No's 1 & 2. Jan/April 1972. IPC, Quezon City, 1972 pp. 79–100. The article includes comments by David Christenson of AID, Jose Drilon Jr, then Director of the Southeast Asian Regional Center for Graduate Study and Research in Agriculture, Los Banos; Akira Takahashi, Japanese geographer at the Institute of Oriental Culture, University of Tokyo; and Assa Marom, Israeli rural organization and farm management specialist. Gleeck and Koone observed in their 1970 AID study: "Objectives were not quantified in 1963, but when ... Marcos became President in 1966, he announced that he would convert 350,750 tenants into lessees by the end of 1969. As of September 30, 1968, 13,377 farmers had obtained leasehold contracts, and on December 31, 1969, 28,616 farmers had such contracts." p. 47. "This is far too few to affect the basic land tenure structure. The ownership pattern in Philippine agriculture has not changed appreciably over the past 20–30 years." p. 79. "The most significant development during this period has been the growth of disillusionment approaching the mutinous with the political system as it exists and functions today and with its capacity to achieve not only justice for the farm tenants, but to move society in the direction that modernization requires." p. 77.

50. De los Reyes op. cit. pp. 83–84.

51. ibid. p. 84.

52. ibid. p. 84.

53. Lewis E. Gleeck Jr., Consultant, Office of Rural Development, Memo. 2–3 August 1971, ORD to Director Thomas Niblock ' For Mission Use Only': "One Year After: Land Reform in Nueva Ecijia" p. 2. This memorandum as a whole, running to six pages, is an interesting document, worth citation at some length. Gleeck remarked to Niblock:

> "From the Mission's end of the telescope, it is clear that the principal value of the project thus far has been again to document ... how many are the obstacles faced by an external agency in promoting Philippine economic development ... They include the all-pervading political atmosphere, the gap between resources and proclaimed government objectives, the viciousness of inter- and intra-bureaucratic struggle, the by now ingrained skepticism of both officials and voters towards the government's intentions and the motivations of officials, the strength of traditional social relations and behaviour in rural areas, the operation of new factors —technological, economic, social and political —which have

disturbed but not changed these relations, and finally, the in-
tractable problem of marrying specific Mission goals to ongo-
ing government programs which are only partially compatible
with these goals." pp. 1–2.

" ... To us, increased mobility, visibility and activity on
the part of land reform teams are evidence both of the new
project and of a new determination; to the official and farmer
it is more generally assumed to be preparations for a new
electoral campaign, from which he is accustomed to expect
favors, if he votes or promises to vote properly. The real
substance of power is in the hands of the mayor, his heavily
armed bodyguards and the chief of police." p.4.

Masaka, the PRRM and the Catholic Church's social organizations were
all lacking in firm direction and influence, Gleeck observed: "All of these
elements function as a leaven in the ... dough of tradition, but none offer
the prospect of becoming true engines of development or change." p. 6.

54. See, in particular, the string of articles that appeared in the *Philippines
Free Press* in 1965, before and after the Presidential elections. Until very
recently, the only full-scale political biography of Ferdinand Marcos was
the eulogistic and unscholarly political pulp work by Hartzell Spence,
Marcos of the Philippines World Publishing Co., New York, 1969 (2nd
edition), much of which reads almost like a parody in retrospect. Raymond Bonner, in his critical exposé of U.S. relations with Marcos, first
published in New York in 1986, put things in a more sober light. The
first serious attempt at a political biography is Lewis Gleeck's *President
Marcos and the Philippine Political Culture.* Gleeck appears to lean over
backwards to depict Marcos as a hero who fell into corruption. A later
biographer, if the subject finds one, may well dispute Gleeck's findings
on the achievements of Marcos, but the book is a valuable historical
document and far more serious than Spence's.

55. Filemon C. Rodriguez *The Marcos Regime: Rape of the Nation* Vantage
Press, New York, 1985 pp. 36–122, provided a detailed and closely rea-
soned account of Marcos's declaration of martial law as a *coup d'tat.*
See also, Raul Manglapus *Philippines: The Silenced Democracy* Orbis
Books, New York, 1976, p. xii: "Marcos posed as a democrat, but at
his first chance he subverted the Philippines' democratic tradition, sus-
pended civil liberties, instituted a rule of force and extinguished the sole
American implant of democratic government in Asia." See also, Robert
B. Stauffer "The Marcos Coup in the Philippines" *Monthly Review* Vol.
24. April 1973 pp. 19–27.
Gleeck, in the eighth chapter of his biography of Marcos, entitled "A
Stalemated President Despairs of Democracy (1969–Sept. 21 1972)",
characteristically attributed motives of anguish and statesmanship to

Marcos, which are difficult to credit:

> "Some time during 1969–71, the attacks on his regime by
> the corrupted alliance of politicians and press, as well as
> the revolutionaries and subversives, forced Marcos not only
> to develop more effective countermeasures against the latter
> groups, but to dream of a transformation in the political cul-
> ture which had checkmated his efforts to promote national
> development. Martial law could probably quell the revolu-
> tion and cripple the subversives, but the idea of a garrison
> state was unattractive to the President's thinking and tem-
> perament. On the other hand, since the faults of society were
> widely acknowledged, and the conflict between its values and
> the objectives of national development and modernization
> were crystal clear, it was tempting to envisage a reconstruc-
> tion of society ..." p. 113

The Lopez owned *Manila Chronicle* seems to have been a particular
target of Gleeck's assertions concerning the corruption of the Philippine
press. *The Philippines Free Press* he described as having waged a cru-
sade against corruption "unceasingly, unsuccessfully, and finally nihilis-
tically and self-destructively" (p. 13) and as having vented a "visceral
hatred" toward Marcos in 1970–72 (p. 24). Certainly the *Philippines
Free Press* was candid and unsparing in its questioning of the case for
martial law in August and September 1972. Thereafter, it was suppressed by Marcos.

On the armed left and martial law, see Armando Malay Jr. *Maoisme,
Loi Martiale Et Insurrection Aux Philippines 1966–1980.* Unpublished
PhD dissertation Université de Paris VII 1985.

56. *Vital Documents On Agrarian Reform In The New Society.* Manila. No
date or publication details supplied. p. 1.

57. ibid. p. 2.

58. Eduardo C. Tadem *Handbook On the Reorganization Proposals of the
Ministry of Agrarian Reform.* Presidential Commission on Government
Reorganization. Manila Dec. 1986 p. 4. Tadem's Table 5 supplies 1971
and 1980 data compiled by the National Census and Statistics Office
which, not very surprisingly, agrees with Kerkvliet's data, which was
drawn from basically the same source.

59. Simbulan 1965 pp. 81–88. See especially the data assembled by Simbulan
at p. 88.

60. NEDA *Statistical Yearbooks 1975* p. 141 and 1984 pp. 320–21.

61. Joel E. Rocamora/David O'Connor "The U.S., Land Reform and Rural
Development in the Philippines." in Walden Bello/Severina Rivera *The*

Logistics of Repression and Other Essays. Friends of the Filipino People, San Francisco, 1977. pp. 72–74.

62. NEDA *Statistical Yearbook 1984* pp. 320–21.

63. ibid. pp. 322–24.

64. Tadem Dec. 1986 op. cit. p. 4.

65. Olson 1974 p. 93.

66. ibid. p. 83.

67. ibid. p. 83.

68. ibid. p. 84.

69. ibid. p. 84.

70. ibid. p. 84.

71. ibid. p. 84.

72. ibid. p. 93.

73. Rocamora/O'Connor 1977 loc. cit. p. 63.

74. ibid. p. 63.

75. ibid. p. 70.

76. ibid. p. 76.

77. ibid. p. 76.

78. Benedict J. Kerkvliet "Land Reform: Emancipation or Counterinsurgency?" in David A. Rosenberg (ed) *Marcos and Martial Law in the Philippines* Cornell University Pres New York 1979 pp. 113–144. (p. 116).

79. ibid. pp. 113–14.

80. ibid. p. 121.

81. ibid. p. 122.

82. ibid. pp. 126–28.

83. ibid. p. 119.

84. ibid. p. 119.

85. ibid. p. 119.

86. Interview with Roy Prosterman, Seattle, 20 October 1984.

87. *Solidarity* No's 106 & 107 1986 "Agrarian Reform Now!" p. 8. Tavanlar asserted: "U.S. Ambassador *[sic]* Niblock, with the presence of U.S. Senator Inouye, who was the chairman of foreign aid in the U.S. Senate and Senator Magnusson, who was the chairman of finance in the U.S. Senate, were here. We talked to Marcos together and they were willing

to give us [a] $7 billion grant to buy this land from the landlords. We did not take it. Marcos said to me in the privacy of his office: 'Tavy, ... we don't want to use their money'." Tadem exclaimed incredulously: "7 billion and Marcos rejected it?" Tavanlar rejoined: "$7 billion and Marcos rejected it."

88. Olson 1974 p. 90 would seem to have got some vague sense of this startling episode. He wrote: "It was reported that the United States would provide the necessary funding if Manila seriously pushed the program. This public statement [which he attributed to 'one local AID official', whom he did not name, or otherwise identify] touched off a furor within higher levels of the agency in Washington, because it was both unauthorized and untrue." See also ibid. p. 101 n73.

89. Roy L. Prosterman *Revising the Approach to the Retention Limit.* mimeo AID Manila 29 April 1973 pp. 5–6.

90. Lewis E. Gleeck Jr. Memo. to Keith W. Sherper 10 July 1974. AID Manila. *Some Accomplishments and Problems of the Agrarian Reform Project 1971–1974.* Gleeck had been in the Philippines for twelve years by then, since 1962, and had been one of the U.S. officials most closely connected with the land tenure question for a number of years, co-authoring a paper on it, with Harold Koone, for AID's Spring Review conference on land reform in 1970.

91. ibid. pp. 2–3. According to Gleeck, Estrella, at a chance meeting with AID's Thomas Niblock, in Davao, reproached Niblock "for the alleged antipathy or indifference AID had shown towards land reform in the Haraldson years, neglecting to add that Haraldson had carefully investigated the GOP [Government Of the Philippines] program as it then existed and found it without real substance, stagnating under the weight of political sloganeering, inadequate funding and a charter of activities which seemed mainly to provide employment for a large number of government employees." *Bulletin of the American Historical Collection* Vol. V. No. 2. Manila April 1977 pp. 63–67.

92. Gleeck to Sherper 10 July 1974 p. 1. Niblock attended the meeting, as did "most of the leading lights in the field, including Roy Prosterman, but not Wolf Ladejinsky."

93. ibid. pp. 2.

94. ibid. p. 3.

95. Wolf Ladejinsky, letter to Lew Gliech (sic) 25 May 1974. Gleeck Papers, Los Banos.

96. Gleeck to Sherper AID Manila 10 July 1974 *Some Accomplishments and Problems of the Agrarian Reform Project 1971–1974* p. 3.

97. ibid. p. 3.

98. ibid. p. 3.

99. ibid. p. 4.

100. Jack Doughty "Land Reform Expert Assaills Marcos Delay" *Seattle Post-Intelligencer* 3 March 1975 p. 1. See also *Pacific Stars and Stripes* 5 March 1975 "Speed Up Land Plan, Yank Tells R.P.": "An American advisor to the Philippine government's land reform program said Sunday that the government's failure to make progress in the last two years is paving the way for revolution."

101. ibid.

102. ibid.

103. Roy L. Prosterman "The Philippine Land Reform: What Needs To Be Done." mimeo AID Manila 12 March 1975. p. 1.

104. Gleeck to Sherper AID Manila 10 July 1974 *Some Accomplishments and Problems of the Agrarian Reform Project 1971–1974* p. 2.

105. Wolf Ladejinsky, letter to Robert S. McNamara, 14 Oct. 1974. Gleeck Papers, Los Banos.

106. Wolf Ladejinsky, letter to Conrado Estrella, 3 Dec. 1974. Gleeck Papers, Los Banos.

107. Wolf Ladejinsky, letter to William Sullivan, 5 Dec. 1974. Gleeck Papers, Los Banos.

108. Paul Montgomery "Wolf Ladejinsky, Land Reformer, Dies: Helped Break Feudal System in Japan" *New York Times* 4 July 1975.

109. Duncan Harkin *Some Distributional Considerations in the Philippine Land Reform.* ARI/UPLB 14 Jan. 1975 pp. 6–7.

110. Lewis E. Gleeck Jr. *Program Opportunities in the Agrarian Reform Project.* AID Manila 31 Jan. 1975 p. 2.

111. ibid. p. 3.

112. Harold D. Koone/Lewis E. Gleeck Jr. *Land Reform in the Philippines.* Spring Review of Land Reform. AID Washington D.C. June 1970 2nd edition Vol. IV p. 47.

113. Sonya Diane Cater *The Philippine Federation of Free Farmers: A Case Study in Mass Agrarian Organizations.* Data Paper No. 35. S. E. Asia Program, Dept. Far Eastern Studies Cornell University 1959 p. 129.

114. Mark A. Van Steenwyck *A Study of Philippine Farmers' Organizations* AID Manila Feb. 1975. p. 8. Gerardo Bulatao survived the Marcos years and in 1986 joined the Ministry of Agrarian Reform under the new Aquino Administration. Writing in December 1987, Manila journalist Malou Mangahas described him as one of a group of "frumbies" (former radical upward moving bureaucrats) working with the Aquino

Administration. *Manila Chronicle* 6 Dec. 1987 p. 11 "What 'Frumbies' Could Do For the Aquino Government."

115. This purge, which included Ludovico Villamor, Gerry Bulatao, Charlie Avila, Noel Mondejar, Luis Jalandoni and others, was protested in a long collective letter to Jeremias Montemayor, drafted at the Divine Word Mission Seminary in E. Rodriguez Ave, Quezon City, on 18 July 1973. The letter referred to the arrest by the Philippine Constabulary of the above-mentioned FFF militants and others between 28 June and 1 July 1973. Following the first wave of arrests, an FFF executive meeting voted Montemayor "full and complete emergency powers to safeguard the security of the organization, to cleanse its membership and leadership of all taint of infiltration/subversion and to make arrangements with the government for this purpose ..." The signatories of the letter charged Montemayor with "deceit and bad faith", gross nepotism (in that seven members of his family were receiving salaries from the FFF) and receipt of funds from undisclosed sources abroad, the amounts and their uses being concealed.

116. Lewis E. Gleeck Jr. *Evaluation of USAID's 1970–1978 Agrarian Reform Projects in Support of Philippine Agrarian Reform.* AID Manila mimeo 5 Dec. 1978. p. 6.

117. Jerome T. French, Jonathan Silverstone, John D. Montgomery *Report on Evaluation of Agrarian Reform Project to AID Manila.* mimeo AID Manila May 1975. pp. 3–4. This document hereinafter referred to as the *French, Silverstone, Montgomery Report.*

118. ibid. p. 5.

119. ibid. p. 6.

120. ibid. p. 10.

121. Lewis E. Gleeck Jr. *Evaluation of USAID's 1970–1978 Agrarian Reform Projects in Support of Philippine Agrarian Reform.* AID Manila mimeo 5 Dec. 1978 p. 14.

122. *French, Silverstone, Montgomery Report* p. 24.

123. ibid. p. 24.

124. ibid. p. 25.

125. ibid. p. 25.

126. James Price Gittinger "United States Policy Toward Agrarian Reform in Underdeveloped Nations." *Land Economics* Vol. XXXVII No. 3. 1961 p. 200.

127. Interview with Richard Hough, Washington D.C., 8 Feb. 1985.

128. Michael Korin, letter to the author, 17 Dec. 1987.

129. Lewis E. Gleeck Jr to Keith W. Sherper *Misinformation on Land Reform.* AID Manila mimeo 3 Sept. 1975.

130. Interview with Lewis Gleeck, Los Banos, 30 April 1985.

131. Michael Korin, letter to the author, 17 Dec. 1987.

132. Lewis E. Gleeck Jr. "Twenty Five Years of USAID in the Philippines." *Bulletin of the American Historical Collection.* Vol. V No. 2. Manila April 1977. p. 66.

133. Michael Korin, letter to the author, 17 Dec. 1987.

134. Jewett Millard Burr, AID Washington D.C. to Michael Korin, Agrarian Reform Officer, AID Manila 27 May 1977. Gleeck Papers, Los Banos.

135. Michael Korin, letter to the author, 17 Dec. 1977.

136. Referring to it as the "Rand Report", then AID Manila Agriculture Division chief James Beebie presented this document to the author in December 1986 as the point of departure for an inquiry into the problem of land reform in the Philippines. His appreciation of the Hickey Report was refreshing, but entailed the startling implication that the "history" of the problem could be dated from 1978. Beebie's successor, Robert Resseguie, in November 1987, expressed boredom with the land reform debate and appeared to have no historical grasp of it at all. Interview with Robert Resseguie, Magsaysay Center, Manila, 24 November 1987.

137. Interview with Gerald C. Hickey, East West Center, Honolulu 5 Sept. 1984.

138. Peter M. Cody, AID Manila Director to David Newsom, Acting Ambassador. Information Memorandum. AID Manila Jan. 1978 p. 7.

139. ibid. pp. 8–9.

140. Gerald C. Hickey/John L. Wilkinson *Agrarian Reform in the Philippines.* Report from a seminar held at the RAND Corporation offices, Washington D.C. Dec. 16–17 1977. RAND Corp. 1978. p. 14. This report will hereinafter be referred to as the *Hickey Report.*

141. ibid. p. 22.

142. ibid. pp. 15, 22–23, 25, 28,31.

143. ibid. p. 10.

144. ibid. p. 11.

145. ibid. pp. 33–34.

146. Lewis E. Gleeck Jr. *Evaluation of USAID's 1970–1978 Agrarian Reform Projects in Support of Philippine Agrarian Reform.* AID Manila mimeo 5 Dec. 1978. p. 37.

147. Roy L. Prosterman "For Filipinos, Democracy Will Mean Land Reform" *International Herald Tribune* 11 Feb. 1986.

148. Bruce Koppel *Agrarian Problems and Agrarian Reform: Opportunity or Irony?* East-West Center, Honolulu. mimeo. 1986. p. 41.

Bibliographic Essay:

Sources and Problems in The Study of American Involvement in The Land Tenure Issue in The Philippines

There is a good deal of searching scholarship being pressed to completion by American and Australian students of Philippine rural and internal security affairs, which should contribute substantially to the opening up of these hitherto largely neglected subjects. Over the next twelve months or so, Ian Coxhead, Viberto Selochan, James Putzel and Vincent Boudreau will all complete doctoral work of great interest to those concerned with these matters. Ian Coxhead has been studying rural incomes in the Philippines; Viberto Selochan is putting together a study of the development of the Philippine armed forces; James Putzel is working on land tenure issues under the Aquino administration; and Vincent Boudreau has investigated the diffusion of political ideologies among Philippine peasants. In addition to these, the work of Owen Lynch, on land law and its evolution in the American colonial era in the Philippines will be of great interest when it becomes available in print.

Background reading of a secondary nature is limited. Those wishing to plunge into the subject from scratch should start with two PhD dissertations, neither of which is easy to obtain, but each of which is more immediately useful than any single book published so far. The first of these dissertations is David Sturtevant *Philippine Social Structure and Its Relation to Agrarian Unrest* (Stanford University 1958), a version of which was published by Cornell University Press in 1976, under the title *Popular Uprisings in the Philippines, 1840–1940*. The second is a Philippine dissertation, completed at the Australian National University in 1965: Dante Cantos Simbulan's *A Study of the Socio-Economic Elite in Philippine Politics and Government 1946–1965*. Simbulan's thesis is extremely difficult to obtain, as, for some reason, even the copy in the Menzies Library at the A.N.U. was on restricted access for twenty years after its completion. It is, however, replete with invaluable data and should be read by those wanting to form a picture of the Philippine oligarchy in the decades before and after the Hardie Report was written. Indeed, Simbulan's tables serve to demonstrate most usefully the extent to which the very families who dominated the Philippine economy and society before the advent of Ferdinand Marcos have reasserted their hegemony since the overthrow of the corrupt dictator in February 1986. In terms of general background reading, these dissertations should be supplemented by the superb collection of essays edited by Alfred McCoy and Ed de Jesus under the title *Philippine Social History: Global Trade and Local Transformations* (Asian Studies Association of Australia, Allen & Unwin, Sydney, 1984).

For the impact of American colonial policies, it is Glenn A. May's *America In The Philippines: The Shaping of Colonial Policy, 1898–1913*, a PhD completed at Yale University in 1975, that is the most incisive single study. Various works by Lewis Gleeck provide a good deal of detail on the American period. Perhaps the most useful is his recent study *The American Governors-General and High Commissioners in the Philippines: Proconsuls, Nation-Builders and Politicians* (New Day, Quezon City, 1986). In most respects, the historiographic method and historical perspective of Gleeck are to be found in a much older work of reflection on the American legacy to the Philippines, a bulky tome entitled *The Philippines: Past and Present* by Dean Worcester and Joseph Ralston Hayden (Macmillan, New York, 1930).

The standard work on the Huk Rebellion is still Benedict J. Kerkvliet's *The Huk Rebellion: A Study of Peasant Revolt in the Philippines* (University of California Press, Berkeley, 1982). Kerkvliet has his critics, but none of them has so far written a better account of the social roots of peasant rebellion in Central Luzon in the decade after Philippine independence was declared. The reader interested in setting Kerkvliet's findings within a broader literature on peasant rebellion under radical leadership, should read some of the major texts on the phenomenon as it manifested itself in Vietnam in the 1950s and 1960s. The work of James Scott, clearly influential on Kerkvliet, is required reading. His best known work is *The Moral Economy of the Peasant*. Alongside it, one should read Samuel Popkin's *The Rational Peasant* and Jeffrey Race's *War Comes To Long An*, both written and published in the last years of the Vietnam War, by men who had worked for the U. S. Government in its bloody and unsuccessful efforts to "pacify" the Mekong delta in the 1960s.

The more recent periods are not as yet covered by an adequate scholarly literature. Once again, an obscure and hard to obtain PhD dissertation seems to me probably the single best introduction to the root issues of peasant attitudes, radical methods of mobilizing rebellion and the impact on both of the martial law rule of Ferdinand Marcos. I refer to a study completed at the University of Paris VII in 1985, by Armando "Buddy" Malay Jr, *Maoisme, Loi Martiale et Insurrection 1966–1980*. In English, there is little that directly bears on the problems discussed in this monograph. Certainly, from the standpoint of investigation into U.S. policies in the Philippines during the Marcos years, the most thorough and stimulating is Raymond Bonner's *tour de force Waltzing With a Dictator: The United States and the Marcoses*, published in New York in 1986 and republished in Manila in 1987. As indicated above, there is a crop of serious literature ripening at present which should add more weight to discussions about the developments of the Marcos years and their implications for the coming decade.

The primary materials used in this study make up its real substance and most of them are not readily available to prospective readers of this monograph. Chief among them, of course, is the Hardie Report itself. Most of the copies originally made of this document have been swallowed up without trace over the past thirty six years. Three copies, however, were found by the author in the Communications and Media Division Resource Library of U.S.A.I.D., at the Magsaysay Center, Manila. A copy had earlier been procured and xeroxed by the author at the Ateneo de Manila University Library, in Quezon City. While there may well be copies buried in an archive in Washington D.C. somewhere, the author was unable to locate one on his research trip there in the northern winter of 1984–85. Unfortunately, it is not possible to reproduce the whole of the Hardie Report between these covers, for it runs to nearly 300 pages. However, the main findings, conclusions and recommendations of the report are reprinted here, so as to become more widely available to students of Philippine affairs and American involvement therein.

Other, related reports, notably the McMillan/Rivera Report of 1952, the Davis Report of 1954, the Sorongon Report of 1955 and the end of tour reports by Raymond Johnson (1955), James Emerson (1956) and Frate Bull (1958), are almost as rare and hard to come by as the Hardie Report. They are, however, less interesting or controversial, for the most part, than the Hardie Report and unless a research institute should arrange to gather and reprint copies in some historical documents series, it seems probable that they will become progressively harder to recover for research purposes. One such, of more recent origin, is the Hickey Report of 1978, sometimes referred to as the Rand Report. The author's copy of this document was obtained in the U.S.A.I.D. Library, Arlington, Virginia. Other copies are in circulation, but not in places that make them easily accessible to scholars or students.

The same applies to a number of other studies, reports, memoranda and the like utilized in this monograph, but nowhere gathered together and preserved. Two of these, in particular, merit attention and would repay a reading by any serious students of these matters: Sonya D. Cater *The Philippine Federation of Free Farmers: A Case Study in Mass Agrarian Organizations* (Data Paper No. 35, S.E. Asia Program, Department of Far Eastern Studies, Cornell University, 1959) and Mark A. Van Steenwyck *A Study of Philippine Farmers' Organizations* (AID Manila, February 1975). Many other papers, from the 1970s chiefly, were discovered by the author among the collection of materials kept by the aging Lewis Gleeck at his home in Los Banos, or in the American Historical Collection, now at the Jefferson Cultural Center, Makati, of which he has been the curator for a number of years. One can only hope that he will lodge his papers in the American Historical Collection library before long, so as to make them more readily available to scholars.

Finally, the personal testimonies of participants in historical events must be regarded as especially valuable, the more so if they can be obtained by interview or correspondence rather than merely in the form of inert documents. Only recent history, of course, can take advantage of such testimonies. In this instance, the recollections of a number of individuals reaching the end of their years made a decisive difference to the inquiry. Chief among these, of course, was Robert Hardie himself. It is sobering to consider that, had Hardie been unavailable for interview, much of the account presented in these pages would have been more uncertain, more speculative than it is. It is the nature of the fate of peasants that, being illiterate and repressed, they seldom enter into "history" in the active voice. Such is also, most often, the fate of minor and unsuccessful specialists and reformers such as Robert Hardie. That his voice has been activated in this study is almost fortuitous. It is to be hoped that it will, after more than three decades, contribute in the 1990s to activating the voice of the much-abused peasants of the Philippines, whom Hardie vainly aspired to assist in 1951 to 1953.

ANNEX : THE HARDIE REPORT OF 1952

Special Technical and Economic Mission
Mutual Security Agency
United States of America

PHILIPPINE LAND TENURE REFORM

ANALYSIS AND RECOMMENDATIONS

- Manila, 1952 -

PREFATORY STATEMENT

The problem of Land Tenure Reform in the Philippines is an exceedingly complex one, involving practically every phase of social, economic, and political life. As a consequence, implementation of the land tenure aspects of the Agreement between the Governments of the United States and the Philippines requires a careful analysis of the problem, the establishment of well-defined objectives, and a determination of the most appropriate means for achieving those objectives.

This paper is intended to serve as the basis for policy discussion and program planning. It attempts to give a brief though conclusive picture of existing tenure patterns and practices; of the implications of these practices for agriculture, industry, and democracy; of the adequacy of existing laws and administrative structures as corrective agencies. Finally, it offers recommendations for remedial action.

With respect to the recommendations, we want particularly to emphasize the fact that while we feel quite definite about principles and aims, this does not imply an arbitrary position respecting such specific elements as land retention limits, land prices, and the cut-off date. These are matters appropriate for further discussion. Final decisions must, of course, be made by and through discussions with Philippine Government officials responsible for finding the best solution to this most vital and difficult problem.

It is recognized that existing problems respecting land taxation, cadastral survey and the issuance and registration of land titles are closely allied with that of land tenure reform. Each of these problems is considered so important as to warrant individual analysis of a type similar to that contained herein. It is planned to commence analysis of these problems at an early date and when complete, to present suggestions for remedial action based on findings.

GENERAL INDEX

SUMMARY STATEMENT

General: This paper, an analysis of the land tenure situation in the Philippines, is divided into five parts: (I) A statement of the scope of the report; (II) A compilation of certain selected facts which bear on the land tenure problem; (III) Conclusions, in which is discussed the implications of the problem and proposals, attitudes and official efforts respecting correction; (IV) Recommendations for remedial action; and (V) Appended supporting documents.

The Philippine Land Tenure Problem: In the Philippines, agriculture furnishes a livelihood to nearly three-fourths of the population and accounts for about three-fifths of the national income. The industry is plagued, however, by a pernicious land tenure system which thwarts all efforts for technological improvement in agriculture. Chronic poverty and unrest among tenants has culminated in open and violent rebellion which the Communists are exploiting to the full. That tenants seek to become owners of the land they cultivate is prima facie evidence against their adherence to, or their understanding of, the basic principles of communism. This knowledge affords little comfort, however, for the fact remains that misery and unrest among tenants is being used to advance the goal of communism in Asia. The problem is not a postwar phenomenon; it has been developing for years, deeply rooted in feudal customs.

Causes for Agrarian Unrest: The causes of rural poverty and consequent unrest are not far to seek. (a) The smallness of farms acts to limit potential gross income. As a national average, the tillable land area per farm is 3 hectares. Farms containing less than 2 hectares of tillable land, constituting more than 1/2 the total farms, occupy less than 1/5 the tillable land area. (b) Tenant frequency is high, averaging about 35\% for the nation as a whole and soaring to more than 70\% in those areas where unrest is greatest. (c) Farm rentals are oppressive. Most tenants pay 50\% of the gross product (after planting and harvest costs) as rent. (d) Net family incomes derived from farm operations are woefully inadequate for a decent standard of living. Farm family income from outside sources is insignificant. (e) Interest paid by tenants on borrowed money is grossly onerous. Annual rates of 100\% are common and rates of 200\% and even higher are not unusual. The majority of small farmers borrow regularly from year to year. (f) A lack of adequate and economic storage, marketing and buying facilities forces farmers to sell in a low price market and buy in a high. (g) Guarantees against ruinous prices are non-existent. (h) The development of institutions conducive to the growth and strengthening of democratic tendencies has long been neglected in the rural areas. (i) Other factors bearing on rural economic instability include minimum wages, taxation, and inheritance.

The thought that the solution to Philippine agrarian unrest is to be found in the settlement of underdeveloped areas is based on a false appraisal of the problem. Firstly, world experience proves that increases in population will alone serve to neutralize the planned effects of emigration. Secondly, the acquisition and settlement of such land by one in the status of a typical Luzon tenant requires cash reserves he does not have. Lastly, and most basic, is the fact that these newly developed areas are after all a part of the Philippines and subject to the laws and customs of the land. If not corrected, pernicious land tenure practices which have led to violent rebellion in Luzon will continue being transported to the newly developed area, thus spreading the misery and unrest. Land tenure reform is needed quite as much for Mindanao as for Luzon. Settlement of new areas is an imperative but it is no substitute for land tenure reform. Early accomplishment of both programs is vital to the nation's economic and political stability.

Implications of the Problem: The land tenure system affects every phase of the nation's social, economic, and political life. Its correction is a matter of vital importance to numerous interests other than those of tenant farmers alone. (a) Political Stability: Open and violent rebellion, rooted in and fed by tenant discontent threatens the very existence of the Republic. (b) Agricultural Production: Generally speaking, in the Philippines concentration of land ownership is inimical to maximum production: abilities and incentives for efficient management tend to decrease as the size of holdings increase; tenants grow indignant of the marginal effort when half the gains derived thereby accrue to the interests of others. (c) Industry: Development suffers so long as rentier wealth lies dormant in land and is thus denied to the needs of industrial investment. (d) Fiscal Management: Tax burdens mount with increasing costs for maintaining law and order while initiation of fiscal policies vital to the entire economy must be held in abeyance for want of funds. (e) Morale: And then there are the effects of misery and unrest and violence on the individual citizen -- his family -- his church -- which history will for many years continue to measure.

The Problem Restated: The existence of the agrarian problem thwarts agricultural improvement, inhibits the development of industry and the growth of stable and democratic institutions. The size of the ordinary farm enterprise in the Philippines so limits potential farm family income as to make the institution of tenancy inimical to the establishment of economic and political stability. Correction of the land tenure aspects of the agrarian problem is therefore basic. The need to eliminate landlordism, establish the maximum practicable number of owner-operators on family-sized farm units, and guarantee just and fair tenancy practices for those who will continue to operate the land as tenants is urgent and must be given top priority among measures to quell unrest and establish peaceful, prosperous and democratic life in the rural areas. But remedying the tenure problem -- although basic -- will not along solve the whole agrarian problem. Other maladies require correction. Leading the list is credit. Since the landlord group is at present an important source of tenant credit, institution of land tenure reform will necessitate simultaneous action respecting provision for credit. The development of adequate marketing facilities, agricultural cooperatives, rural community activities, and improved production techniques, and the elimination of practices prejudicial to agriculture and farmers also require attention.

Public Opinion Respecting Reform: Public opinion appears appreciative of the land tenure problem as the root cause of rural unrest and possessed of a genuine desire to create an environment within which a peaceful and prosperous economy can develop. Among elements expressing an opinion are the Churches, private realty interests, and the press. The problem has received considerable recognition from abroad.

Official Action to Date: The Philippine Government, sensitive to unrest in rural areas, began as early as 1933 to enact legislation and frame resolutions designed, ostensibly, to protect the interests of tenants and to aid tenants on landed estates to become owner-operators. Respect for this aim is specifically stated in the Constitution. The term "social justice" has seen much service in written and spoken form. But all such implementing laws are weak in structure and limited in scope. They have been rendered ineffective by feudal culture, by lax enforcement, and through failure on the part of Congress to provide funds necessary for the accomplishment of stated aims.

Responsibility for the enforcement of existing legislation is scattered through several Departments with little or no coordination of related interests. Administrators, strained by efforts to enforce ambiguous and piecemeal legislation, often appear to have adopted apathetic and indolent attitudes respecting remedial action.

Remedial Action: Remedial action necessary to satisfy land tenure objectives envisaged by the Bell Mission Report and the related Agreement between the Governments of the United States and the Philippines conditioning extension of ECA assistance, as recommended herein, includes:

1. Establishment of a Land Tenure Authority with exclusive responsibility for drafting legislation, formulating operational procedures and administering a program designed to eliminate

inequities in the Philippine land tenure system and to initiate such socio-economic patterns and practices respecting land tenure as are necessary for the creation and maintenance of a peaceful, prosperous and democratic agricultural economy. Specifically, the Authority would be directed to take action necessary to:

    a.   Abolish, insofar as practicable, the institution of tenancy.

    b.   Establish, to the maximum practicable degree, a rural economy based on owner-operated family-sized farm units.

    c.   Establish and guarantee fair tenancy practices for that portion of farmers who will continue to work the land as tenants.

    d.   Eliminate hindrances to the fruition of objectives set forth in a, b, and c above.

2.   Establishment of a Land Commission system at national, provincial and local levels through which the program would be administered; membership on individual commissions to be selected by an from among farmers at a ratio of three (3) landowners to two (2) owner-cultivators to five (5) tenants.

3.   Repeal of existing law respecting acquisition by the government of privately owned agricultural lands, and the enactment of legislation providing for:

    a.   Purchase by the government of agricultural lands in certain specified categories, together with buildings, equipment, livestock, etc. relating thereto.

    b.   Acceptance by the government of responsibility for disposing of claims which may exist or be developed respecting prior ownership or rights to such properties.

    c.   Transfer, by sale, of clear and legal titles to properties so acquired by the government to bona fide cultivators in accordance with specified priorities.

    d.   Price determination, and methods and terms of payment for land so purchased and sold.

4.   Amendment or repeal of existing law pertaining to the establishment, regulation, and litigation of a farm lease contract (inclusive of a contract of share tenancy), hereinafter called contract, and the establishment, within a single law of principles set forth below:

a. The law would apply to all contract irrespective of crop or location of the undertaking.

b. A contract and parties thereto, should be accorded the same prestige and treatment as is accorded to any other contract or contractor under Philippine law. The landlord and tenant should each be considered as full and equal parties to the contract.

c. A contract should have singular and exclusive relation to rights and responsibilities respecting tenure.

d. The contract should be written and all principal provisions clearly specified.

e. Payment should be in cash only.

f. Assessments and/or fines, except when specifically provided for by contract, would be illegal.

g. Maximum rental on land should not exceed 30 per cent of the gross product except as specified by law.

h. The tenant should be compensated for improvements he has made to the property provided such improvements were authorized by the landlord.

i. All contracts, and any alterations or cancellations thereof, should be subject to approval by the Local Land Commission.

j. The Local Land Commission should act as arbiter in all landlord-tenant disputes.

5. Laws concerned with adjudication of landlord-tenant disputes should be repealed or modified as necessary to provide for:

a. A Court of Agrarian Relations, similar to but separate from the Court of Industrial Relations, with responsibility for adjudicating landlord-tenant disputes.

b. The Court should be authorized to act directly to effect enforcement of its decisions.

6. Establishment of procedures guaranteeing legal representation to litigants in landlord-tenant disputes who are unable to afford the service of private counsel.

7. Law respecting land title clearance, transfer and registration should be revised as necessary to expedite land transfers during the reform.

8. Inheritance law respecting succession to agricultural properties should be so modified as to prevent:

a. Fragmentation of farm units through succession.

b. Development and perpetuation of debt burden in agriculture resulting from succession.

9. Amendment of Minimum Wage Law so as to provide that:

a. Any person employed in the production and/or the first stage of processing agricultural products who is neither an owner nor tenant operator (nor a member of the immediate family) of the enterprise in which he (she) is so employed would be defined as a farm laborer.

b. The law would apply to all farm laborers except those employed on farms operated by tenants or cultivating owners as defined in the laws recommended for enactment in paragraph 3, page viii.

c. Farm laborers, other than those excepted in paragraph b. above, would receive a minimum wage equal to that established for other laborers or equal skill.

PHILIPPINE LAND TENURE REFORM

ANALYSIS
AND RECOMMENDATIONS*

PART I

THE PROBLEM

1. To survey conditions respecting land tenure in Philippine Agriculture and weigh the implications; examine options, policies, legislation, and activities relating thereto; and determine appropriate action.

PART II

FACTS BEARING ON THE PROBLEM

2. Statistical data on land tenure is attached as enclosure No. 1. Source is Volume II, Census of the Philippines, 1938[1], unless otherwise specified. It is assumed that the existing situation does not differ greatly from that which prevailed in 1938 -- particularly insofar as size of farms and the relative frequencies of the different tenure groups are concerned. Salient statistics relating to tenure are: (See Appendix "A".)

a. The 1,634,726 farms occupy a total farm area approximately 6,691,000 hectares. Of this total area, about 59 per cent is under cultivation. Some 17 per cent, although immediately tillable, lies idle. The balance is devoted to pasture, forest, and "other" uses. (See Appendix "A", specifically A4 and A8.)

---

* Prepared by Robert S. Hardie, Land Tenure Specialist, MSA-STEM

[1] Compilation and publication of 1948 census data respecting agriculture, long delayed for lack of funds, is progressing with the aid of ECA assistance.

1

b. As a national average, about 49 per cent of all farms are operated by owners (those who own all land operated), 16 per cent by part owners, and 35 per cent by tenants (those who rent all land operated), less than 0.1 per cent by farm managers. Overall averages, however, fail to give a true picture of the tenancy situation. The frequency of tenancy varies as between provinces from 1.8 per cent to 70.4 per cent.[2] Tenancy frequency exceeds 40 per cent in 16 provinces, 50 per cent in 7, and 60 per cent in 4. Tenancy tends to be most frequent in Central Luzon. (See Appendix "A", page A3.)

c. Owners operate about 55 per cent of the total farm area, part owners 12 per cent, tenants 25 per cent, and farm managers 8 per cent. (See Appendix "A", page A2.)

d. Of the cultivated land in all farms, farms operated by owners account for about 49 per cent, by part owners for 15 per cent, by tenants for 32 per cent, and by farm managers for 4 per cent. (See Appendix "A", page A12.)

e. Of the idle land in all farms, farms operated by owners account for about 72 per cent, by part owners for 8 per cent, by tenants for 14 per cent, and by farm managers for 5.7 per cent. (See Appendix "A", page A12.)

f. The overall average area of farm land per farm is about 4.1 hectares; for farms operated by owners 4.6; by part owners 3.2; by tenants 3.6; and by farm managers 320.3. Overall averages, however, fail to give a true picture of the distribution of farm lands among farmers; e.g., in terms of cultivatable land (cultivated plus idle land capable of cultivation) 22.5 per cent of all the farms contain less than 1 hectare and occupy 5.9 per cent of all cultivatable land; 41.5 per cent less than 1-1/2 hectares and occupy 12.9 per cent of the land; 52.4 per cent less than 2 hectares and occupy 18.4 per cent of the land. Or, conversely, operators of farms exceeding 5 hectares (constituting only about 1/8 of the total farms) account for more than one-half of the cultivatable land, whereas operators of farms of less than two hectares (constituting more than one-half of total operators) account for less than one-fifth of the cultivatable land. (See Appendix "A", pages A6 and A7.)

g. On a value basis, owners account for about 37 per cent of farm equipment on all farms, part owners for 17 per cent, tenants for 36 per cent and farm managers for 10 per cent. (See Appendix "A", page A15.)

---

[2] Figures exclude Manila

h. Of carabaos on all farms, about 45 per cent are on farms operated by owners, 18 per cent by part owners, 35 per cent by tenants, and 1 per cent by farm managers. (See Appendix "A", page A15.)

i. Farms operated by owners have a disproportionately greater number of cattle and hogs than do farms operated by tenants. (See Appendix "A", page A15.)

j. In comparison to their frequency among farm operators in all tenure groups, owners operate a disproportionately large number of abaca, coconut, fruit, vegetable, livestock, and "other" farms; tenants operate a disproportionately large number of rice, corn, sugar cane, tobacco, and poultry farms. (See Appendix "A", page A14)

k. Persons not citizens of the Philippines operate only 0.2 per cent of the total number of farms and cultivate 1.6 per cent of the total are of cultivatable land. (See Appendix "A", page A16.)

3. The land tenure pattern is an integral part of Philippine culture. The Americans inherited the situation from the Spaniards who, in the beginning of the 17th century, had carefully adjusted their colonial methods to harmonize with the social and economic structure of an earlier Asiatic form of feudalism. Although not satisfied with the situation, the Americans failed to take effective measures to correct it. (See Appendix "C", specifically pages C1 and C5.)

4. Some 72 per cent of the population of the Philippines derive their livelihood from agricultural production which accounts for 58 per cent of net national income at factor cost. Thus a breadwinner in agriculture receives an income equal to 53.3 per cent of that of his urban counterpart.[3] (See also Appendix "B", pages B1, B2 and B18.)

5. Some 95 per cent of all tenant farmers are share tenants. As a minimum, they pay 30 per cent of the gross product (after harvest costs) as a rental, but the majority pay 50 per cent or more. (See Appendices "A". "C" and "G", specifically pages A11, C6, C13, G1, and G24).

6. The size of farms severely limits income potentials. At the present price of P10 per cavan (the small producer rarely realizes the "official price"), an owner operator of the average rice farm (cultivated area = 2.16 hectares), requiring no credit, and producing 27.4 cavans per hectare (national

---

[3] Calculations by Mr Dimas A. Maulit, Department of Agriculture and Natural Resources.

average) would gross P590 per annum. Expenses of production and harvesting (exclusive of the operator's own and family labor cost) being estimated at P45, would cause net annual income to approximate P545. A share tenant operator, working on a 30 per cent rental basis and borrowing no money (uncommon condition), would net approximately P365.70, with no allowance being made for pay of labor of the operator or his family.[4] (See also Appendix "C", pages C19 and C22.)

7.   Farm family income from sources other than the farm is small -- being estimated as probably not exceeding from 30 to 90 pesos per annum.[5]

8.   The average farm family numbers 4.99 persons.[6]

9.   Farm family living costs are estimated at P1,087 per annum for owner-operating farmers and P626 for tenants.[7]

10.   The situation described in paragraph 6 above is further aggravated by grossly usurious rates of interest on borrowed monies, lack of an economic marketing system, a regressive tax system, and vicious tenancy practices. (See Appendix "C", specifically pages C6, C14 and C15.)

11.   Implication of the above situation notwithstanding, Filipino tenants seek first of all for security of tenure. (See Appendix "C", page C21.)

12.   Philippine inheritance law is based on the principle of equal distribution among heirs. (See Appendix "G", page G7.)

13.   Philippine land tenure patterns and practices act to render ineffective all efforts to improve agricultural production and distribution; to impede the development of industry; to foster the growth of communism; and to threaten the United States position in Asia. (See Appendices "D" and "E". Also, since the validity of this statement is best illustrated by argument, it has been developed as paragraph No. 23 under CONCLUSIONS.)

14.   The Philippines Government, sensitive to increasing unrest in rural areas, began as early as 1933 to enact legislation and frame resolutions designed ostensibly to protect the interests of tenants and to aid tenants on "landed estates" to become owner operators. Respect for this aim is stated specifically in the Constitution. The term "social justice" has seen much service in written and spoken form.

---

[4] Estimated in collaboration with Mr D.A. Maulit.

[5] Based on limited field observation

[6] Mr D.A. Maulit, Department of Agriculture and Natural Resources.

[7] Ibid

They have been rendered ineffective by legal tests of ambiguities, by the Common Law based on feudal concepts, by bureaucrats who are lax in enforcement, and through failure on the part of Congress to provide funds necessary for the accomplishment of stated aims. (See Appendices "G" and "K".)

15. Numerous studies and reports on the Philippine Land Tenure problem have been prepared by qualified and properly constituted bodies since the origin of American Government interest in the Philippines. All have noted its pernicious character, recognized its implications and recommended remedial action. None have found to the contrary. (See Appendix "D".)

16. Important organizations and individuals constituting important political elements have stated, either officially or implied, through official publications, the need for remedial action respecting land tenure patterns in the Philippines. (See Appendix "E".)

17. The announced policy of the Philippine Government, the United States Government, and the Economic and Social Council of the United Nations (chaired by Cornelio Balmaceda, the Philippine representative) favors ownership of family-sized farms by persons who actually till the soil, and the initiation of a Land Reform Program as a means of attaining this goal.

18. The Agreement between the Governments of the Philippines and the United States which served as the basis for the installation and continuation of ECA-STEM in the Philippines, specifically obligates the Philippine Government to initiate and carry out a thoroughgoing Land Reform Program. (See Appendix "F".)

19. Officials in the Philippine Government and others with long experience in working with tenants report them aware of their problems and capable of working through their accepted leaders toward solution; that in the absence of intimidating elements they are quite articulate; that some have been lax in paying for lands acquired from the government; that collection experience on government farm operating loans was satisfactory. They also report Filipino farmers to be inveterate adherents of cock-fighting and perfectly capable of going heavily into debt in order to meet the costs of "social obligations" connected with a wedding, funeral, or etc.

20. Estimated administrative costs involved in eliminating tenancy (to the maximum extent possible) and for the establishment of fair tenancy practices approximate P23,000,000 per annum for a two year period. This cost is low as compared to increasing costs for the "enforcement" of law and order. (See Appendix "I".)

21. Real and potential lethargy, ignorance, and graft require that any program of amelioration respecting land tenure be supported by a full-scale information program.[8]

---

[8] This statement is based on an overall evaluation of the situation.

PART III

CONCLUSIONS

22. <u>Preface</u>: The question of Land Tenure in the Philippines is broad and exceedingly complex. It involves every phase of the nation's social, economic, and political life. It also is possessed of international implications. A written analysis is therefore subject to possible criticism on grounds of redundancy and reiteration. In an attempt to avoid this pitfall and thus lend succinctness to the effort, conclusions to facts presented in the preceding section are presented in the form of answers to basic questions which we believe confront the policy-maker and the administrator who would deal with the problem.

Valid conclusions are by nature but logical deductions based on factual information and become therefore facts in their own right. Thus, it is impossible to draw an arbitrary line dividing this section of the paper from the one preceding and the one to follow -- as, perhaps, should be the case anyway. It is hoped that each section will be considered, in a sense at least, as a complement to the others.

23. IS IMMEDIATE LAND TENURE REFORM JUSTIFIED?

   a. <u>General</u>: Agriculture far exceeds all other industries in importance. It furnishes a livelihood to some 72 per cent of the population and produces some 58 per cent of the national income. The industry, however, is plagued by poverty, disease, and unrest which are but logical products of a pernicious land tenure system fraught with gross inequities. The problem is not a postwar phenomena but has been developing for centuries, deeply rooted in feudal custom, undauntedly withstanding demands imposed by a money economy, increasing population pressures, and a growing consciousness on the part of tenants of political significance and individual dignity. Tenant family income, limited by the size of the farm operation, rack rentals,* usurious rates of interest, and an uneconomic marketing system, is insufficient to meet minimum requirements for subsistence living. The land tenure system prevents industrial growth and the development of stable and democratic institutions, threatens the very existence of the Republic of the Philippines, and bodes evil for United States and other Western interests.

---

* Excessive or unreasonably high rent.

b. Political Implications: Chronic economic instability and political unrest among farm tenants has culminated in open and violent rebellion. The rebellion derives directly from the pernicious land tenure system; it is but the latest in a long and bitter series. Communists have acted quickly and directly to exploit the situation as a part of the general movement against capitalism in Asia -- as they did in China and Korea. In championing the cause of tenants, communism wins their sympathies -- just as governments (or supporters of government), careless of causes -- whose actions are limited to the suppression of symptoms and maintenance of the status quo -- are bound to win their enmity. That the rank and file of tenants seek to become individual owners of the land they cultivate if proof against their adherence to, or their understanding of, the basic principles of communism. This knowledge, however, adds little comfort, for the fact remains that the strength and bulk of rebellious tenants are being used to support the communism which champions their cause. Taking into consideration the landless as well as tenant farmers, it is possible that the sympathies of at least 35 per cent of the population are open for bid -- and this in the rural areas alone.

Open rebellion and murderous violence rooted in and fed by tenant discontent is at present endemic to Central Luzon and a few scattered areas, but the causes of discontent characterize the whole of Philippine agriculture. There is no reason to believe, unless the cause be remedied, that rebellion will not spread. Neither is there any reason to believe that the rebellious spirit, nurtured by years of poverty and strife, will be broken by the force of arms or appeased by palliatives in the form of a questionable security in Mindinao. Relief from the oppressive burden of caciquism has been too long sought -- and too long denied. Years of privation, suppression, and empty promises have served, apparently, to endow tenant demands with a moral as well as an economic character. Tenants demand correction of the basic inequities which characterize the agrarian pattern. Growth and development of a peaceful and democratic rural economy will come into existence only when these basic inequities have been eliminated.

c. Agricultural Implications: Even though law and order prevailed (which it does not), existing land tenure patterns are inimical to maximized production. Concentration of the ownership of farm lands into the hands of a few implies uneconomic management: firstly, because life of relative ease and comfort deadens the incentive to owners to introduce and enforce practices conducive to maximizing production;

secondly, because the ability of management to render effective surveillance decreases as the number of units under supervision increases. Tenants have little incentive to increase production through a greater expenditure of effort or the introduction of technological improvements when landlords claim some half the gains resulting from the increased effort; and interest rates deny the feasibility of employing fertilizer, insecticides, etc. At present an unascertainable amount of tillable land lies idle as owners, through fear of violence, have given up farming operations and moved to the relative safety of urban centers. Efficiency in distribution currently suffers in that a disproportionate amount of indigenous production is consumed in the rural areas and is thus denied to the industrial non-producer.

d. Industrial Implications: The bulk of Philippine wealth is concentrated in the hands of a few and invested in land. This group enjoys an adequate and stable income (excepting only the possibility of political upheaval). So long as rentier wealth is invested in land, it is thus denied to needs attending the development of Philippine industry. In this regard, existing potentials for investible funds for industry diminish as rentier wealth, apprehensive of the political chaos which derives from the tenure system itself, is being moved out of the Philippines.

e. International Implications: From what has been said above, it is apparent that, until remedied, the land tenure system stands as an obstacle thwarting all efforts of the United States to foster the development of a stable and democratic economy. But over and above all this, continuation of the system fosters the growth of communism and harms the United States position. Unless corrected, it is easy to conceive of the situation worsening to a point where the United States would be forced to take direct, expensive, and arbitrary steps to insure against loss of the Philippines to the Communist block in Asia -- and would still be faced with finding a solution to the underlying problem. The military implications of a Communist Republic exceed the competence of this paper, but it seems that majority opinion among military strategists regards the Philippines as a major fortress denying the Communists access to the whole of Australasia.

f. Further Study: Suggestions for "further study of the problem" and fears of "hastily conceived remedies" ring hollow and as something less than original in light of the fact that officially constituted bodies have been recommending remedial action since the time of Taft; and that, even now, open rebellion threatens the very existence of democracy in the Philippines. This is hardly a time when, to borrow from Tacitus, "indolence stands for wisdom." Any action on the part of the Philippine Government that would convince tenants of an honest intent to correct basic inequities in the land tenure system could not but serve to strengthen the political and economic well being of a democratic Philippine Republic. Any action (or inaction) capable of interpretation by tenants as more procrastination would be an aid to the Communists.

g. Settlement versus Reform: It has been argued that a solution to the agrarian problems of the Philippines is to be found in Mindanao and other undeveloped areas -- that the opening up and development of these areas will serve to satisfy demands of tenants for land ownership and thus create a peaceful and productive rural economy. While there is, of course, much to be said for the settlement of undeveloped areas, inflation of the argument to a point where it becomes a sort of panacea for the treatment of rural ailments must be rejected flatly on the grounds that it fails utterly and miserably to evaluate the political, economic, social, and moral implications of existing agrarian problems -- and, in that it bespeaks a myopic attitude respecting the future of farmers now being settled in these new areas. It is emphasized that this is not to condemn the settlement of new areas. Mindanao, for example, represents vast and unexploited natural resources. Unemployment exists in the Philippines -- particularly in the rural areas. To delay the development of new areas would be utterly uneconomic and anti-social. But, this development will have little effect on quelling or eliminating the causes for unrest in Central Luzon and other established areas. As mentioned elsewhere in this paper, agrarian unrest, while deriving from economic and social inequities, has now taken on a political and moral aspect. The objective is to change the very structure of tenure -- a position affording little or no room for compromise and hardly subject to abortion by substitute offers. Furthermore, settlement policies, procedures, and regulations currently employed in Mindanao would render extremely questionable the "opportunities" being offered to one in the status of a typical Luzon tenant. He is financially unable to purchase the land being sold. The waiting involved for a homestead right is long, requiring of reserves he does not have, and even if granted is subject to the hazards imposed by a questionable title. Even is these obstacles be successfully negotiated, he is still subject to the economic parasites which plague him in Luzon. And this leads back to the true and basic argument. These newly developing areas are, after all, a part of the Philippines -- and must some day, in their turn, become old and densely populated districts. If not corrected, the inequities which exist in Luzon will (as even now has started) characterize the situation in Mindanao and other undeveloped areas -- and thus spread unrest. Appropriate portions of reform legislation discussed elsewhere in this paper will, of course, be applicable throughout the Philippines. Indeed, it is needed quite as badly for the undeveloped areas as in any other area. In short, reform and resettlement programs are both imperatives -- neither is a substitute for the other.

(NOTE: Policies and procedures respecting settlement in undeveloped areas are currently reported as being under the close scrutiny of ECA and appropriate officials in the Philippine Government pursuant to improvement.)[9]

h.   Summary: The evidence favoring an immediate and thorough land reform in the Philippines is overwhelming.

24.   WHAT SHOULD BE THE NATURE OF THE REFORM AND WHAT ELEMENTS REQUIRE PRIORITY IN CONSIDERATION?

Inadequacy of Exist-Concepts: In reviewing the record respecting the need for the abolition of tenancy and the establishment of owner farmers on privately owned tillable lands, one is struck by the fact that the thought behind such consideration has been confined almost exclusively to "landed estates". The term (and concept) permeates Philippine law and even writers of the Bell Report incorporated it into what might otherwise have been a specific recommendation. However satisfying the phrase may be to those who would "abolish feudalism", the term is absolutely ambiguous and has in the past served only to becloud apparently benevolent legislation with charges of discrimination. Existing law respecting the subject is, therefore, totally ineffective. Aside, however, from the ambiguity of the term "landed estates", the concept is subject to

---

9.   Implications of statistics on population distribution, size of existing farms, area of public lands capable of development for agriculture, and population growth, presented on pages B20, A7, B21, and B17, respectively, would seem to counteract widespread optimism respecting the capacity of undeveloped public lands to absorb vast numbers of families seeking to establish themselves as owner-cultivators. Based on conservative assumptions, calculations made from 1948 census data indicate the existence of some 4,148,446 individuals composing an estimated equivalent of 755,636 families who, though employable, are for all practical purposes unemployed. In addition to this group, some 857,956 (1938 census data) farm families operate less than 2 hectares. Thus it would appear that there are already in existence, in the rural areas alone, some 1,613,592 families requiring land. The population of the Philippines (reckoned by the Bureau of Census to be increasing at the rate

10

much more basic criticism. In the first place, it places the whole idea of reform in an extremely negative light -- it would destroy large (?) estates rather than create over-cultivators -- the idea becomes one of "soaking the rich" just because they are rich and to help the poor just because they are poor. Secondly, it would confine opportunities for becoming an owner-cultivator to those "fortunate" enough to have leased from an estate owner. Aside from other faults involved in this criticism, the proposition becomes even more disturbing when one remembers that it is no more glorious to be a tenant of a small owner than of a large -- that as a matter of fact, tenants of the larger and more economically secure owners the world over are usually subject to much more favorable treatment than are those who rent from small owners whose meager incomes make benevolence to their tenants a luxury they can ill afford. Thirdly, it limits what should be a vital and necessary reform to a haphazard, piecemeal, discriminatory program. The courts have quite justly questioned the validity of considering such law as serving to improve "public welfare", have condemned it as a measure to satisfy few and selfish interests, and have, therefore, named action under it unconstitutional. Fourthly, the concept would not eliminate tenancy -- but only "landed estates". A great deal of land capable for use as a source upon which to establish owner-operators of family-sized farms would be left untouched. Conversely, the problems of tenants on this land would go unsolved. Lastly, the concept fails to consider optimum (or even existing average) farm sizes based on productivity within the areas.

Footnote 9 continued

of 1.9 per cent per year) rose from 16,191,200 in 1939 to an estimated 21,120,500 in 1952. As compared to the magnitude of this unemployment problem the Bureau of Lands estimated that of all the lands released to it for disposal by the Bureau of Forestry, only some 400,000 hectares of approximately 785,458 hectares remaining unobligated are fit for agricultural development. The Bureau of Forestry estimates that of the 19,739,828 hectares of land remaining to be classified, only some 7,224,638 hectares will be classifiable as suited for agriculture. Thus, in all the Philippines there remains but an estimated 7,624,638 hectares of public lands capable of settlement for agricultural development. To divide the total of public lands ever to become available for agricultural development among the estimated number of rural families requiring land who are already in existence would mean an average allowance of but 4.72 hectares per family -- an amount slightly in excess of the existing average farm size. Or, in terms of a flow of population, settlement of undeveloped areas at a rate of at least some 52,400 families per year would be required to neutralize the annual increase in population in the rural areas alone.

11

In light of the above, the whole idea of breaking up the "landed estates" should be discarded as ambiguous, impracticable, and inadequate. It should be replaced by a positive program aimed at creating the maximum practicable number of owner-operated family-sized farms. In short, with exceptions as specified in Part IV, RECOMMENDATIONS, page 25, all tenant-operated farm land and all owner-operated farm land exceeding specific and legally fixed retention allowances should be purchased by the government and sold to tenant-operators.

Basic Causes For Discontent Among Small Farmers In The Philippines Listed In Accord With Demands For Prior Consideration:

a. Tenancy: The size of farms so limits potential revenues as to make the institution of tenancy inimical to the development and maintenance of a stable, peaceful, and democratic rural economy.

b. Insecurity of tenure: High and mounting population pressures on limited tillable areas, high social and economic costs involved in developing virgin areas, excessively low standards of living, and pernicious land tenure practices combine to foster an ever-increasing competition for land currently under cultivation and serve to intensify insecurity of tenure.

c. Rack-renting:* Farm rentals are excessively high. This is more than the counterpart of the problem cited in paragraph a. above. It has special significance in light of the fact that irrespective of the need to establish owner-cultivators, maximized production dictates the need for the possibility of some land remaining under tenant operation. This will be discussed in more detail below.

d. Unfair tenancy practices: This heading covers a multitude of since ranging from truck payments** to abuses of contract imposed by customary practices steeped in feudal culture. Tregao a very great extent, these problems could be corrected by employment of a written lease contract and application, by the courts, of principles characterizing established contract law in litigations involving farm lease contracts.

e. Inadequate farm credit: Credit is ordinarily available to farmers only at excessively high rates of interest ranging from approximately 30 to 400 per cent per annum. Under the Kasama system (involving the vast majority of tenants),

---

* Excessive or unreasonably high rent
** Payment of wages in kind

12

interest rates of from 100 to 200 per cent per annum are common. It is common for small and tenant farmers requiring money for subsistence during the production period to sell their crops to a buyer prior to harvest at prices grossly inferior to prices which would otherwise have been paid had sale been accomplished at the time of harvest. Losses to farmers resulting from this practice are rarely regarded as interest charged on what are in reality short-term loans.

f. Inadequate distribution facilities: Small farmers, indebted and without protective marketing facilities, are customarily forced to sell at harvest in a buyers' market. Conversely, subsistence and input requirements are necessarily purchased in a sellers' market. Ultimate relief in this respect will require increased physical facilities for processing and storing farm products, but development of an adequate credit system would go far toward alienating the problem. Consideration should be given to the development of agricultural cooperatives with initial emphasis being placed (provided an adequate credit system be established) on consumer activities. It would appear that this must necessarily be a long-term program.

g. Regressive taxation: The tax structure existing in 1950, dependent as it was for 85 per cent of the revenues on excise and sales taxes and other forms of revenue that paid little respect to the ability-to-pay principle, placed a disproportionately heavy burden on small farmers as consumers. Revision of the tax laws in 1951 was designed to make the system more progressive. The success of the new law remains to be proven.

h. Inheritance: Philippine inheritance law is based on the principle of equal sharing in an estate. The deceased, even though he leaves a will can control no more than one-half of his estate. Intestate property is divided equally in accord with priority of status of heirs -- lineal heirs taking priority over collateral -- a widow's right being essentially usufructuary during her lifetime.

However ingrained in our mores may be the principle of equal rights of heirs, knowledge of the fact the the principle has been applied in a country where the average farm approximates 4 hectares and the average farm family 5 persons is somewhat less then comforting. The system offers alternative choices in the settlement of an estate -- either of which is rather terrifying. Assuming the relative flexibility of a first succession to an average farm, then the estate might be (10 divided physically into 5 parcels of 0.8 hectare each, leaving each heir in a position of being either (a) the operator of an area grossly inadequate for the support of his family or (b) forced to lease the plot to a going farmer and thus contribute to the perpetuation of tenancy -- an institution generally unacceptable for Philippine agriculture; or (2) one heir, in order to settle claims of other heirs, might take physical possession of the farm by assuming a burden of debt equal to

13

80 per cent of the estate. Inasmuch as the life expectancy of an inheriting heir does not, in all probability, exceed by many years the time required to amortize a mortgage equal to 80 per cent of the value of an average-sized farm, it is plain that under such procedures each generation of farmers would pass through life bearing a heavy burden of debt. In the event of rapid succession, the burden would be, in all probability, so intolerable as to cause loss of the land to the family altogether. The above deals only with the first succession. Consider the implication of succeeding successions -- the second, third, ad infinitum! This assumes, of course, that agricultural property will dominate the estate -- that there will be little else with which to satisfy the claims of "other" heirs and thus avoid the problems cited above. This appears to be a very fair assumption for the vast majority of Philippine farm families -- particularly if a reform to establish owner-cultivators is the be carried out.

We appreciate that we are here arguing in a manner totally foreign to American ideas and ideals, but we believe the implications of existing inheritance law to be so disturbing (particularly in relation to land reform objectives) as to demand consideration of basic changes in the Civil Code.

i. Land Consolidation: While data adequate for determining the extent of farm fragmentation in the Philippines are non-existent, it appears to be the consensus of opinion that the majority of farms exist as contiguous areas. The situation no doubt results from the fact that ownership of much of the land has long been concentrated in the hands of a few and operated by tenants. If the required study of this question justifies the need, action to remedy farm fragmentation should be initiated.

j. Rural Community Improvement: There is a marked need for what we shall here call "community improvement" in the rural areas, even though tenants have apparently made no coherent demands for it. Under this heading should be included an extension service, health facilities (both formal and adult), cooperative enterprises, recreational facilities, etc. Such a program will take years for achievement, but its ultimate establishment is basic to the full realization of democratic living.

Land Reform Defined: From the foregoing, it is clear that the term "Land Reform", while inclusive of, is not limited to the transfer of land ownership to cultivators and stabilizing the position of tenants. It must ultimately pay respect to all elements which exercise important roles in determining rural life values. It is entirely possible, of course, that simultaneous prosecution of all elements would prove both impossible and impracticable, but it is emphasized that eventually attention must be given to all. Only then will the groundwork be laid for solving the institutional problems which plague rural areas.

Top Priority of Tenure Reform: Of all the reform measures enumerated above, those dealing directly with land tenure are basic and requiring of top priority in remedial action. Opinion in this regard is based on two facts: firstly, security of tenure (ownership is practically a synonym) is the cause behind which revolts have been rallied -- its attainment basic to the establishment of law and order; and1 secondly, (and it proceeds logically from the first) the existence of a peaceful, industrious, and law-abiding community is absolutely basic to the establishment of institutions adequate for the achievement of other objectives (including technological innovations).

Importance of Credit Reform Considerations: The above argument requires, however, that something be said immediately on credit. Philippine small farmers customarily borrow in order to finance family subsistence and farm operating costs during the production season. They usually borrow from either landlords or merchants. Interest rates are usurious in the extreme. This situation demands correction irrespective of whether other activities be undertaken or not, but initiation of a program to correct land tenure problems makes immediate attention to the credit problem mandatory. The elimination of tenancy as an institution would in all probability eliminate the present landlord group as an important source of credit for the newly established owner-cultivators. Without arrangements for a substitute source of credit, prosecution of the basic element in land reform (land transfer) would be accomplished only with marked disruption in agricultural production.

Owner-Operated Family-Sized Farm Defined: Throughout this paper repeated mention has been made of "establishing owner-cultivators" and "family-sized farms". Perhaps a word of clarification of these objectives is necessary. Thought has been based on the assumption that a stable, democratic, and efficient agricultural economy is most easily achieved and maintained in a society composed of farmers who own the land they cultivate. In short, the need is for the establishment of owner-operated family-sized farms. This, of course, raises the question as to the size of a "family farm". Although the average existing farm is small (a factor materially limiting income) serious questions arise as to (1) what the optimum size may be, and (2) the feasibility of increasing the size, even though, from the point of view of family income, such a move is indicated. First, the existence of idle tillable land raises the question of the ability of the average farmer (given existing technology) to operate a larger area efficiently. Second, even though it may be established that individual farm areas are too small, displacement of surplus population which would result from a program to correct

15

the situation might easily (in the absence of alternative occupations which do not exist) jeopardize the stability of the whole economy. Third, there is the question of the validity of the so-called "optimum-sized farm" for national planning purposes. While the concept may have at least an evanescent validity for the individual farm family, it is at best possessed of but theoretical significance and vaporizes into an economic will-o-the-wisp immediately the attempt is made to apply it for national planning purposes. Recognizing the need for consideration of measurable variables in accord with production potentials as between areas, the dynamics of other factors -- markets, technological innovations and the human factor -- are so great as to cause calculated optimum farm sizes to be at all times questionable and only temporarily valid. Last, there is always the fact that existing farm sizes (maximum frequencies within areas) did not, in all probability, "just happen" -- but rather represent the product of years of adjusting farm size to all other factors in an effort, on the one hand, to maximize profits, and on the other, to avoid frictions. It would be difficult to conceive of generations of landlords, however, careless of efficiency, deliberately subdividing their holdings in such a manner as to reduce profit potentials. Thus, it is entirely possible that the established farm-size pattern may be the best indicator of optimum farm size under existing conditions.

In summary, mention in this paper of the establishment of owner-operated family-sized farms implies, broadly speaking, the immediate objective of transferring ownership from the landlord to the tenant the land the latter now operates, with appropriate provisos respecting maximum ownership retention rates based on regional productivity and modified by individual family requirements and capabilities. Ultimate objectives for Philippine agriculture may well envisage an increase in the size of farms but always with the proviso that such action harmonizes with efficient production and the nature of the overall socio-economic structure.

Total Abolition of Tenancy is Impracticable: While the aim should be to create the maximum number of owner-cultivators, consideration must be given to the fact that continuous operation of the maximum farm area requires provision for the possibility of a portion of the land being tenant operated. A too rigid law, totally abolishing tenancy, would cause land to stand idle during periods when personal circumstances of owners temporarily prevent operations if to rent out the land would cause its being classified as "tenant-operated" and precipitate its permanent loss to the owner. Conversely, the temporary circumstances of an owner operator may be such as to enable and justify his operation of additional land as its tenant -- even though normally his work capacities would limit operations to the smaller area of his own land.

Specific Elements of a Land Tenure Reform Program are set forth in Part IV, RECOMMENDATIONS. Basic economic, legal, and fiscal considerations involved in the formulation of a program are discussed in Appendix "K".

25. WHAT IS THE OPINION OF THE PUBLIC RESPECTING THE NEED FOR LAND TENURE REFORM AND WHAT IS OFFICIAL POSITION ON THE QUESTION? Public opinion in the Philippines, apparently appreciative of the root causes of rural unrest and motivated by a deep and sincere desire to create an environment within which a peaceful and healthy economy can develop, seems overwhelmingly favorable to land reform. Those who might oppose or inhibit its accomplishment appear as a small minority which owes its position to the wealth and prestige which derives from land ownership in a feudalistic culture. The political strength of this minority group has in the past proved dominant and its potential opposition would be a factor to be reckoned with. It is entirely possible, however, (as indicated by appended editorials and other documents) that possession of arms by the "dissidents" (a material shift in power as compared to the prewar situation) and worldwide publicity given the need for reform may be causing this group to modify its position -- as an act of expediency in harmony with political and economic prudence.

Important organizations and individuals of international stature, whose other interests may be in conflict, recognize the need for correcting inequities in the land tenure system. The official position of the Catholic Church favors establishment of owner-cultivators. The United States state department has adopted an unequivocal position respecting the need. Land reform has been adopted as an objective by the Economic and Social Council of the United Nations.

The Bell Report specifies and gives high priority to land reform.

The Agreement establishing ECA(MSA)-STEM assistance to the Philippines, under date of 27 April 1951, makes land reform an imperative conditioning continued MSA assistance to the Philippines. This is further strengthened by an agreement negotiated by President Quirino in person and Mr. Foster of ECA.

26. ARE AVAILABLE DATA RESPECTING LAND TENURE PATTERNS ADEQUATE FOR THE PLANNING AND ADMINISTRATION OF THE REFORM? Official records now available are adequate for preliminary planning purposes and for the drafting of legislation. Census data for 1948 (anticipated as being quite adequate for detailed administrative purposes) should be available for use by the date needed.

27. WHAT WOULD BE THE PROBABLE SCOPE OF A REFORM AIMED AT CREATING THE MAXIMUM PRACTICABLE NUMBER OF OWNER-OPERATING FARMERS? How Many Hectares, Tenants, and Owners Would be Involved? The scope of the reform will depend directly on allowable retention rates (for the several categories of owners) as fixed by law. These will in turn depend on top policy decisions to be made by the Philippine Government.

17

Philippine statistics, while good with respect to farm areas and the tenure of operators, are deficient (as is the case in many countries) with respect to (1) nature of ownership and residence of owners of tenant-operated lands, and (2) actual tenure status of "workers" on farms listed as operated by "farm managers". As a consequence, final estimates of the amount of land to be transferred must await (1) establishment of legal retention rates and (2) collaboration with Philippine statisticians. In order, however, to give some idea of the magnitude of the transfer program, attention is invited to the following rough and partial estimates based on retention assumptions as shown:

Category of Owner	Retention Allowance (Hectares)	Number of Owners Affected	Purchasable Area (Hectares)
Absentee landlord	None	909	255,484
Resident non-cultivating owner	4	No estimate	No estimate
Owner-cultivator	8	83,293	1,282,733
Part owner	8	No estimate	No estimate
Other owners	No estimate	No estimate	No estimate
Total purchasable Area			1,538,217

The number of tenants established as owners is estimated at 398, 295. Owners so established would constitute about 69 per cent of present number of tenant farmers. Lands made available would equal about 91 per cent of the total farm area operated by tenants. (See Appendices "A", page A17, and "J", in relation to the above calculations.)

Notes on Above Estimates:
a. Figures given in above table are subject to downward bias since they do not take into account: (1) Absentee landlord-owned farm lands owned by owners of less than 24 hectares and owners who, although residing within the municipality in which the land is located, are nevertheless absentee as defined below; (2) certain tenant-operated farm land owned by resident owners (inclusive of both cultivating and non-cultivating owners) in excess of allowable retention limited; (3) farm land owned by part owners in excess of the allowable retention limited; (4) farm lands listed under a farm manager that may actually be tenant-operated; and (5) farm lands owned by institutions ineligible to retain such lands. (See Part IV. RECOMMENDATIONS, page 25.)

b. Estimates relate to farm lands. Actually, retention rates should be fixed in terms of tillable lands only (cultivated plus cultivable though idle land -- constituting 75.5 per cent of the total national "farm land" area). It is planned that the law will provide for such land in other categories -- pasture (10.9 per cent of total farm land area), forest (9.7 per cent), other (3.7 per cent) -- as is attached to and an integral and necessary part of the farm to which the tillable land relates, being purchased (within limited) along with the tillable land. Farm implements, livestock, buildings, and other "improvements" on the farm land thus purchased would also be purchased as appurtenances necessary to the operation thereof.

c. Existing national average tillable and farm land areas per farm by tenure operator are:

	Tillable Land	Farm Land
Overall average	3.1 hectares	4.09 hectares
Owner-operator average	3.4 hectares	4.58 hectares
Part owner average	2.7 hectares	3.21 hectares
Share tenant average	2.49 hectares	3.86 hectares

d. Definitions:

(1) "Absentee landlord": An owner of farm land who resides neither in the barrio nor in the barrio adjacent to the barrio in which that land is located.

(2) "Resident non-cultivating landlord": An owner of farm land residing either in the barrio or in the barrio adjacent to the barrio in which the land is located.

(3) "Owner-cultivator": An owner of farm land who actually operates that land with his own or immediate family labor; provided that for purposes of fixing retention rates, an area not to exceed one-half the area of the allowed retainable area (fixed for the general area in which the farm is located) may be leased for tenant operation.

(4) "Cut-off date": Requirements of administration will demand, for purposes of fixing the tenure status of individual land parcels under the law, that a cut-off date be established. (It is suggested that June 30, 1952 apply.)

28. CAN REFORM BE CARRIED OUT UNDER EXISTING LEGISLATION? WHAT CHANGES ANY ARE REQUIRED? The brief answer to this question in NO. However, inasmuch as neither existing nor necessary legislation to be proposed is possible of combination within one law, specific comment on the

different categories of land tenure law follow:

a. All existing legislation respecting the acquisition of privately owned <u>farm land</u> by the government <u>for the purpose of establishing owner-operating farmers</u> should be repealed, and replaced by legislation incorporating principles set forth in Part IV, RECOMMENDATIONS.

b. Existing law and procedures respecting title registration and transfer should be modified in accordance with principles set forth in Part IV, RECOMMENDATIONS. As relates to the land transfer phase of the reform, such modification will involve rather radical changes in concepts respecting the role of government in order to expedite the establishment of clear titles.

c. All existing legislation governing relationships between landlords and tenants should be combined into one single law, purged of ambiguities, extended to include all crops (and other kinds of agricultural produce) and geographical areas in the Philippines, and modified to incorporate principles governing landlord-tenant relationships as set forth in Part IV, RECOMMENDATIONS.

d. Legislation respecting landlord-tenant litigations should be so revised as to include principles set forth in Part IV, RECOMMENDATIONS.

e. Administrative procedures governing participation of Public Defenders in landlord-tenant disputes should be revised in accordance with principles set forth in Part IV, RECOMMENDATIONS.

f. Consideration should be given to so revising those section of the <u>Civil Code</u> relating to inheritance of agricultural property as will prevent fragmentation of farms and the perpetuation of farm debt resulting from succession to agricultural estates.

g. Recently enacted Minimum Wage Law, particularly when considered in relation to existing tenancy law and practices, appears possessed of some extremely questionable elements -- elements which could lead to widespread evasion. The law should be thoroughly studied and modified as necessary to comply with principles set forth in Part IV, RECOMMENDATIONS.

29. ARE EXISTING ADMINISTRATIVE AGENCIES ADEQUATE FOR THE FRAMING AND CARRYING OUT OF A PROGRAM OF TENURE REFORM? The existing administrative structure is considered inadequate in that::

a. Responsibility for surveillance over the various aspects of tenure are scattered through three Departments with little or no coordination of related interests;

b. Responsibility for enforcement of piecemeal and impotent legislation has contributed to a failure on the part of administrators to see the problem as a whole -- to the development of a capacity for apathy and indolence respecting remedial action;

c. Attitudes respecting tenure in the Bureau of Lands are dominated by considerations relating to the settlement of newly developed areas, whereas the Division of Landed Estates (not recognized in the budget) appears as but a newly born foster child created to do a housekeeping job on what is predominantly urban property acquired by the discredited Rural Progress Administration;

d. No arrangement exists whereby farmers assume responsibility and authority in the regulation of matters pertaining to land tenure.

Particularly insofar as the land transfer phase of tenure reform be concerned, the situation requires an Authority created specifically for the purpose, working directly under the President, constituted in accord with principles set forth in Part IV, RECOMMENDATIONS. Once land transfers and title clearances are complete, the "government" side of the structure, materially reduced in size, may well become what might be called the Land Tenure Division in the Bureau of Lands. Responsibility for settlement of actual litigation in landlord-tenant cases should, of course, remain with the Department of Justice and responsibility for Public Defenders with the Department of Labor. But, general responsibility for administering land tenure law should eventually (though not until land transfers are practically complete) be fixed in the Department of Agriculture and National Resources.

30. WHAT ESTIMATE CAN BE GIVEN AS TO THE TIME REQUIRED TO CARRY OUT THE TENURE REFORM ENVISAGED IN THIS PAPER? The answer to this question is dependent on many variables, but in our opinion, in deference to political as well as administrative considerations involved, such an answer should be strongly influenced by a policy of speed. Experience in other countries would indicate that the land transfer phase of the reform -- the purchase and sale of lands effected by the law -- could be accomplished within about two years from the date of the enactment of enabling legislation. Completion of title registration will probably require in the neighborhood of another three years. Amortization of tenant payments and retirement of bonds should require about 30 years, though the law should make provision for an extension of this period in instances of adversity beyond control of land purchasers.

Assuming that principles to characterize reform legislation are decided in the relatively near future and in accordance with the foregoing, it would appear that the following time schedule is possible of attainment::

a. Assuming early settlement of policies and principles, and establishment of an appropriate administrative authority, legislation could be drafted in time for consideration by the Congress convening in January, 1953;

b. Provided legislation is enacted during the session opening in January, 1953, a Land Commission System could be established and ready to start operations by July, 1953;

c. Provided the above schedule is met, land acquisition and sale could be accomplished by July, 1955;

d. Then, title registration could be completed by July, 1958;

e. And bonds should be retired and purchase contracts settled by about 1980 -- the latter not later than 1985.

A major portion of the administrative staff required for the land transfer phase of the program could be retired upon its completion (July, 1955).

31. How Should the Reform Be Financed? Costs involved in establishing owner-cultivators and regulating conditions of tenancy fall into two categories: administration and land acquisition.

Estimates for administrative cost muct necessarily be considered as rough approximations pending decision on the nature and scope of the program. One the asumption that (1) tenants are to become owner-operators, (2) the land transfer phase can be carried out in about two years, and (3) a continuing organization to regulate land tenure and land tenure relationships will be established, it would appear that administrative costs would approximate P23,000,000 per annum for the two (transfer stage) years, and P4,000,000 per annum as a continuing charge. As a program of interest and benefit to the welfare of the general public, administrative costs attending tenure reform and regulation are a logical public expenditure and should therefore be paid from appropriated funds. (See Appendix "I".)

Costs of land acquisition, however, financed, would necessarily be met in a manner involving no additional burdens on the Government. This situation is made manifest by certain basic economic considerations: (1) potential purchasers are, by and large, without cash reserves and would necessarily have to pay for lands purchased from future production; (2) since, if the Government was to finance land acquisition, (a) the magnitude of costs involved would grossly exceed possible tax revenues, and (b) intolerable inflation would result from immediate payment with newly created money, it becomes mandatory that actual delivery of cash payments for lands acquired be accomplished through the years at a rate approximately in harmony with collections from tenant purchasers.

If land acquisition was to be "financed" by the Government it would appear that the process could best be accomplished through the use of non-negotiable, interest-bearing bonds, payable to former owners in a number of equal annual installments equal to the number of years permitted tenant purchasers to amortize their payments to the government. Interest paid by tenants would equal interest on the bonds. Under such a plan, annual collections from tenants would serve to neutralize the effect of monies paid out to former owners as annual increments in the retirement of bonds. The plan would, of course, involve fixing a price for land.

An alternative method for covering costs of land acquisition would be that of paying former owners (in kind, or the cash equivalent thereof) a certain percentage of future production for a specified number of years -- the price paid for the land thus coming eventually to equal the cumulative sum of payments made during the amortization period. The chief advantages of this method are two:

a. It automatically relates the value of land to the value of farm produce, and

b. It might avoid the difficult and thankless job of fixing a land price.

On the other hand, the method has the disadvantages of:

a. Being much more difficult and expensive to administer;

b. Needlessly continuing landlord-tenant frictions; and

c. Creating uncertainties among a potential investor class -- a situation inimical to the interests of industrial growth.

On balance, the first method described above (non-negotiable bonds) is favored over the second, but under either method, the expensive part of the reform could be accomplished without cost to the public -- and without disruption to the economy.

Attention is invited to Appendix "K" in which this whole question is discussed in more detail.

32. WHAT WOULD BE THE EDUCATIONAL AND INFORMATIONAL REQUIREMENTS FOR A TENURE REFORM? Several facts combine to focus attention on the fact that a thoroughgoing information-education program most of necessity be an integral part of any successful tenure reform program. One-half of the people in the Philippines are illiterate; the number of small farmers (particularly tenants) with experience in being able to decide their own questions -- let alone to act officially in the solution of those of others - is negligible; many are without experience as members of organizations; few have access to current periodicals; many are awed by the law; many will be subject to the sabotaging arguments and acts to be expected from some landlords and all communists. And yet, it is this very group who must be made to understand what the program holds for them -- of the need for vigilant and intelligent cooperation if the program is to be successful.

Land reform cannot be carried out in Manila. Decisions respecting status of individual land parcels and farm operators must be made on the spot by persons thoroughly acquainted with the real situation. Decisions must be so made as to guarantee full protection of tenant and former owner interest. In short, it is on properly constituted groups of farmers, equally representative of tenant and owner interest, that we are forced by the very nature of the problem to place responsibility for actually doing the job. These groups will need to be informed -- and their constituents will need to be kept abreast of what is, and should be, going on.

Furthermore, the record shows public officials to have at times been subject to graft, and that the acts of Congress, although ostensibly favoring reform, have been weak and ambiguous. Inasmuch as a majority of the public appear to favor reform, continuing and widespread publicity on the nature and accomplishments of the program is mandatory if the program is to accomplish its objective.

There is another consideration respecting publicity. The Communists have championed land reform as a means to gaining adherents from among the ranks of discontented and landless farmers. They have worked hard to associate land reform with Communism -- to associate western democracies with reaction -- and in Asia, and particularly in the Philippines, they have met with some success. Full publicity should be given to the fact that genuine land reform is actually possible only within the concept of a political framework based on the principle of private ownership; that land reform is recognized by the western democracies as a primary objective; that they are making a genuine and effective effort to accomplish that objective.

24

PART IV

RECOMMENDATIONS

33.

a. In accord with implications of the factual information presented in Part II of this paper and conclusions reached in Part III, action by the Philippine Government to correct these conditions is vital if the objectives cited and implied by the Bell Report as a condition of MSA assistance to the Philippine Government, to which the Philippine Government has agreed, are to be achieved. A recommended course of action is submitted herewith, making certain suggestions as to steps that should be considered by the Philippine Government in achieving these objectives.

b. An Authority should be created by the Government of the Republic of the Philippines. The Authority should be an action agency directly responsible to the President and should have representation at a national, regional, and provincial level. It should have full and exclusive responsibility for drafting legislation, formulating operational procedures, and administering a program designed to eliminate pernicious characteristics in the Philippine land tenure system and initiate such socio-economic patterns and practices respecting land tenure as are necessary for the creation and maintenance of a peaceful, prosperous, and democratic economy. The Authority should concern itself exclusively with the attainment of the aforementioned objectives. Specifically, it would act in a deft manner in order:

1. To abolish, insofar as practicable, the institution of tenancy in Philippine agriculture.

2. To establish to the maximum practicable degree a rural economy based on owner-operated family-sized farms.

3. To establish fair tenancy practices for that portion of farmers who continue to work the land as tenants.

4. To eliminate hindrances to the fruition of objectives set forth in 1., 2., and 3. immediately above.

In pursuance of its objectives, the Authority should at all times be guided by the principle of:

1. The fundamental dignity of man, and

2. Private rather than state, individual rather than collective ownership of land.

25

This Authority should be a temporary agency and, when the land transfer program has been substantially completed, become a part of a regular Department of the Government. For example, it might be made a Division of the Bureau of Lands of the Department of Agriculture and Natural Resources.

c. The following action should be taken respecting the establishment of owner-cultivators:

1. So much of all existing legislation as relates to the acquisition by the government of privately owned agricultural lands for the purpose of establishing owner-cultivators (inclusive of, but not limited to, appropriate provisions of Commonwealth Acts Nos. 20, 260, 378, 420, 538, and 539) should be repealed, and all applicable procedures, instructions and other operational documents relating thereto should be rescinded. All other laws, rules, or regulations so constituted as to conflict with provisions of proposed law described in par. 2. following should be repealed or amended in a manner appropriate for compliance and harmony with such law. Agricultural properties now in possession of the government which were acquired pursuant to provisions of the above-named laws, should be disposed of in accord with applicable provisions of law to be drafted in accord with principles set forth below.

2. Legislation providing for the acquisition of certain privately owned agricultural properties by the Philippine Government for sale to farm tenants and other *bona fide* purchasers, as a means of eliminating the institution of farm tenancy to the maximum possible extent and supplanting it with a pattern of owner-cultivators of family-sized farm units, should be given top priority by Congress. Specifically, such legislation should respect objectives set forth in par. b., page 24, and incorporate the following principles:

a. Status of farm lands, owners, and tenants should for purposes of this law, be fixed in accord with the tenure situation maintaining on a date not later than June 30, 1952.

b. Farm land areas which owners should be permitted to retain should be calculated in terms of cultivable land (tilled land plus idle land capable of cultivation) as defined by the Philippine census for 1938; however, provision should be made that in purchasing such tillable land, such other lands including pasture, forest and "other" (as defined in the aforementioned source) as are attached to, and constitute a necessary and integral part of the "farm" to which the tillable land relates, should (within specified limits) be purchased together with the tillable land. Farm implements, livestock, buildings, and other improvements on the farm land thus purchased should also be purchased as appurtenances necessary to the operation thereof.

3.   All lands and other properties subject to purchase under the law should be purchased by the government from the landowner as a singular and complete transaction, and the government, irrespective of any claims which may exist or be developed respecting prior ownership or rights on such lands, should proclaim itself as legal owner of said land in fee simple and thereby able to transfer clear and legal titles to such land; provided, that the government, as the sole person (juridical or natural) responsible for the settlement of such claims by former right holders may, if it deems them deserving of consideration, settle such claims by paying such compensation as it may consider fair and just. After having acquired land and other property subject to purchase under this law, the government would sell such properties to bona fide purchasers in the manner described below, and should immediately transfer title to said buyer in fee simple subject only to a first mortgage favoring the government, or a tax lien equal in value to the purchase price of the land plus interest, and safeguards specified in par. c. 11), page 34. Under no circumstances would prospective final buyers of property being transferred under this law negotiate with owners of properties subject to purchase for any purpose whatsoever as relates to the sale and purchase of said properties; nor would any claim to these properties based on the status of said properties prior to the date of their acquisition by the government, which may be brought against the final purchaser, be considered valid.

4.   For purposes of this and other laws to be enacted with respect to land tenure, the following definitions with appropriate clarification should be considered:

a.   Categories of farm land are to be defined as in the 1938 Philippine census; supplemented only by the fact that the word "tillable" shall be used interchangeably with the word "cultivable."

b. "National average": use of this terms implies that in application of a law in which the term might be employed, the numerical value to which it relates would be broken down for each province, municipality and barrio in accord with the ratio between the numerical value of the "average" for the whole or the superior unit and that of each of its immediate subdivisions. Example: As a "national average", farms in the Philippines contain approximately 4.1 hectares of farm land, while the "provincial average" farm land area per farm (discounting "managed" farms) in the provinces of Cebu and Masbate approximates 2.8 and 13.6 hectares, respectively. Application of a "national average", the numerical value of which is 4.1 hectares, would mean a "provincial average" of approximately 2.8 hectares (2.8/4.1 x 4.1 hectares) in Cebu and 13.6 hectares (13.6/4.1 x 4.1 hectares) in Masbate. Subsequent determination respecting numerical values for municipalities and, in turn, for barrios would be accomplished in a similar manner. Application of this concept is further illustrated in a footnote to par. 5. b., page 30.

c. "Bona fide cultivator": A person capable and desirous of devoting himself to agriculture and who will personally, or with the aid of labor from within his own immediate farm household, cultivate or operate the land.

d. "Farm household": The immediate members of the family of a bona fide cultivator and other person residing with him who are dependent upon him for support.

e. "Absentee landlord": An owner of farm land who resides neither in the barrio or in the barrio adjacent to the barrio in which the land is located.

f. "Resident non-cultivating landlord": An owner of farm land residing either in the barrio or in the barrio adjacent to the barrio in which the land is located, who does not cultivate (operate) at least 0.3 hectare (national average)[10] of said land.

---

10. See definition of "national average" in par. 4. b., page 27. While clarity requires inclusion of a numerical value in this and the definitions which follow in pars. 4. g. and j., page 29, the 0.3 hectare and the 0.4 hectare figures, employed as examples in these three paragraphs, are not to be interpreted as representing an arbitrary stand on what such numerical values should be. These are questions to be settled by appropriate officials within the Philippine Government. The objective in fixing such numerical values is to eliminate from consideration under the reform, those agronomic and livestock interests, the smallness of which render them unworthy of inclusion. An explanation of the application of a numerical "national average" is presented as a footnote to part 5. b., page 30.

28

g. "Tenant": Any person who is actually cultivating land which he does not own, the cultivated portion of which exceeds 0.3 hectare [10] or farm land portion 0.4 hectare [10] (as a national average), with his own or family labor and who shares in the risk of the venture in which he invests his labor or capital.

h. "Cultivating owner": An owner of farm land who actually cultivates (operates) a substantial portion (to be defined by law) of that land with his own or immediate family labor.

i. "Juridical person": Any legal person, inclusive of, but not limited to, corporations, legal partnerships, and private schools, hospitals, churches, organizations, who may own or operate land.

j. "Farm": Any parcel or group of parcels of farm land involving a minimum of 0.3 hectare [11] of farm land (national average), the operation of which contributes substantially toward the support of its operator.

k. For purposes relating to the election and composition of Land Commissions:

1 - "Owner": An owner of farm land the area of which is more than twice the area of the land he personally operates.

2 - "Tenant": A cultivator of farm land, the area of which is more than twice the area of the land he owns.

3 - "Owner cultivator": A cultivator of farm land whose tenure status would exclude him from inclusion in either category 1 - or 2 - above.

5. Land and properties subject to purchase by the government under this law should be as follows:

---

11. Ibid

a.   All farm land owned by absentee landlords.

b.   All <u>tillable lands</u> owned by resident non-cultivating landlords in excess of three (3) hectares [12] (as a national average [13], provided that the excess over four (4) hectares (as a national average) of all <u>farm lands</u> owned by a landlord in this category should be purchased.

c.   All tillable lands owned by a cultivating owner in excess of six (6) hectares (as a national average); provided, that the excess over eight (8) hectares (as a national average) of all farm lands owned by owners in this category should be purchased; provided, further, however, that the established retention rate may, for specified individual farmers in this category, be increased upon recommendation of the Local Land Commission and with the approval of the Administrator of the Authority, when in the opinion of the recommending and approving body the individual farmer has demonstrated his ability and intention to cultivate a larger area efficiently and where subdivision of property into smaller farm units could not be accomplished without serious damage to agricultural production, but no such exception should be granted in instances where more than four (4) hectares (national average) of the farm land owned by such cultivating owner is tenant operated.

---

12. To avoid ambiguities inimical to existing laws (see par. 24, page 10) it is vital that a law to implement adequate land tenure reform be quite definite on the question of retention allowances. Use of 3 and 4 hectares in this paragraph and 6 and 8 hectares in paragraph c. following, is not however, to be construed as representing and arbitrary position on the question of what the numerical value of the retention allowance so fixed should be. These are questions to be settled by appropriate officials of the Philippine Government. Since, however, the size of the average farm in the Philippines approximates 4 hectares, about 3 hectares of which is cultivable, for reasons set forth in paragraph 24, subparagraph "Owner-Operated Family-Sized Farm Defined", page 15, it would seem that retention allowance rates herein used as examples, might well serve as a starting point for a discussion of the question.

13. See definition of "National Average", page 28. Use of 3 hectares does not mean, of course, that each and every resident non-cultivating owner through the Philippines would be permitted a retention allowance of exactly 3 hectares of tillable land. It rather means that the retention allowance for a given

d. All farm land owned by a juridical person:

1 - In excess of requirements for the accomplishment of the primary purpose for which such juridical person was constituted; or

2 - Which is operated by tenants; or

3 - Which is not operated directly by that juridical person.

Footnote 13 continued

area would be determined by the ratio of the weighted average size of existing farms in that district to the weighted average size of existing farms in the region of which that district is an immediate subdivision. Example: Assume that the retention rate is set at 4 hectares of farm land as a national average; that the weighted average farm size for the Philippines as a whole (national average) is 4.1 hectares; that the weighted average farm size for the province of Cebu is 2.8 hectares (provincial average) and 13.6 hectares in Masbate. Then the retention rate for Cebu would be about 2.73 hectares (2.8/4.1 x 4) as a provincial average, and about 13.3 hectares (13.6/4.1) for Masbate. Next assume that within Masbate province the weighted average size of farms in one municipality is 8 hectares (municipal average) and in a second municipality, 15 hectares. Then the retention rate for the first municipality would be about 7.8 hectares (8/13.6 x 13.3), for the second about 14.7 hectares (15/13.6 x 13.3). A retention rate for application within a barrio (i.e., the rate which would actually apply to a given owner within that barrio) would, in turn, be fixed in a similar manner. In paragraph 24, subparagraph "Owner-Operated Family-Sized Farm Defined", page 15, it was pointed out that such factors as land productivity and cropping systems serve to determine the farm size pattern for any given area. Thus, when the weighted average size of farms in a given barrio is averaged with the weighted averages for other barrios in the municipality, the resulting "municipal weighted average" farm size would then reflect the accepted norm farm size for that municipality. And just as the weighted average size of farms for all municipalities within a province would be reflective of productive potentials and cropping patterns within that province, so would a weighted average size of farms for all provinces, when combined into a weighted average for the nation as a whole, make consideration for variations as between districts in relation to productivity and cropping patterns. Conversely, in breaking down national and regional weighted average farm sizes in accordance with the method described above, provision for variability as between districts in relation to crops and productivities is accomplished automatically.

4 - Except that portion which could not, in the opinion of the Local Land Commission and the administrator of the Authority, be accomplished without serious damage to agricultural production.

e. Any farm land which, in the opinion of the Local and Provincial Land Commissions, is not being cultivated in a productive manner.

f. Any farm land which the owner may offer for sale to the government.

g. Any other farm lands designated by the law.

6.   The method for fixing prices to be paid for farm lands and other farm properties purchased should be decided by the Philippine Government and clearly stated in the law.

The formula should:

a. Be based upon the productivity of the land;

b. Minimize the opportunity for human error in fixing the price for individual tracts of land;

c. Result in a price not so high as to be inconsistent with the ability of the tenant purchaser to pay;

d. Result in a price high enough to give owners fair compensation for their land.[14]

7.   Payment for lands purchased by the government should be made in taxable, non-negotiable government bonds bearing a reasonable rate of interest and payable over a period of time in equal annual installments (An interest rate of 4 per cent and

---

14. It is suggested that the price established should not exceed an amount equal to a 6 per cent capitalization of 30 per cent of the cash value of the average annual gross product less harvest costs computed in terms of average annual prices expected to prevail during the amortization period. Local Land Commissions should be permitted a specified measure of flexibility in pricing individual properties. Attention is invited to Appendices "H" and "K" for suggestions respecting certain considerations in connection with price determination and payment-collection methods.

a period of 25 years is suggested), provided that the government may retire such bonds at its discretion by paying the balance of the unpaid value. It is suggested that at the discretion of the government, such bonds might be declared eligible as collateral for productive investment.

8. Only persons capable of demonstrating an intention to devote themselves to the cultivation (operation) of the land with their own and immediate family labor should be eligible to purchase land purchased by the government under this law, provided potential purchasers shall be given priority to purchase said lands in accordance with the following:

   a. Tenant on the land as of 30 June 1952;

   b. Any other tenant farmer;

   c. Any owner-cultivator who owns and operates land in the immediate vicinity; or

   d. Any *bona fide* owner-cultivator otherwise eligible to purchase land under this act;

and provided further that no person shall be able to purchase land

   a. When the farm land purchased, together with any other farm land he may own, would cause his total farm land holdings to exceed the farm land area which an owner-cultivator in the immediate vicinity may legally retain.

   b. When in the opinion of the Local Land Commission he is incapable (either by ability or desire) of farming land within reasonable limits of efficiency.

9. Purchasers of land from the government shall pay a price equal to that paid by the government for such land and in addition shall pay interest on the unpaid balance of their purchase contract. An interest rate of 4 per cent is suggested.[15]

---

15. It is suggested the government might, fiscal conditions permitting, use appropriated funds to reduce payments from purchasers, though it is emphasized that accomplishment of the reform is not contingent upon such action.

10.   Purchasers of land from the government under this law should pay for the land in equal annual installments amortized over a period of time (25 years is suggested); provided that the government would, in periods of adversity beyond the control of and rendering land purchasers unable to meet their obligation to the government, postpone payments respecting the period of adversity; and provided further, that under no circumstances would the annual payment (including interest) be so fixed as to cause it, when added to other costs attending landownership (taxes, etc.), to exceed an amount equal to 30 per cent of the gross annual product less harvest costs, provided, however, that a purchaser should be given an opportunity to pay for land purchased at a rate faster than that fixed by the payment schedule in the event he may elect to do so.[16]

11.   No lands nor properties purchased from the government under this law should be used as collateral for a loan prior to the date when purchasers shall have liquidated their indebtedness to the government respecting such lands and/or properties. Any contract negotiated with a purchaser during the amortization period and involving said purchased properties as collateral, should be considered null and void.

12.   This law should constitute a permanent instrument for the control and regulation of land tenure patterns and land values. No land purchased by a farm operator under this law, nor any other privately owned land should be sold without the approval of the Local Land Commission having jurisdiction over the area in which the land is located. The Commission, in giving its decision on these matters, would be guided by the objectives relating to the nature of tenure, size of farms and land values established by this law. If it should develop that no eligible buyer is available to purchase land from the one wishing to sell under conditions fixed by the Commission, the Commission, acting as an agent of the government, may purchase said lands for eventual disposal in accord with procedures outlined above. A commission in possession of land relative which there is no eligible purchaser, would rent such land to any farm operator on a year to year basis, provided that such lease would be cancelled at the end of a year in which an eligible purchaser has been located and the land should at that time be sold to such eligible and willing purchaser.

---

16. It is suggested that collections for lands and properties sold by the government under the law be accomplished through the agency of a Special Tax levied on purchasers, the annual levy equalling the annual installment on principal plus interest.

13. Provision should be made for appeals on decisions to higher echelons within the administrative system in relation to application of this law to particular land parcels, purchase price, eligibility of purchasers, etc., and access to established courts should be insured in cases where questions are raised respecting the validity of decisions made by the Authority or agents thereof who would, by the nature of its constituting authority, serve as an administrative agency (as compared to an agency of the judiciary).

d. The following action should be taken in relation to the establishment and maintenance of fair tenancy practices for those who continue to till the land as tenants:

1. So much of existing law and supporting rules and regulations as pertain to the establishment, regulation, and litigation of farm tenancy agreements, inclusive of, but not limited to CA 271, CA 4113, CA 4054, CA 461, CA 178, CA 608, RA 34, and RA 44, should be repealed or so amended as will result in a single, concise, and administrable law incorporating principles set forth below:

a. Application to all landlord-tenant agreements in the Philippines, irrespective of product or location of undertaking.

b. A farm lease contract (hereinafter called contract) and parties thereto should be accorded to any other contract or contractor under Philippine law. The landlord and the tenant should each be considered as full and equal parties to the contract.

c. A contract should have singular relation to rights and responsibilities respecting tenure. Disputes arising in relation to compliance with conditions of the contract should not be inferred to warrant action exceeding provisions specified in the contract proper. Conversely, a dispute between a landlord and a tenant involving matters other than those previously specified in the contract should have no effect on the contract itself, provided however that this should not be construed as violating the right of either party to take such action in the settlement of other differences as is provided by law.

d. All landlord-tenant agreements should be bound by written contract and all principle provisions thereof should be clearly stated. (The model farm lease currently used by the Philippine Government when revised to provide for principles recommended herein should be given wide publicity and its use encouraged vigorously).

e. Payment considerations within the contract should provide exclusively for payment in cash. Provisions for payment in kind would be declared illegal.

f. The practice of truck payments [17] and/or the payment of fines, except when specifically and previously provided for in the contract, should be considered illegal.

g. No contract should be considered legal which provides for an annual rental exceeding an amount equal to 30 per cent of the gross value of the annual crop; provided that lower ceilings may be fixed by law for less productive and remotely situated land; and provided further that in applying these ceilings additional and separate consideration may be made for perennial crops on the land, the existence and employment of which relates directly and necessarily to the type of farm operation intended by the lease.

h. Provision should be made for compensating the tenant for any improvements on the property made by him, provided that such improvements were specifically authorized by the landlord.

i. All contracts and any alteration or cancellation relating thereto should be subject to approval of, and a copy filed with, the Local Land Commission.

---

17. Payment of wages in kind.

j.   The Local Land Commission should investigate and act as arbiter in landlord-tenant disputes involving questions relating to the lease contract; however, if either or both parties signify an unwillingness to accept the findings of the Commission, the question should be referred by either party or the Commission to the Court of Agrarian Relations for disposal; provided, however, that the Court would hear the findings and recommendations of the Commission before making its decision.

2.   Law respecting the adjudication of landlord-tenant disputes (inclusive of but not limited to CA 271, CA 4113, CA 4054, CA 461, CA 178, CA 608, RA 34 and RA 44, and appropriate portions of the Civil Code) should be repealed or modified so as to:

a.   Create a Court of Agrarian Relations which should be similar and parallel to, though completely separate from, the Court of Industrial Relations. The Court of Agrarian Relations should deal exclusively with settling landlord-tenant disputes and such other problems as affect socio-economic relations in agriculture deemed appropriate to its jurisdiction.

b.   The Court of Agrarian Relations should be given authority to act directly to effect enforcement of its decisions.

3.   Law, regulations, or procedures respecting participation of Public Defenders in the settlement of landlord-tenant disputes coming before the Court of Agrarian Relations for adjudication should be revised as necessary to make it mandatory that a litigant, unable to afford the expense of counsel, would receive adequate legal representation before such courts.

e.   Law respecting the transfer and registration of farm land titles should be revised in accord with principles set forth in paragraph c. 3), page 27. Furthermore, appropriate laws, regulations, and practices should be modified to provide for streamlined administrative procedures necessary for the expeditious handling of the great number of land title transfers and registrations which will be involved in a thoroughgoing tenure reform program.

f.   To eliminate threats to farm family economic stability cited in paragraph 24. h., page 13, law respecting inheritance as pertains to agricultural properties should be revised in such manner as will prevent:

1. Fragmentation of farm units through succession.

2. The development and perpetuation of debt burdens in agriculture resulting from succession.

g. Minimum Wage Law should be studied thoroughly in light of, and amended as necessary to comply with, principles set forth in paragraph 33 d, page 35, and following:

1. Persons employed in the production and/or the first stage of processing agricultural products who are neither owner not tenant-operators (nor members of their immediate families) of the enterprise in which they are so employed should be defined as farm laborers.

2. The law should apply to all farm laborers, except that it should not apply to those farm laborers employed on farms operated by tenants or cultivating owners as defined in paragraph 33 c.4) g) and h), page 29.

3. Farm laborers should be paid a minimum wage equal to that established for other laborers of equal skill.

h. The administration of Land Tenure Reform involves two general functions, distinctly different in character. The first has to do with program formulation, the enforcement of implementing law and the performance of such administrative duties as relate thereto, the collection and disbursement of funds, and the acceptance and issuance of titles. The second has to do with application of implementing law to individual persons and specific lands and other properties, and the formulation of such policies and the making of such decisions relating thereto as are authorized and otherwise provided for by law. While these two general functions are mutually interdependent, they so differ in relation both to vested responsibility and the abilities and interests of personnel, as to preclude their being combined within a single chain of authority. The first function implies the exercise of duties, responsibilities and authorities of a type which might ordinarily be expected to characterize a public action agency. The second function, however, requires not only a unique knowledge of agricultural operations and of individual characteristics of persons resident within particular farm communities, but also an assurance that conflicting interests will receive equitable attention in reaching decisions respecting such questions as the application of the law to a given piece of land, the value of that land, and the selection of the most eligible purchaser. As a consequence of the dissimilarity between these two general functions involved in the prosecution of a Land Tenure Reform Program, provision should be made for the establishment of an administrative structure composed of two coordinated, though separate, administrative systems, each responsible to the Administrator of the Authority suggested in paragraph 33b, page 25; one system, hereinafter referred to as the Authority proper, being responsible for activities described under the "first" general function discussed above; the other system, hereinafter referred to as the Land Commission System, responsible for duties described under the "second" general function.

1. It is suggested that the Authority recommended in paragraph 33b, page 25, and described above, be constituted as an action agency with existence at three echelons: National, Regional, and Provincial. As example of a functional organization plan for such as Authority, attention is invited to the following:

a) National level: Headed by the Administrator, responsible for overall planning and administration, inclusive of the preparation of legislation and supporting regulations; issuance of operational policies and procedures; nationwide tenure reform information and education; intergovernmental negotiations; and immediate supervision over its regional offices.

b) Regional level: To the maximum extent consistent with control and coordination, responsibility for actual administration of the reform should be decentralized into about five regional offices, each headed by a Deputy Administrator. Primarily, a Region would supervise the work of each province in the area under its jurisdiction to insure compliance with the law and the thorough and expeditious prosecution of the reform. It would deal directly with the "Bank" and should be the office of record for all financial matters respecting land purchases, sales, and collections. It should have a legal staff, equipped to investigate and prosecute cases of evasion and malfeasance arising in the provinces.

c) Provincial level: Headed by a Provincial Director, this office would maintain surveillance over the work carried out by the Local Land Commissions in the barrios pursuant to effecting a thorough and vigorous prosecution of the law. This office, acting for the Philippine Government, should be responsible for final approval of all purchase and sale plans submitted to it by the Provincial Land Commission. Responsibility for accomplishing transfer and registration of titles should center in this office. The Director should have authority to order a recall election respecting the whole (but not just a part) of a Local Land Commission.

2. It is further suggested that the Land Commission System, described above should be composed entirely of bona fide farmers and such non-voting experts as are specifies by law, and should have existence at three echelons: National, Provincial, and Local. As an example of a functional organization plan for the Land Commission System, attention is invited to the following:

a) The National Land Commission should be composed of three (3) owner, two (2) owner-cultivator, and five (5) tenant, voting members: [18] such other voting members within the limits of five (5) [18] who by their training and experience would enhance the effectiveness of the Commission; and the Administrator, who would act as chairman. It would decide questions fixed for its jurisdiction by law and matters relating to overall policy. It should be the body of highest appeal of decisions made by Provincial Land Commissions. Members of the Commission should be appointed by the President of the Philippines with the advice of the Secretary of Agriculture and Natural Resources and such other persons as he may deem appropriate. The Commission should serve without pay but should be reimbursed for actual expenses incurred in connection with service. The Commission should meet in Manila at least as often as once each year.

b) A Provincial Land Commission should be similar in composition to that of the National Commission except that non-voting expert membership should be limited to three (3), [18] and that the Provincial Director should serve as chairman. Voting members of the Commission should be elected by and from among members within their own category on the Local Land Commissions within the province, provided that when a member of a local commission is elected to the provincial commission, he should resign his membership on the local commission and the vacancy thus created on the local commission should be filled by an immediate election. The Commission would decide questions fixed within its jurisdiction by law,

---

18. While the question as to the size of Land Commissions should be decided by those responsible for drafting the implementing law, it is suggested that the basic principles guiding this decision should be that of assuring that tenant representation (purchase interest) will equal owner representation (seller interest).

questions and appeals forwarded to it by the Local (or National) Land Commissions for decision, and should be responsible for first approval of all purchase and sale plans originated by the Local Land Commissions. It might act directly in the purchase of eligible lands which exceed the jurisdictional limits of a single Local Land Commission. The Commission members would serve without pay but should be reimbursed for actual expenses incurred in service. The Commission should meet at least as often as once each month.

c) A Local Land Commission should be composed of three (3) owners, two (2) owner-cultivators, and five (5) tenants. [18] All members should be voting members. The chairman should be elected by and from among the members; except that if the question of the chairman cannot be decided, a member should be designated as chairman by the Deputy Administrator. [19] Members should be elected by and from among voters in their registered category as described in paragraph i.1), following. The Commission should be responsible for drawing up purchase and sale plans respecting land subject to purchase, price, and eligibility of purchasers). The Commission should also regulate landlord-tenant agreements and serve as the arbiter of their disputes as provided for in paragraphs d.1)i) and j), page 36. The Commission should serve without pay but should be reimbursed for actual expenses incurred in service. The Commission should meet at least as often as once each two weeks. The Commission should be furnished with clerical assistance.

i. To insure that members of Land Commissions, recommended in paragraph 33h, page 38, and described in subparagraph 33h.2), page 40, discharge their responsibilities in an equitable and effective manner, provision for the establishment and maintenance of a Land Commission System should include:

1) Provision for the registration of voters and the election of members. (Note: As an example, such provisions might adhere to the following pattern: All persons of

---

18. Ibid (above)
19 See par.33h.1)b), page 39.

twenty-one (21) years of age or over, who are immediate members of families owning or operating tillable land exceeding three-tenths (0.3) hectare or farm land exceeding four-tenths (0.4) hectare [20] would be registered in accord with tenure categories as defined in paragraph c.4)k), page 29. All persons so registered would be eligible to vote in the election of representatives of their particular tenure group on Local Land Commission. Any eligible voter might hold office on the Commission. Eligibility to represent, or vote for, or recall representatives of a given tenure group should be confined exclusively to registrants within that tenure group. In the event any category of electors should fail to elect its representatives to a commission, the existing vacancies should be filled by persons appointed by the Deputy Administrator. Such appointments might be made from among voters registered within the area in any of the three categories, irrespective of the category in which such vacancy exists.

2)   Establishment of election procedures and schedules appropriate for the reform, with special attention to the abilities and experience of the electorate involved.

3)   Ample provision for the dissemination of information respecting the Land Tenure Reform Program in general and the establishment, maintenance, and responsibilities of the Land Commissions, with special attention to procedures respecting recall elections.

---

20. See definition, par. c.4), page 27